MW00991480

Dreams, Nightmares, and Reality

A Family Memoir

 MASCOT
BOOKS

www.mascotbooks.com

Dreams, Nightmares, and Reality

©2022 Helga Hatvany. All Rights Reserved. No part of this publication may
be reproduced, stored in a retrieval system or transmitted in any form by any
means electronic, mechanical, or photocopying, recording or otherwise without
the permission of the author.

For more information, please contact:
Mascot Books
620 Herndon Parkway, Suite 320
Herndon, VA 20170
info@mascotbooks.com

Library of Congress Control Number: 2021916572

CPSIA Code: PBANG0921A
ISBN-13: 978-1-64543-982-0

Printed in the United States

Cover image: The author with her father in Paris, 1965.

Innovation is a pleasurable, satisfying, arduous, prickly, sometimes suicidal, but always adventurous activity (somewhat like love). It always begins with a period of euphoria, almost always followed by one of disappointment and disillusionment, finally—if successful—to proceed to tranquil prosperity, where the cycle begins again.[1]

József Hatvany, *Dreams, Nightmares and Reality*

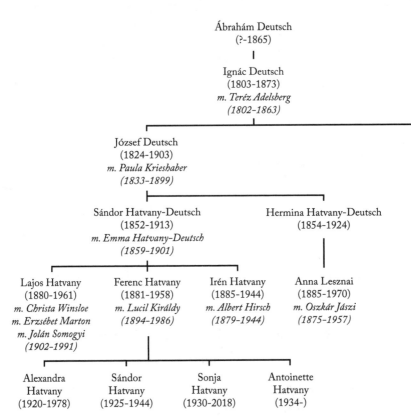

Ábrahám Deutsch
(?-1865)

Ignác Deutsch
(1803-1873)
m. Teréz Adelsberg
(1802-1863)

József Deutsch
(1824-1903)
m. Paula Krieshaber
(1833-1899)

Sándor Hatvany-Deutsch
(1852-1913)
m. Emma Hatvany-Deutsch
(1859-1901)

Hermina Hatvany-Deutsch
(1854-1924)

Lajos Hatvany
(1880-1961)
m. Christa Winsloe
m. Erzsébet Marton
m. Jolán Somogyi
(1902-1991)

Ferenc Hatvany
(1881-1958)
m. Lucil Királdy
(1894-1986)

Irén Hatvany
(1885-1944)
m. Albert Hirsch
(1879-1944)

Anna Lesznai
(1885-1970)
m. Oszkár Jászi
(1875-1957)

Alexandra
Hatvany
(1920-1978)

Sándor
Hatvany
(1925-1944)

Sonja
Hatvany
(1930-2018)

Antoinette
Hatvany
(1934-)

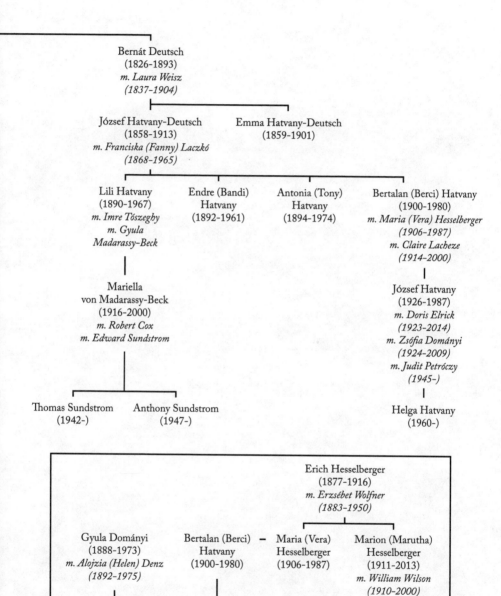

Dreams, Nightmares, and Reality

A Family Memoir

Helga Hatvany

Chapter One
Salt

"The sea is salty," he said. *Salty? How can the entire sea, such vast amount of water, be full of salt?* I wondered, picturing a giant from the tale of *Gulliver's Travels* wading in the water, saltshaker in hand. *Will I be able to see the salt when we arrive at the beach? Will I taste it when we go for a swim? Will my skin remain salty after emerging from the water?* My young mind was full of questions and confusion, but most of all, anticipation.

It was a beautiful summer day in 1965. My parents and I boarded a Caravelle jet at Paris-Le Bourget Airport, bound for the Côte d'Azur. The prospect of seeing the Mediterranean filled me with tremendous excitement. On our way to the French Riviera, my father pointed out some of the most important differences between the sea and Hungary's Lake Balaton, my only reference for a large body of water at the time. He explained to me that the sea was much bigger and deeper, and it always had waves on its surface, unlike Balaton, the shallow lake that often appeared as smooth as a mirror once the winds died down. In my mind, the most fascinating part was when he told me that seawater was salty. I found the idea very hard to imagine. As our plane descended toward Nice-Côte d'Azur Airport, my face was glued to the window. At last, I could see the beautiful blue sea with my own eyes. The water's surface, glistening in the bright sun, was feathered by the wind. I was mesmerized. My father gently put his hand on my shoulder as he leaned over from his seat so we could share the view. With the enthusiasm of a child who has just discovered something magical, he pointed at the whitecaps dancing on top of the waves and said, "Look, my little angel, there's the salt." At the age of four and a half, I had no reason to doubt him. I hung on every word he said, not because he was very smart, which he was, but because he was my father. It didn't cross my mind, not even for a split second, that he might have been joking. I will never know whether he realized at the moment that I took him seriously, but it doesn't really matter. It was a perfect moment, one of my earliest, clear memories of the two of us.

My father often addressed me *angyalkám*, which literally translates as "my little angel," but the word *sweetie* may come closer in flavor. It was meant as a sign of affection, not that I needed a verbal reinforcement of the obvious. I knew he adored me, and he knew I adored him. He was the center of my universe. In his presence I felt completely safe, happy, and content. At such a young age, I didn't know anything about his background, how he had grown up, what kind of experiences and influences had shaped him into the man I came to know as my father. It wasn't until decades later that I slowly started to peel back the countless layers of a story and untangle some of the knots, in an attempt to put together a puzzle, trying to find answers to my questions about his fascinating, extremely complex, and often controversial personality.

◠

József Hatvany was born in 1926 in Budapest, Hungary. His family was one of the wealthiest, most prominent, and highly respected Hungarian-Jewish dynasties before World War II. Besides proving themselves as exceptionally successful industrialists, his ancestors played a significant role in Hungary's cultural life as talented writers, artists, and legendary philanthropists.

The family's fame outlived its fortune. Our name, one that had evolved from Deutsch to Hatvany-Deutsch and finally to Hatvany, remained very well known decades after World War II, even during the communist era that followed. Growing up, I remember so many people asking me whether I was a member of *that* Hatvany family. Some of my friends insisted on calling me baroness in the 1970s, as if they were trying to bring this aristocratic title back from hibernation, when in fact we all knew it was gone forever. As a teenager desperately trying to fit in, especially in a society that considered the former bourgeoisie a class enemy, I felt rather uneasy with this label. Nevertheless, I have always been proud to be one of *the* Hatvanys.

But I must digress. To shed some light on my father's heritage and background, we should start our journey all the way back in the eighteenth century.

Chapter Two
Sugar

IN THE LATE 1700s, my four times great-grandfather, Ábrahám Deutsch, left his hometown of Kőszeg and moved across Hungary to settle in the town of Arad in today's Romania. Soon after his arrival, he opened a small store for mixed goods, making a living as a rural merchant. Arad was the center for Hungarian grain production, and it didn't take long before Ábrahám saw an opportunity to expand his business. During the Napoleonic Wars at the beginning of the nineteenth century, he shifted his focus primarily toward grain, in order to supply French soldiers with this essential food source.

His son, Ignác Deutsch, joined the family shop at an early age. By the time he turned nineteen in 1822, he played a key role in establishing a company that blossomed into one of the most prestigious crop-trading enterprises in southern Hungary. Ignác's wife, Teréz Adelsberg, also came from a successful Jewish crop merchant family. Most likely it was

an arranged marriage, but one can only speculate. If indeed it was a calculated business merger, it might have been the first of many more to
come in the history of my family.

Inspired by his quick success, and yearning for more, Ignác broad-
ened his horizons. He became one of the earliest pioneers of the
Hungarian insurance business. By 1843, he assumed a key position in
the First Savings Bank of Arad.

Ignác and Teréz had four children: József, Bernát, Róza, and Ernes-
tine. Both József and Bernát joined the family business, but it was Bernát
who truly followed in his father's footsteps. Actively involved in the
enterprise from the tender age of fifteen, he officially became his father's
business partner when he turned twenty in 1846.

As Hungary's transportation system rapidly improved with more
railroads and steamboats available for shipping merchandise across the
country, the large city of Pest became a major hub for the country's grain
trade. Ignác Deutsch saw his chance, and decided to move the company's
headquarters from Arad to Pest. In 1856, he and his son Bernát established Ignác Deutsch & Son, a crop merchant enterprise that received
wholesale rights from the magistrate of the city of Pest. They acquired a
building in Nádor Street in the heart of downtown. The house in Nádor
Street served as the headquarters for Ignác Deutsch & Son as well as
their new private residence, while they also kept the Arad operations
running.

In 1864, a new chapter opened for the family enterprise when Ignác
Deutsch & Son became a publicly traded company. As the center of crop
trade shifted from the countryside to Pest, the one and only noteworthy
mill in the city was no longer sufficient to support the booming grain
business. The Deutsch family joined forces with other entrepreneurs to

establish the First Buda Steam Mill Association, as well as Concordia Steam Mill. Most of their business partners had already been related to the Deutsch family as spouses, cousins, or in-laws.

Three years later, in 1867, Ignác Deutsch once again demonstrated his outstanding entrepreneurial skills. He invested in land, paving the road toward the fortune of future generations. He purchased a baroque castle sitting on a twenty-acre property in the town of Hatvan, about forty miles northeast of Pest, just as the new railroad was being completed between the two cities. This lavish thirty-two-room mansion, justifiably called a castle, would play a major role in the family's life up until World War II.

Ignác Deutsch died in 1873, the same year when Hungary's old capital, Buda, was united with Óbuda (old Buda) and the city of Pest, creating a new metropolis: Budapest. Ignác left behind a very prosperous company, Ignác Deutsch & Son, the Concordia Steam Mill, over ten thousand acres of land, the castle in Hatvan, and further properties in Arad and its vicinity and in Budapest.

Eighteen seventy-three also brought a serious financial crisis to the Austro-Hungarian Empire, and a depression to Europe and North America that lasted for the rest of the decade. The crash of 1873 forced many out of business. In this turmoil, Ignác's son Bernát took the helm of the company, aided by his brother József. They were trading in a commodity that was essential even during the economic depression: grain. The Deutsch family had significant liquid assets, and didn't shy away from taking risks. At a time when the majority of companies were forced to sell their shares, the family started buying. By the end of the decade, most of the country's capital was concentrated in the hands of just a few entrepreneurs, the Deutsch family being one of them. Bernát Deutsch served on the board of the Pest Branch of the Austrian National Bank, the Hungarian Commerce Bank, the Hungarian Mortgage Bank, the United Budapest Savings Bank, and the Salgótarján Coalmine Corporation, becoming one of the wealthiest taxpayers in Budapest.

Eighteen seventy-nine marked a significant milestone in the history of the Deutsch family, as Austro-Hungarian emperor Franz Joseph elevated Bernát and his brother József to the ranks of Hungarian nobility.

It was sugar that catapulted the Deutsch family into the economic stratosphere. Once a rare and exotic luxury item shipped from countries with tropical or subtropical climate, cane sugar was a highly sought-after condiment in Europe. In the early 1800s, supplies from the Caribbean were cut off by the English shipping blockade during the Napoleonic Wars. This gave rise to the cultivation of sugar beets throughout continental Europe.

The first sugar factory Bernát Deutsch and his brother József purchased in 1879 was in Nagysurány, a town in the former Austro-Hungarian Empire, today Slovakia. Two members of the next generation, József's son Sándor and Bernát's son, my great-grandfather József Jr., soon joined the enterprise. I wish my ancestors were more creative with names than recycling Bernát and József, using them repeatedly in alternating generations. This practice certainly adds an extra layer of difficulty when trying to navigate through the labyrinth that is my family tree.

Sándor and József Jr. both proved themselves as very talented entrepreneurs, making one good business decision and investment after the other, successfully expanding the family's sugar and grain empire.

Without a doubt, Sándor was the most brilliant businessman in the entire family. He started spreading his wings and producing considerable financial gains for the company soon after he finished his economic studies. By 1879 he was already co-owner of Ignác Deutsch & Son with his uncle Bernát and was deeply involved in the start of sugar production at the Nagysurány factory. He demonstrated a great deal of flexibility toward the market and its constantly shifting demands while also being a natural risk taker, a true entrepreneur in every sense of the word.

Sándor took calculated risks not only in business, but in his private life as well. As scandalous as it may seem, he married his first cousin Emma. They had three children: Lajos, Ferenc, and Irén.

In the late 1880s, Sándor and his cousin József Jr. started the construction of a huge factory on their family estate in Hatvan, where sugar production commenced within a year. In less than a decade, two more sugar factories followed, one in Sárvár in western Hungary and another in Oroszka, in today's Slovakia. Sándor became president of the Association of Hungarian Sugar Factories.

This business success was recognized in 1897, when the Deutsch family was given permission by Emperor Franz Joseph to use the hyphenated name: Hatvany-Deutsch (Deutsch of Hatvan).

At the dawn of the twentieth century, members of the Hatvany-Deutsch family were on the board of directors of all major banks in Budapest. Under the leadership of Sándor, the family business had become the sole owner of Concordia Steam Mill, was the principal shareholder in five other steam mills, the Grain Trust, several banks, and four sugar factories. Sándor Hatvany-Deutsch was reported to be the fourth richest person in the country at the time. In 1902, he cofounded the Association of Hungarian Industrialists and became its first president.

In 1908, Austro-Hungarian Emperor Franz Joseph granted my great-grandfather, József Hatvany-Deutsch Jr., and all his family members, including his living and future descendants, the title of baron. Sándor Hatvany-Deutsch, along with his family and descendants, received the same rank two years later. All members of the Hatvany-Deutsch family were now eligible to use the gender-appropriate title baron or baroness in front of their names. They were also given the right to use the newly granted family crest, complete with an extensive list of places and methods of its possible display, as suggested and described meticulously by the emperor himself. This honor was given to the Hatvany-Deutsch family as an acknowledgment of their loyalty, patriotism, and diligence, as well as their economic and charitable contributions to society.

The family's vast agricultural properties, close to twenty thousand acres by 1910, primarily served the sugar factories and mills by supplying the majority of sugar beets and grains grown locally, but they also played a role in other agricultural enterprises such as an animal feed factory and the Hatvan Seed Company. In the early 1930s, the family business expanded again to launch the very profitable Hatvan Tomato Canning Factory. Ignác Deutsch & Son also had interests in timber, textile, asbestos, brick, and shingle manufacturing.

Hungary was one of the last countries in Europe to let go of its feudalistic system, vestiges of which lingered well into the early twentieth century. While many land owners and early industrialists were notorious for the terrible treatment and widespread abuse of their farm and factory workers, the Hatvany-Deutsch family was much liked and respected by locals in Hatvan and surrounding towns. They were known for treating their employees quite well and for contributing to various charities helping those in need. Whether it was in the form of donating food, milk, and clothing items to their workers; distributing Christmas packages among them; organizing cultural events; or making financial contributions to the town's development, the generosity of the Hatvany-Deutsch family was often mentioned in local newspapers. Sándor's will included, among other charities, a foundation for helping widows and orphans of Ignác Deutsch & Son employees, the orphanage of the Israelite parish in Arad, and a significant amount donated to building the women's wing in the Israelite hospital.

When Sándor died in 1913, the newspaper *Pester Lloyd* dedicated an entire page to his obituary. Relatives arrived from Munich, Cannes, Monte Carlo, and Cairo to attend his funeral. Sándor had dedicated his life to the business. He considered it a big game, in which success was not necessarily measured strictly by the resulting profits, but also in the joy of risk-taking.

∽

In three generations, a rags-to-riches story had unfolded. From a corner store, an industrial empire came to life. The transformation of our family name was also complete. As my ancestors became synonymous with the town of Hatvan, members of the next generation gradually dropped the hyphenated *Deutsch* and started using the simplified surname: *Hatvany*.

The family saga did not remain focused solely on building industrial might. Sándor's children, despite their father's prowess in business, pursued different lives. With the exception of his elder son, Bandi, József Jr.'s offspring also chose to pave their own road.

Chapter Three

Splendor

JÓZSEF JR.'S WIFE, my great-grandmother Fanny, was the embodiment of glamour and luxury, an emblem of what it meant to be a wealthy baroness in Hungary in the early 1900s. She was also famously strict and intimidating as the most dominant matriarch in the family's history.

My father never had the chance to know his grandfather József Jr., who died before the First World War, but he remembered his grandmother very well. As a small child, he often visited Fanny in her lavish mansion at 7 Werbőczy Street, today Táncsics Mihály Street, in the Buda Castle District. My father's older cousin Mariella, who had lived with Fanny herself, described details of the house as follows:

> My grandmother had re-decorated and furnished the house
> in the most ornate baroque and rococo style. It was a three-
> story mansion with eight tall windows on the street level
> and a massive center door large enough to accommodate

an automobile. This door had a small door that was used for those on foot. These doors led into a courtyard and the family's living quarters. At the opposite end of the courtyard a door led into a small garden overlooking the Danube River. Houses of this size were often called palaces.

Two sides of the courtyard, on the street level, contained the apartment where my mother and I lived. On the other two sides were the garages and servants' quarters… the small apartment Aunt Tony used when she visited from America and the porter's quarters…

The center door at the end of the courtyard led to the apartment occupied in sumptuous style by my Grandmother and uncle Bandi. These apartments were on the floor above, reached by a museum-wide marble stairway hung with two large Goblin tapestries…. The walls were lined with pillars on which playful amorini, flowers, trailing vines, and frescoes were done in painted stucco, and enhanced by delicate gilded wood and filigree ornamentation. Close to the walls were conversational settings of large upholstered sofas and chairs interspersed with ornate marble-topped tables that held large porcelain urns from grandmother's collection. The ceiling, like ceilings in all the rooms, held lavish glass chandeliers. The room reminded me of the large formal reception rooms I had often walked through in small European palaces….

Next to this large room was an exquisite little sitting room into which no one ever went—at least to my knowledge. It had unusually beautiful walls covered with pieces of oddly shaped silk, each piece in a narrow gold frame. The furniture was dainty rococo, upholstered in silk. It was a silly room because it had no purpose. I can't remember anyone ever using it.

Next came the dining room with its large oval table and interesting frescoes. They were hand-painted to my Grandmother's specifications with landscapes and mythological subjects.

From there one walked into the paneled library. Above its huge fireplace was a ceiling-high mirror that reflected the elaborately decorated ceiling. On either side were bookcases through whose glass doors one could see my Grandmother's priceless collection of books on porcelain. The library was also used as a sitting room, and was comfortably furnished with an arrangement of overstuffed chairs and a large coffee table placed in front of the fireplace, with other chairs and tables in conversational settings.[2]

My father remembered the library that served as the centerpiece for this lavish residence. It was also the place for frequent and elaborate social gatherings. Endless rows of beautiful leather-bound books lined the walls. A lot of them were fine-art related, catering to Fanny's primary interest. Another part of the book collection represented a quite eclectic selection, their age being the only common denominator. Old books had prestige and value, just for being old. Some of them were in German, some in English, others in French, and of course, some were in Hungarian.

A small but very important room was devoted to my Grandmother's famous porcelain collection, consisting mostly of Sevres and Meissen china. It was displayed behind glass on glass shelves. In addition to her porcelain china, there were also exquisite figurines of the daintiest, loveliest figures in all sorts of settings and dress. One typical piece depicted an Austrian Emperor, and his wife and children.

Underneath the glass shelves were slanted open drawers covered in glass that held her special collection of cups and saucers. Each drawer contained a complete tea set—cups, saucers, teapot, sugar and creamer; there were also coffee sets and sets for hot chocolate. I particularly loved looking at a tea set that showed the Empress Theresa with her husband and children.[3]

Some of the many rooms in 7 Werbőczy Street left lasting memories in my father's mind. One was the porcelain room, where he was only allowed to pass through very slowly, with his hands behind his back. Another one was a large, pink-marble bathroom with a huge bathtub in the middle, deep enough to have stairs leading into it. This was an unusual luxury at the time in Hungary, even among the exceptionally privileged.

What enchanted me most were the two large wash basins, side by side, and between them a tiny basin for brushing one's teeth. I was told the reason for the tiny basin was to prevent the big basins from being polluted by teeth cleaning. I've always thought this very funny.

The kitchen was on the top floor so that the cooking odors would not permeate the rest of the house.[4]

His grandmother's sewing room also mesmerized my father as a young boy. I remember him describing it to me with a childish fascination. There was a life-size mannequin, made to Fanny's exact shape and measurements, slightly adjusted as needed, should her figure change. Her dresses were handmade by her seamstress, right there in this dedicated sewing room, but the baroness never had to be disturbed for fittings. The seamstress simply used the mannequin and presented Fanny with the finished product, which fit like a glove.

Those were the days when the wealthy traveled in style, with numerous pieces of matching custom-made luggage and hatboxes, all monogrammed and bearing the family crest. Fanny always traveled with a member of her extensive domestic staff, called *társalkodónő* (a lady companion for conversation). This position was a feudalistic heritage and could be best described as someone providing companionship to a woman of nobility by engaging in sophisticated conversations with her. This lady, a well-read and refined personal assistant, was to arrive at the railway station ahead of Fanny, in order to fit their private first-class cabin with custom-made, monogrammed seat covers. Anecdotally, Fanny once said, she would rather stop traveling altogether should she not be allowed to follow this routine anymore. Of course, she would later adapt to changing times and continue traveling without these allures.

Besides her avid interest in literature and fine art, Fanny successfully ingrained something else in her grandson. My father was subjected to endless and extremely strict lessons in table manners at her house. Every time he visited and stayed for a meal, he had to sit with his feet square on the floor, knees together, his wrists off the table, holding a book under each armpit to keep his elbows by his side, while balancing a third book on top of his head for proper posture. The napkin had its place in his lap, while a sequence of specific silverware was dedicated to each course. My father was not to hold the knife or the fork pointing upward at any time, and he had to place them neatly next to each other on one side of the plate when he finished eating. Talking with his mouth full or touching the food with his hands was just as unimaginable as leaving the table before asking to be excused and being granted permission to do so. Her methods may have been Spartan, borderline cruel, but Fanny's efforts certainly paid off. Perfect table manners became second nature to my father at a very early age. When it came to teaching me the same, he would be just as thorough and consistent as his grandmother had been, though with a much kinder and gentler approach.

Chapter Four

Gift

MEMBERS OF THE NEXT GENERATION were known for their talent and passion for the arts, and for their notable work as philanthropists. Born into privilege and incredible wealth between 1880 and 1900, they all had the opportunity to receive the best education, travel abroad, learn multiple foreign languages at an early age, and be exposed to the finest forms of art and culture. Of course, that alone would not have been enough. Good taste, inherent talent, diligence, and dedication were also crucial ingredients in the making of such remarkable and noteworthy contributors to early-twentieth-century Hungarian literature and fine art.

∽

Lajos was arguably the best-known Hatvany of his generation. Sándor's firstborn son showed little interest in the family business; he was drawn to literature instead. Educated both in Germany and Hungary, Lajos became a writer, a playwright, a critic, a historian of literature, and one of the most significant patrons of contemporary Hungarian prose and poetry. He traveled around Europe, "conversed with Rodin in Paris, Reinhardt in Berlin, published a successful book in Leipzig (*Die Wissenschaft des nicht Wissenswerten* [*The Science of Things Not Worth Knowing*] in 1908), and had his play shown in Munich (*Die Berühmten* [*The Famous*] in 1913)."[5]

Lajos founded several literary journals, the most influential being *Nyugat* (*West*). This progressive periodical became a platform for numerous talented, upcoming writers and poets in the early twentieth century, most notably Endre Ady, one of the greatest Hungarian poets of all time, with whom he developed a very close friendship. In 1915 Lajos moved from the family's house in Nádor Street to his own residence in the Buda Castle District, which served as a venue for several grand intellectual gatherings, so-called salons, frequented by the most prominent actors, painters, writers, and composers of that era. Gizi Bajor, Merse Pál Szinyei, Frigyes Karinthy, Ernő Szép, Thomas Mann, and Béla Bartók were recurring guests.

"In 1917, Lajos became the founder and editor-in-chief of *Pesti Napló* [*Pest Journal*]…that paved the road to Károlyi's [1918 bourgeois-democratic] revolution. It was also here, that he started the literary periodical *Esztendő* [*Year*] with Frigyes Karinthy, Dezső Kosztolányi and Árpád Tóth."[6]

As World War I came to an end, the Austro-Hungarian monarchy collapsed. Hungary went through a chaotic series of political upheavals, starting as a brief flirtation with liberal democracy and quickly devolving into an equally brief Soviet-style communist regime, before finally settling on a conservative nationalistic government.

Count Mihály Károlyi was a member of Parliament during World Word I, becoming the war's most notable critic. In 1916, he formed the United Party of Independence. He argued for peace and looser ties between Austria and Hungary. Károlyi married countess Katinka Andrássy, a member of another very influential Hungarian family. During the so-called Aster Revolution that followed, Károlyi became a leader of the nation. On November 16, 1918, he proclaimed Hungary a democratic republic and became provisional president. On January 11, 1919, he was officially recognized as president. One of Károlyi's main allies during the Aster Revolution was his minister of nationalities, Oszkár Jászi, who himself became a member of the Hatvany family when he married Lajos's cousin, Anna Lesznai, an accomplished poet and artist. Lajos published Anna Lesznai's first poem in *Nyugat*. Anna was also known for her Hungarian folk-art inspired textile and book cover designs. Lajos Hatvany was one of the leading figures in the Aster Revolution along with Károlyi and Jászi. As many of the Hatvanys, he was a leftist, liberal thinker who valued democracy. While he supported Károlyi's ideas, Lajos described the shortcomings of his leadership as follows: "From the discussion no decisions arose, and from the decisions—no actions. A cabinet? No, it was a debating club."[7]

Károlyi's short-lived Hungarian Democratic Republic came to an end with a communist takeover, led by Béla Kun. Károlyi accepted his defeat, retired from politics, and left the country.

The breakup of Austria-Hungary and the resulting 133 days of the communist Hungarian Soviet Republic, which on 21 March 1919 followed the democratic government, destroyed the pact between the ruling political class and Hungarian Jewry. The fact that the leaders of the communist regime were overwhelmingly of Jewish origin, such as Béla Kun, the strong man in the Revolutionary Governing Council, provided a convenient pretext for equating Jews and communism, even though most Jews had rejected Bolshevism. When in November 1919 Admiral Miklós Horthy entered Budapest on a white stallion at the head of the White National Army, he called the Hungarian capital in his speech "the sinful city." That was the signal for vehement anti-Semitism. The Red Terror of the Soviet dictatorship was quickly superseded by the even more relentless White Terror of the right-wing officer detachments and paramilitary organisations.... Having risen to unique heights in the Monarchy, the Hungarian Jewish community now found itself the first anywhere in Europe after the First World War to be subjected to anti-Jewish legislation. In 1920 parliament passed a law [Numerus Clausus] restricting the entry of Jewish students to University.[8]

Like Károlyi, Lajos Hatvany also chose immigration. For the next eight years he lived in Vienna, but became terribly homesick and decided to return to Hungary in 1927, risking humiliation and imprisonment. Lajos Hatvany opposed the communist regime, but he was also a harsh and very outspoken critic of Horthy's conservative nationalist administration. For his role in the Aster Revolution, he was sentenced to a year and a half in prison. Due to health reasons, he was released after nine months. The family worried about their business and reputation suffering because of Lajos's involvement in the Aster Revolution, so they bought him out of Ignác Deutsch & Son.

Lajos Hatvany's most famous novel, *Urak és emberek* (loosely translated as *Lords and Men*) was written in 1927, and was partially translated into English in 1931 as *Bondy Jr.* Though technically a fiction, the book contains many autobiographical elements and is often compared to Thomas Mann's family saga, *Buddenbrooks*.

Ferenc Hatvany, Lajos's younger brother, did not show much interest in the family business either. A very talented and accomplished painter, he studied from various masters in Hungary as well as in Paris. His works still surface from time to time at auctions in Budapest. Ferenc was an outstanding painter in his own right, but most people associate his name with his legendary art collection. Some even called him the Rockefeller of Europe. His baroque mansion in the Buda Castle District was the home of exquisite furniture, sixteenth-century tapestry, and countless decorative items he carefully hand selected during his travels throughout Europe.

Ferenc became famous for his incredible collection of paintings by Ingres, Pissarro, Delacroix, Constable, Bonnard, Degas, Corot, Courbet, Renoir, Manet, Cézanne, Chassériau, Daumier, Gauguin, Picasso, El Greco, and Tintoretto, along with the works of contemporary Hungarian artists such as Szinyei, Csontváry, Rippl-Rónai, Munkácsy, Mednyánszky, Derkovics, Fényes, Lotz, Ferenczy, Czóbel, and Paál. His collection expanded to more than seven hundred pieces. It was not the largest in the country, but was widely considered to be one of the finest.

According to family anecdotes, the monumentally rich sugar baron and illustrious philanthropist Sándor Hatvany-Deutsch invited former and future Prime Minister Sándor Wekerle to his country estate in 1904. In the awe-inspiring park surrounding the castle in Hatvan, the host introduced his sons to Hungary's head of government…"This one"—pointing to Lajos, who had just received his doctorate summa cum laude—"is a philosopher, and that fellow with his starveling looks"—gesturing toward Ferenc, the outstanding painter and art collector—"is even worse."[9]

Irén Hatvany was the youngest of Sándor's three children. Like all her relatives, Irén grew up learning foreign languages, traveling around Europe, and maturing into a well-read and well-cultured person. She married an ambitious young university graduate, Albert Hirsch in 1905. Unlike her brothers Lajos and Ferenc, who didn't express any interest in pursuing the family business, Irén would have liked to be involved, but as a woman, she was neither accepted nor encouraged to do so. Hence her husband, Albert Hirsch, stepped in. "After the death of her father, Irén occupied herself with raising her daughter Emma, decorating the Castle and developing the park, spending more and more time in Hatvan. She witnessed tremendous backwardness and poverty, and identified with the problems of the town and the estate. Her own wealth weighed heavily on her mind, as well as the knowledge that she, as a woman, was unable to make changes. Her social sensitivity was very highly developed. She helped those in need with sincere empathy."[10]

∽

My great-grandfather József Jr. and his wife, Fanny, had four children: Lili, Endre, Antonia, and my grandfather Bernát, who used the name Bertalan, a slightly different version of Bernard, probably in an effort to distinguish himself from his grandfather, Bernát Sr.

Lili was the oldest, blossoming into a talented writer as a young girl. As her daughter Mariella writes in her memoir: "My mother started writing stories as a small child and at the age of eight my grandfather had one of her stories printed, which infuriated my grandmother, who favored her two sons."[11] Lili Hatvany grew up to become a successful playwright and novelist, publishing her works in Hungarian, German, and Italian during the 1920s and '30s.

> My mother was not only beautiful and talented, she was very witty; when she was in the mood, she could be hysterically funny. She lived a scintillating social life while keeping up her reputation as one of Hungary's most popular playwrights.
>
> There was hardly a week that she didn't give a magnificent party—either a luncheon, a formal dinner party, or a dinner dance followed by a buffet. These entertainments were attended not only by Budapest's literati, actors, musicians, concert stars and members of embassies and legations, but also by any luminaries from Hollywood visiting in Budapest.

A frequent caller at our house, both in person and by telephone, was my Mother's friend, the playwright Ferenc Molnár. He served as a barometer for the success or failure of her plays. If, on the morning after an opening night Ferenc phoned to congratulate her on her new play, she knew it was a failure. If there was no telephone call, she felt assured the play was going to be a success. Those telephone calls became a standing joke in Budapest.[12]

Endre (Bandi) joined Ignác Deutsch & Son in 1916. In his generation, he was more involved in the family business than any of his siblings or cousins, with the exception of Irén's husband, Albert Hirsch. Bandi's idea, the Hatvan Tomato Canning Factory, became a very successful enterprise by the 1930s, despite Albert's initial hesitation and disagreement. The tomatoes were mostly grown in the family's estate in Hatvan, the sheet metal was imported from England, and the cans were manufactured at the factory. The tomato puree, processed and canned locally, was not only popular in Hungary but was also exported to England and to the Benelux countries. Bandi was also an avid sportsman, spending a lot of time in Hatvan, riding horses and enjoying country life, but there seems to be a consensus among descendants referring to him as one with a rather difficult personality. Apparently, Bandi and my grandfather Bertalan did not get along very well.

Antonia (Tony) studied architecture, a rather unusual choice for a woman in early twentieth century Hungary. "Aunt Tony had been a Red Cross nurse in Budapest during the first World War. By the early 1930s, well aware of the storm clouds forming over Europe and eager to detach herself from her dominating Mother, she migrated to the United States."[13]

Chapter Five

Leather

My grandfather Bertalan Hatvany was born in 1900, on the family estate in Hatvan. Growing up, he was exposed to city life in Budapest, with its culture, theaters, museums, and frequent social gatherings, as well as to a much quieter country life in Hatvan. Unlike his older brother, Bandi, he never developed the slightest interest in outdoor activities or sport; therefore, Budapest was a much more suitable playground for him.

When it came to choosing a profession, he had absolutely no idea which road to take, so his family made a decision for him. Bertalan studied chemistry and business in Budapest and continued his education in Hamburg and Berlin before briefly working in New York. To say he was not at all enthusiastic about any of these potential career paths would be an understatement. As he would later reminisce, "I was wasting the time of my employer in a New York office in 1925, and writing sad Hungarian poems to pass time." My grandfather had a life-changing experience when he embarked on a long tour of Asia before returning to Hungary. Something immediately touched him about that continent. The rich and mysterious history, the works of art, their philosophy resonated with him more than anything else in the first twenty-five years of his life. Exploring Asia became his real passion, something he remained deeply drawn to for the rest of his life.

Soon after returning to Hungary, Bertalan did another thing his family expected him to do. He married a perfectly suitable woman chosen for him by his mother and future mother-in-law. There is no doubt it was an arranged marriage. Fanny was a good friend of Erzsébet Wolfner, whose family owned Gyula Wolfner & Co. Leather Factory. Erzsébet Wolfner's own marriage was an arranged union as well. Her husband, Erich Hesselberger, a German industrialist, was also in the leather business. It seemed a brilliant idea to add a prosperous sugar dynasty to the two previously merged leather factories. It was also a very practical idea, since my grandmother was a handful as a teenager, and her mother Erzsébet was worried she would ruin the family's reputation should she stay single and continue her scandalous behavior. Anecdotally, she would sneak out of her parents' house on weekends to spend time with boys, once going as far as hiding in the overhead rack of a train. She also entertained the thought of becoming an actress, which was considered unacceptable in those days in her family's elite circles. My great-grandmother Erzsébet Wolfner was relieved to give away her older daughter at the age of nineteen to a respectable and very eligible groom, thus merging three wealthy conglomerates.

My grandmother, Maria Veronica (Vera) Hesselberger, was born in Munich in 1906. Her sister, Marion Ruth (Marutha) Hesselberger, remembered their early childhood as follows:

> I was born December 31, 1911—New Year's Eve—in my parents' apartment…in Munich. My mother was Hungarian, and had moved to Germany…when she married my father. My father was German, from a large family in Munich. I had an older sister, Vera, who was born nine months after my parents were married. I remember my father only vaguely because he was killed at Verdun in March of 1916 at the age of 39. He joined the German army early in the war, so I hadn't seen much of him. My strongest memory of him is he coming into my room to kiss me goodnight, like all parents do, to say goodnight to their small children. I remember he was smoking a cigarette, and that was very intriguing because the room was dark and he could make circles and sort of figurines with the cigarette. Then he kissed me good night and went out. Also among my earliest remembrances is my Grandmother Hesselberger, who…was always called Bertchen, which means "little Bertha". Her husband…and his brothers had founded a leather business, Gebrüder Hesselberger [Hesselberger Brothers], in the 1870s, and by the time I was born it had become quite a large firm…My mother's family, the Wolfners were very different. They were also in the leather business, but on a larger scale than my father's family. Wolfner & Son, the family business, had

been founded in the early 1800s, and by the time I was born was one of the larger industrial groups in Hungary. The business was run by my mother's father, who was the senior member of the, by that time, large extended family.[14]

Vera and Marutha grew up very privileged, surrounded by governesses and a domestic staff of eleven, living a luxurious lifestyle in Munich, similar to the lives of the Wolfners and the Hatvanys in Hungary. Just like the Wolfners, the Hesselbergers also made an immense fortune during World War I, since leather was vital for the army. But the war did not spare them from suffering:

> The war and its aftermath brought very difficult times. I remember when the war broke out, not that I understood what it was all about. But I remember that my mother cried and cried and that she was so terribly, terribly upset. I remember my father vaguely at that point, because he kissed me goodnight and then he appeared in uniform. Because the family business was involved in war production and supplied the German Army, it was decided that one of the brothers should enlist. My father volunteered as Lieutenant…I remember the terrible time when the news was brought that he had died in battle and how my mother cried. I remember her crying and crying and that she did not talk to me. My grandmother and the family established a hospital for soldiers in memory of my father.[15]

Dark clouds started gathering in the early 1920s, well before Hitler rose to power. After losing the war, Germany had to pay reparations, which resulted in hyperinflation and an economic disaster. Amid the desperate situation, the Nazi party gained strength, blaming everything from capitalism to trade unions and the communists, but more than anything, they blamed the so-called Jewish conspiracy for all their troubles. The Nazis' undisguised anti-Semitism and rapidly growing influence became painfully obvious to Marutha, my grandmother's younger sister, even at a tender age:

> Both the Hesselberger and the Wolfner families were well known and were considered "Jewish." Members of the families had in many cases married Christians, and many of my generation had converted to Christianity. The Wolfners had been ennobled by Franz Joseph. Two family members had married Austrian Countesses and one was reputed to have had an affair with a member of the British royal family. My father had given his life as an officer in the German Army. My mother was Lutheran and I was a Lutheran. My sister was brought up as a Catholic. There were few Jewish people in the schools I went to, or in my mother's circle. I didn't consider myself Jewish and hadn't given it much thought.
>
> But the Hesselberger family was well known in Munich, they were prosperous, and they had been engaged in war production. There was a lot of resentment of "war profiteers" and a search for scapegoats. Munich was where Hitler started his movement and where Nazism first flourished in the confusion following the war. Hitler had a lot of

adherents in Bavaria and tried to stage a coup in Munich in 1923. By the early 1920s, religion had become an issue for me.

After the war there was a lot of malnutrition and starvation. My mother was asked to take in some people and give them food. She was given two young children, a boy and a girl. The boy was called Hansi. He was about 10 years old. And the girl was, I think, 11 or 12. I have not a good recollection of her because she apparently didn't like the food or didn't like to come and she stayed away. But Hansi came for a long time and became somebody to talk to, for me. He was very friendly. The servants all liked him. Before he went home, they would give him a lot of food to take with him. Hansi also got shoe leather. He got clothing coupons and anything my mother could spare in the way of something warm, that would help him and his family. Eventually Hansi stopped coming. A little while after that he came back to see us, but by that time was already in the Hitler Youth, and appeared in his uniform. From what I hear, he made a fantastic career in the SS and did a lot of harm.

One of my most intimate friends at school at the time was a girl named Inge Pröhl. We saw each other after school—I went to her house and she came to my house, to spend the rest of the afternoon. Suddenly, one day when I visited her, her mother came into the room, and she said, "Please don't come to the house anymore. You're not really very welcome here." I couldn't understand what she was talking about. I didn't know why. I hadn't done anything wrong. Certainly Inge hadn't told me anything. Inge went on to marry the brother of Rudolf Hess, who was an early and prominent member of Hitler's entourage. [Rudolf Hess was Hitler's deputy, not to be confused with Rudolf Höss (Hoess), who was commandant at Auschwitz. Ingeborg (Inge) Pröhl married Alfred Hess, Rudolf Hess' brother. Rudolf Hess married Inge's sister, Ilse Pröhl.] At the time I just puzzled and puzzled. But then it started to dawn on me. Other people started to withdraw. I read the newspaper and I started to see pictures of Mr. Hitler in the newspaper, and I understood what was going to happen. At that time I was very involved in the Turnverein, an athletic and gymnastic club. I was always a good athlete, and very good at gymnastics. I loved going to the Turnverein, which was sort of a 20-minute bicycle ride from the apartment. I had a lot of friends there and loved to do the exercises and the trampoline (I was very good at jumping). One day my mother came to me and said "No more. If you really want to do gymnastics, I'll arrange for private lessons, but you can't go to the Turnverein anymore. It's not suitable." I understood that I was going to be excluded from a lot of other things. Friends withdrew. We dropped out of the Tennis Club. My mother didn't want me to go to dances. I felt very isolated and very sad about things.

In 1925, around the time all this was happening, my sister Vera, got engaged to, and married a Hungarian, Baron Bertalan Hatvany. The marriage, of course, took place in Munich, Catered by Walterspiel. It was a big, big event. While we weren't very close, I felt very sad of losing her as a good friend and sister and being isolated. The marriage was an unforeseen event in my life because I thought I would always have her close to me, but suddenly she wasn't.[16]

Sometime in the late 1920s, Marutha fell in love with a young man in Munich. They were very happy, and she thought he would make a perfectly suitable husband. One day, they went to a grand party together, where she wore a beautiful new dress made just for the occasion. As the evening progressed, the gentleman asked her to join him on the balcony so they could have a private conversation. Marutha was bursting with excitement. She was convinced that the love of her life would ask for her hand in marriage. Much to her shock, instead of proposing, he broke up with her. He said he couldn't continue seeing her because she was a Jew. She was heartbroken.

Marutha visited Vera from Germany, but unlike her sister, she never learned to like Hungary. Despite making some half-hearted attempts to learn some Hungarian, she did not master the language, remaining an outsider in Vera's adopted country:

> I really never liked Budapest very much, and always tried to go someplace where I would meet people of my own age. Budapest seemed very, very backward to me. In my grandparents' house, there were lots of servants and they

always tried to kiss the hem of your skirt, which I hated. I thought it was terrible. They made curtseys. They retired backward, out of the room. That didn't appeal to me at all. Germany was entirely different. People walked forward, not backwards, like that. When my sister lived there, she loved it. She spoiled me with going to the dressmaker, having clothes made from scratch, of course; and shoes made to measure, of course. Nobody would ever think of buying a pair of shoes that came out of a shop. No, the feet were measured, each foot separately. The leather had to be the finest and the best. Of course, they lasted forever.[17]

Chapter Six
Privilege

NOVEMBER 18, 1926, marked the birth of my father, József Erik István Hatvany. Likely the first in his family to be delivered in a hospital, at the Clinics of Üllői Street in Budapest, he was born with a silver spoon in his mouth. His inherited socioeconomic status was undoubtedly glamorous and enviable, but nobility and wealth came at a price. As a consequence of being born an incredibly rich baron, he was rather isolated from his parents. It was customary for someone in my grandmother's circles to have a wet nurse instead of breastfeeding one's own child, as well as leave him almost entirely in the hands of nannies and governesses. Vera, my grandmother, would sit in the living room midafternoon and ring a little bell. The nanny would bring in my father so she could spend some time with him. When Vera felt she had performed a sufficient amount of her motherly duties, she would ring the bell again, and my father was promptly whisked away. It is hard to tell whether this kind of

daily routine was the first crack in their very fragile and later tumultu-
ous relationship, but it certainly did not serve as a strong building block
establishing a solid bond between mother and son. József had a number
of consecutive nannies and later governesses taking care of him, and they
left him with kinder, warmer memories than he had of his own parents.

József's early memories of Bertalan were much fonder than those of
Vera. Their taste for simple food brought them closer, forming an alliance
against my grandmother. They weren't supposed to eat such a Hungarian staple as white bread with a spread of lard, seasoned with salt and
paprika, and topped with slices of red onions. In Vera's opinion, it was
for "commoners," as she put it, not for barons. My grandfather and my
father entered into a conspiracy with the kitchen staff in order to enjoy a
few bites now and then, behind my grandmother's back. Sadly, the smell
of onions always gave them away.

Sometime in the late 1920s, Vera sent Bertalan to a resort in Switzerland, where he was put on a strictly supervised diet in hopes of losing
some weight. Her attempt failed miserably. Bertalan managed to slip out
of this luxurious but rather restrictive spa unnoticed and enjoyed several
evenings on the town, indulging in decadent dinners washed down with
large quantities of fine wine. When my grandmother came to visit and
check on his progress, he put on a new shirt two sizes bigger than usual
and proudly showed her how loose it was around his neck. He couldn't
fool her. Vera stormed out with utter disappointment. Upon returning
home, she tried to make my grandfather adhere to a lean diet, but it
didn't take. When he finished his small portion of plain, boring dinner,
he asked the cook in secret to bring a plate of real Hungarian food to
his study, something the staff would eat. He hid the empty plates behind
the furniture, but the fragrant smells of heavy, sauce-laden dishes such

as stuffed cabbage, chicken, or beef stew with gnocchi and sour cream betrayed him.

∼

The marriage between Bertalan Hatvany and Vera Hesselberger was very short lived. My father was only four years old when his parents separated, and five when the divorce came through. Even while married, Vera continued to live on the edge, as far as her social behavior was concerned. She was once pictured on the pages of a boulevard magazine engaging in a catfight with a young actress at a bar in Budapest. The two women were tugging on each other's hair, competing for a gentleman's attention. This was a despicable scandal, of course, and for my grandfather the last straw that broke the camel's back. After the divorce, my father lived with, and was primarily raised by, Bertalan, but he also spent some time with Vera, especially summer vacations at Lake Balaton and at various exquisite resorts around Europe.

As a young divorcée and socialite, Vera lived quite a lavish life in Budapest. She took a fabulous apartment in the heart of Pest, where she entertained select members of Budapest's aristocracy during the 1930s. She enjoyed everything the country could offer to a very wealthy, young, and attractive woman. She had numerous affairs, one of them said to be with the son of a well-known political figure, but the relationship was unsustainable because of her Jewish heritage.

Vera was not the only one appearing on the pages of boulevard magazines. Bertalan had his share of public scandals too. As unlikely as it may sound, given his immaculate manners and absolute indifference toward any kind of athletic activity, he was once involved in a bloody sword duel. It was in the fall of 1935. He was spending the evening at a bar in Budapest. A man who undoubtedly had had far too many drinks came up to him and asked if he could dance with the lady accompanying my grandfather. Before Bertalan had a chance to answer, the intruder provoked a fistfight. The waiters promptly removed him from the site, but according to the rather feudalistic etiquette of the time, this type of insult between two gentlemen of nobility called for a duel. Both parties named their assistants, who were responsible for choosing the appropriate weapon and facilitating the duel itself. They decided to settle the difference between the opposing parties with swords and agreed on a format they called "fight until complete exhaustion, without piercing." Both men sustained minor injuries.

Bertalan was expected to be involved in the family business. For a while, he reluctantly showed up at the offices of Corcordia Steam Mill every morning around ten, shuffled papers, made a fuss when he found grammatical mistakes in the firm's foreign-language correspondence, and sat through some business meetings that he found incredibly boring. As he was notorious for speaking extremely slowly, the members of the board needed all their patience to wait for the end of his sentences, even though he possessed a sophisticated vocabulary of a well-read intellectual. Bertalan soon dropped his responsibilities at Concordia and dedicated his time to his true interests: Hungarian literature, Asian history and culture, and, as a young divorced man, late-night culinary delights with fine wine on the town and a colorful social life.

Ever since he stepped foot in Asia, studying oriental history and culture remained my grandfather's real passion. He contacted various respected scholars of history, read everything he could get his hands on, and very diligently educated himself without ever taking a formal course in this topic. He meticulously studied the ancient history of China and India, expressed interest in the origins of these nations, and was especially fascinated by their art and culture. His papers titled *Asia and Nationalism* and *China and its Jews* appeared in Hungarian periodicals in the early 1930s. Bertalan was elected secretary of the Hungarian Oriental Association, where he gave several lectures on Chinese sculptures, paintings, and porcelain. In 1935 his first book, *Ázsia lelke* (*Asia's Soul*), was published. It earned him an honorary doctorate from the University of Pécs.

My grandfather's parental skills, however, left a lot to be desired, as he would only spend an hour with his son every afternoon. Just like Bertalan's colleagues at Concordia Steam Mill, my father's patience was put to the test when he had to listen to my grandfather's endless stories and lengthy explanations, talking very slowly. Nonetheless, he enjoyed Bertalan's vast knowledge of the world's culture and history.

My grandfather had a rather unusual daily schedule. He was deep asleep in the morning when the chauffeur drove my father to school, only to wake up for lunch. He took a long bath in the afternoon, often educating his son from the bathtub. My father would sit outside, listening to him from the other side of the door, which was cracked open just enough for them to have a conversation without actually seeing each other. After finishing his bath and simultaneously fulfilling his fatherly duties, Bertalan got dressed, had a couple of drinks, usually whisky, and went out for dinner, leaving his son with the governess and the rest of the staff. For this, he didn't feel guilty at all, but he felt sorry for his driver having to sit in the car in front of the restaurant all night, waiting for him, especially in the winter. Bertalan sent his chauffeur home by tram, and he himself attempted to drive back to the house. My father recalled a number of occasions when he woke up to a loud crashing noise before dawn. After having one too many drinks, it was quite a challenge for my grandfather to navigate through the narrow gate of their house in the Buda hills. He often missed. Fortunately, there was very little traffic in the streets of Budapest in the 1930s, especially in the middle of the night. Only his automobile suffered damage.

Chapter Seven
Poetry

BERTALAN EMBRACED contemporary Hungarian literature in more ways than one. In 1934 he became acquainted with Attila József, a struggling young poet who turned out to be one of the greatest talents the country has ever seen. Born into extreme poverty, not knowing where his next meal would come from, fighting schizophrenia, and balancing on the border of crazy and genius, Attila József made a very significant mark on Hungarian literature and history during his short life of only thirty-two years. In December 1935, Bertalan Hatvany, Attila József, writer-journalists Pál Ignotus and Ferenc Fejtő, and publisher Imre Cserépfalvi became the founders of *Szép Szó* (*Beautiful Word*), a very progressive literary periodical. Their main goal of creating such a journal was to give Attila József a platform to publish his poems. Bertalan financed *Szép Szó* and also acted as editor. The group met either at his house or at Lajos Hatvany's. My grandfather also contributed to the publication as a writer himself, sometimes under his real name, but mostly using the alias János Mondjuk, which translates to something like John Pretend.

By the time I went to school, an in-depth study of Attila József's life and poems was on the curriculum. His birthday, April 11, would become the National Day of Poetry, and most towns in Hungary have at least one street named after him. Both my grandfather and his cousin Lajos Hatvany supported him financially, as they did with many other upcoming and promising writers and poets of that time. However, it was Bertalan who stood by Attila in his last years, when his schizophrenia took the best of him. It was my grandfather who saved him from being thrown into a mental hospital notorious for its cruel treatments and prisonlike atmosphere. Instead, he placed him in a much more accommodating sanatorium, the *Siesta*, which he, of course, paid for. He visited Attila until his untimely death, a tragedy that is believed to have been suicide, but some consider it an accident. I heard it from my grandfather in person, and also read in interviews he gave in his later years, that he considered his personal friendship with Attila József the biggest and proudest achievement of his life. He wished he had been able to help Attila to a greater extent both financially and in his struggle with mental illness. Bertalan was humbled and deeply honored when Attila dedicated one of his late poems, *Költőnk és Kora* (*Our Poet and His Time*) to him.

My father had his own personal recollection of Attila József. One day, after the chauffeur drove him home from school, he was anxiously waiting for lunch. He was hungry. My grandfather and Attila were sitting in the library, engaging in a heated discussion. It could have been literature, politics, or any other topic for that matter—my father didn't pay attention, nor was he old enough to understand it. All he cared about was lunch. After some time that seemed an eternity, the butler appeared in the library and said, "Mr. Baron, lunch is served." My grandfather and Attila did not want to be interrupted. It was quite some time before they finally got up and walked over to the dining room. Just as they were about to enter, a large chunk of the ceiling's elaborate stucco, together with a heavy crystal chandelier, fell straight onto the dining table. A thick cloud of dust covered the dining room along with plaster and shattered glass. Lunch had to be delayed even further, but the passionate and lengthy exchange of thoughts between these two intellectuals spared everyone from injury or possibly worse.

Along with Attila József and the other cofounders of *Szép Szó*, my grandfather had a close relationship with several representatives of Hungarian literature. Bertalan and his cousin Lajos were also well acquainted with German novelist, philanthropist, and 1929 Nobel Prize in literature laureate Thomas Mann, whom they gladly hosted in their homes both in Budapest and in Hatvan when he visited Hungary. Interestingly enough, Thomas Mann's son Klaus and my grandmother Vera had been classmates at school in Munich. I don't know whether it was Bertalan or Lajos who introduced Attila József to Thomas Mann, but it was certainly at one of the Hatvany salons where they first met. In early 1937 Attila József wrote a beautiful poem honoring his German friend, with the title *Thomas Mann üdvözlése* (*Welcome to Thomas Mann*), expressing his worries about the gathering clouds, foreshadowing the troubled times Europe and Hungary were about to face:

> Appalled we ask: More than what went before,
> What horror has the future yet in store?
> What ravening thoughts will seize us for their prey?
> What poison, brewing now, eat us away?

And, if your lecture can put off that doom,

How long may you still count upon a room?[18]

⌒

My father spent his early childhood in a beautiful, spacious villa in the Buda hills, with a huge private garden and a domestic staff of seven: a butler, a cook, a laundress, a maid, a chauffeur, a gardener, and a governess. Prominent figures of contemporary Hungarian literature were frequent guests at my grandfather's house. Thousands of books lined the walls of their extensive library. Ancient Chinese sculptures from the Ming, Wei, and Tang Dynasties were on display throughout the house along with fourth-century artwork from India, items my grandfather collected and brought back during his first trip to Asia in 1925.

Bertalan was a true polyglot. Not only did he speak fluent English, French, German, Italian, and Spanish in addition to his very refined and sophisticated native Hungarian, he also taught himself Chinese and Hindi and understood some Hebrew as well.

Despite the undeniable emotional distance it created between him and his parents, my father's rather formal upbringing had some inherent benefits. Having been raised by a succession of three governesses who were native speakers of English, French, and German, respectively, József was fluent in three foreign languages before he started fifth grade. After finishing elementary school, he was enrolled in one of the best educational facilities in Budapest: the Hungarian Royal Teacher Training School, which was at the time also known as the Minta or Mintagimnázium (the Exemplar School). This was a combined middle school and high school that students would attend from fifth to twelfth grade.

Ágoston Trefort Teacher Training School, or just Trefort, as it is called today, was established in 1872, and it remains one of the highest-ranking schools in Hungary. Its walls have seen many students who later became famous around the world, such as Theodor Karman, Edward Teller, and Béla Bartók. One of my father's former classmates at the Minta, Peter Lax, would become professor of mathematics at New York University, receiving the prestigious Abel Prize in 2005, the award known as the Nobel Prize for mathematicians. I exchanged emails with him in 2012, and he very kindly wrote to me that he remembered my father as a proper, aristocratic young gentleman. Although he couldn't recall any particular conversation with him after more than seventy years, he remembered attending József's birthday party at my grandfather's exquisite home in the Buda hills.

Besides receiving the best education available in the country, my father also had the opportunity to study music and take horse-riding lessons. I once asked him why and when he abandoned playing the violin. He told me he had cut his left middle finger, severing a nerve, and he couldn't bend the last segment of that finger anymore, hence losing his ability to play this delicate instrument.

He adored his two dogs. One of them was a terrier that loved swimming with him in Lake Balaton, where my father spent most of his summers with his mother. The other dog, a Saint Bernard, earned his respect by keeping strangers away from the house with just a little growl when they came too close to the fence, and impressed him with her laid-back attitude. Sári didn't need to bark, my father reminisced; her mere presence demanded respect from people passing by.

This idyllic lifestyle; this privileged and carefree childhood; the lavish mansion with the chauffeur, the cook, the gardener, the governesses, and all other members of the expansive staff soon became something of the past. Suddenly, as if someone had pulled the rug from under his feet, József's life drastically changed. Everything and everybody familiar to him, including his friends, classmates, and even his beloved dogs, would turn into memory.

Chapter Eight

Exile

THE FIRST JEWISH LAW in Hungary was introduced in May 1938. Emulating the Nürnberg Laws of Germany and following in the footsteps of Hungary's Numerus Clausus of 1920, these anti-Jewish measures set quotas limiting the number of Jews in the press and in various commercial enterprises. Only 20 percent of doctors, engineers, and lawyers, as well as freelance intellectuals, were allowed to be Jewish. In small companies, employing more than ten people in commercial, financial and industrial enterprises, a maximum of 20 percent could be Jewish. These laws of 1938 defined Jews on religious grounds. Although they paled in comparison to the much harsher second and third Jewish Laws that followed in 1939 and 1941, the ones that defined Jews on ethnic grounds and eventually banned marriage and penalized sexual relationships between Jews and non-Jews, these sanctions of 1938 immediately made everyone of Jewish heritage a second-class citizen.

My grandfather Bertalan felt he had no place in Hungary anymore. He feared things would soon turn much worse. His decision to leave Hungary before it was too late turned out to be one of the best decisions he made in his entire life. In the summer of 1938, he took his eleven-year-old son and placed him in a boarding school in England. He himself embarked on a nine-month-long adventure through India, Indochina, and Indonesia.

Bertalan was not the only member of the Hatvany family who felt the urge to leave Hungary in 1938. His cousin Lajos chose immigration for the second time in his life. He settled in England. My grandfather's sister Lili and her daughter Mariella made preparations to leave Budapest. They joined Lili's sister Antonia in New York, where she had been living since the 1920s. Nevertheless, my great-grandmother Fanny, my grandfather's brother Bandi, and two of their cousins, Irén and Ferenc, all stayed in Hungary. So did my grandmother Vera.

◦∾◦

Lili received a contract from Metro-Goldwyn-Mayer to write movie scripts in Hollywood. Before leaving Budapest with her daughter, she gave a lavish farewell party for more than eighty people. The city's crème de la crème was invited, including famous artists, distinguished aristocrats, and diplomats accredited to Hungary. According to a report in the magazine *Futár* (*Courier*), the ambassadors from Greece, England, France, and Poland were present, along with the representatives of the Belgian and American embassies and the Romanian military attaché. Mr. Cartier and his wife were there, as well as Mr. Pallavicini, Mária Kornfeld, Mandfréd Weiss's grandchildren, and such Hungarian dignitaries

as Károly Széchenyi and Gyula Batthyány. Three of the most famous
actresses of the 1930s, if not the history of Hungarian theater itself, Lili
Darvas, Ella Gombaszögi, and Lili Muráti were also present. But it was
obvious to all the guests that fulfilling her contract in Hollywood was
not the main reason for Lili's departure.

> The entire evening was overshadowed by sorrow. People
> were indeed sad, as Lili Hatvany is the most popular
> woman in Pest…It was a rather nice evening, this farewell
> party. Everyone was delighted. This is a rare thing, because
> when two people quietly say goodbye, crying and hugging
> each other, it is a sad and touching event. But mass fare-
> wells are usually not sincere. People gather in an official
> manner and everyone's mind is somewhere else, not much
> to do with one's heart and emotions. But Lili Hatvany's
> farewell was serious and sad. Nobody was joking. Cyni-
> cism was silent this evening. Friends were really sorry for
> baroness Lili.[19]

Upon arrival in America, Lili's daughter Mariella lived mostly in
New York. She occasionally visited her mother in Hollywood and found
herself in social settings reminding her of their former life in Budapest:
"She still gave exciting parties and we occasionally attended them. In
fact, I met Vivien Leigh at my Mother's house one night before *Gone
with the Wind* was released and she became well known. I found her fascinating and glamorous."[20]

Antonia (Tony) learned architecture in Hungary and worked as a nurse during World War I. Soon after her move to the US, she studied law and became a member of the American Arbitration Association. Mariella remembered moving to the United States and reuniting with her aunt as follows:

"Each of us brought with us whatever treasured possessions we could pack or ship…Aunt Tony had a small ground floor apartment with a lovely little patio on East 29th Street between Park and Madison Avenues, and a Czechoslovakian cook, so I was able to adapt slowly to less exotic American food. On another floor lived Miss Frances Kellor, a fascinating old woman who was Aunt Tony's employer."[21]

Miss Kellor was a woman of extraordinary ability. Raised in poverty in a single-parent home, she graduated from Cornell University Law School and became a legal scholar and prominent political activist for immigrant rights and education, women's rights, and prison reform. She assisted in the 1912 presidential campaign of Theodore Roosevelt, helping to write the Progressive Party's platform. Antonia Hatvany worked at the Arbitration Association, which had been cofounded and was being run by Miss Kellor, and in the late 1920s collaborated with her to publish scholarly works on international law and arbitration.

It was Frances Kellor who took Antonia to the White House and introduced her to Eleanor Roosevelt.

My father was thrown into the deep water and quickly had to learn how to swim. Two months before his twelfth birthday, József Hatvany found himself in a prestigious boarding school in Oundle, England. He was probably too young to fully comprehend that this seemingly cruel decision to leave him all by himself in a strange country, away from his family, friends, and everything familiar to him would almost certainly save his life.

Oundle School is a British public school located in the ancient market town of Oundle, in Northamptonshire, near Peterborough. In contrast with the American school system, in the United Kingdom, public schools tend to be more exclusive and more expensive secondary schools than private schools, catering primarily to children between the ages of thirteen and eighteen. Oundle School was established in 1556, but its predecessor, Laxton Grammar School, dated back to the reign of Henry VIII.

The third-largest independent boarding school in England after Eton and Millfield, Oundle School rose to real prominence as an English public school in the late nineteenth and early twentieth centuries. By the 1920s the school had become the leading establishment for science and engineering education, advocating teaching students science, modern languages, and engineering and moving away from the traditional English school system. While it was very progressive as far as its program was concerned, it wasn't until 1990 that the school became coeducational. Apart from the excellent academic curriculum, the boys at Oundle were also taught basic welding, milling, and horseshoeing techniques, which helped build their confidence tremendously. When my father talked about those workshops, his eyes would light up. I could sense a great deal of pride and enthusiasm in his voice. These were among his fondest memories of the years he spent in Oundle.

Not only did my father have to get used to a completely different environment, new classmates, and different food and accommodations, he also had to adhere to the very strict, almost military-style discipline that the daily routine of a British boarding school meant. A famous Old Oundelian, as they call their alumni, evolutionary biologist Richard Dawkins attended Oundle School much later than my father had, between 1954 and 1959. In his memoir, he suggests that the environment he experienced was less cruel than it had been before his days, but he still remembers it as rather intimidating:

> I got to the English public school experience too late—thank goodness—for the real cruelties of the John Betjeman era. But it was quite tough enough. There were ludicrous rules, invented 'by the boys for the boys.' The number of buttons you were allowed to undo on your jacket was strictly laid down according to seniority, and strictly enforced. Below a certain seniority level, you had to carry your books with a straight arm. Why? The masters must have known this sort of thing was going on, yet they did nothing to stop it...Each house prefect at Oundle chose one of the new boys as his personal slave...I was chosen by the deputy Head of House...to clean his shoes, polish the brasses of his Cadet Corps uniform and make toast for him at teatime every day on a paraffin pressure stove in his study. I had to be ready to run errands for him any time... Many things about Oundle were intimidating.... In the Great Hall for morning prayers on my first day, new boys were yet to be assigned places and we had to find empty chairs where we could. I found one and timidly asked the big boy next to it whether it was taken: 'Not as far as I can

observe' was his icily polite reply, and I felt crushed very small.[22]

The practice of using a new student as a personal servant would phase out in British public schools during the 1970s and '80s, and corporal punishment would finally be outlawed in 1986. My father, however, attended Oundle School between 1938 and 1944, when petty rules were very much alive, such as the one allowing only prefects to step on courtyard lawns. While Bramston was relatively more liberal than the other houses, with its highly respected housemaster Dudley Heesom trying to curtail bullying, it is safe to assume József, or Joseph Eric Stephen Hatvany, as he was known at Oundle School, had a rough time in the beginning.

Bertalan arrived in Paris in June 1939, after completing his second journey exploring Asia. My father joined him from England for his summer vacation. They contemplated going back to Hungary for a short visit, but international events abruptly altered their plans. In August, the Soviet Union and Germany signed a nonaggression agreement called the Molotov-Ribbentrop Pact, in which the two countries secretly agreed to split up Poland between them. My grandfather was concerned it would free Germany to continue its hostile advances in other parts of Europe. Rather than risking a visit to Hungary, he put my father on the last commercial flight leaving for England and sent him back to his boarding school. Bertalan remained in Paris. On September 1, 1939, Germany invaded Poland. Two days later Britain and France declared war on

Germany. More than six years would pass before my grandfather saw his son again.

∽

In Oundle, József was far away from his parents, completely cut off from them. The only family members he had some limited connection with, were his maternal grandmother, Erzsébet Wolfner, and his aunt Marutha, who both weathered the war in London. Thankfully, József was already fluent in English, French, and German when he arrived in England, so was he an avid reader and an eager student. Immersing himself in his studies most likely helped him cope with the dramatic change and the absence of his parents.

Being Jewish meant an ethnic and cultural distinction to my father rather than a religious one. All his ancestors on both sides of his family had been ethnically Jewish for as many generations as we can trace back his family tree. He had to learn Hebrew as a child in Hungary, and my grandfather even insisted he continue in Oundle; however, they weren't committed to the Jewish religion. Bertalan identified as an agnostic, my grandmother Vera was raised Catholic, and her sister Marutha grew up Lutheran. My father never developed the slightest affinity toward any religion. He was a nonbeliever from his childhood and became a devout atheist as a young adult. Therefore, it was a first for him in Oundle having to say a prayer before every meal: "For what we are about to receive, may the Lord make us truly thankful." When he would later recite it to me, he said it so fast that I didn't understand a single word. "The faster we said it, the sooner we could start eating," he reasoned.

József had one particularly unpleasant memory during his first year in Oundle. He suffered from a terrible ear infection. He cried in pain but was dismissed for whining. By the time he was taken to the doctor, it was too late. He lost all hearing in one ear. Luckily, he was young enough to adapt, and most people never noticed that he was completely deaf on one side. I myself often forgot about it until he reminded me when I walked on his deaf side and he couldn't hear me. Strangely enough, I would never remember which ear it was.

In Paris, Bertalan joined the French Foreign Legion, a military service wing created specifically for foreign nationals willing to serve in the French armed forces. He soon became terribly ill with bilateral pneumonia and had to abandon the army. Once he recovered, he joined the resistance and left Nazi-occupied Paris for France Libre, a government-in-exile led by Charles de Gaulle, in the South of France. That was where my grandfather met his future second wife, French divorcée Claire Lacheze. Unlike his first marriage to my grandmother Vera, an arranged merger of two highly successful industrial dynasties, this was true love. Claire had two daughters from her first marriage to Robert Alexandre. She entrusted her parents to raise the girls in Nice while she lived an independent life, joining the resistance, just like my grandfather did.

France wasn't a safe place anymore for Bertalan, not even in the South. Together with Claire, they hired a *passeur* and embarked on a difficult journey, often walking all night through the Alps to neutral territory. Passeurs were smugglers who saved hundreds by helping them escape to Switzerland, especially Jews after 1942, when Hitler launched plans to exterminate all Jews in Europe. They worked with the resistance fighters and other organizations to guide people to safety. Claire and Bertalan successfully crossed the French-Swiss border and settled into the Hotel Geneva, the place they called home until the end of the war.

Chapter Nine

Ruin

HUNGARY JOINED THE AXIS powers in 1940. Siding with the Germans, the country managed to temporarily recover some of its territories lost to the Treaty of Trianon after World War I. This made Hungary's leader, Regent Horthy, quite popular in conservative, nationalistic circles.

> An Axis satellite, it was not a wholehearted ally, even though Hungarian soldiers fought on the Russian front, supplying at times about a third of the non-German cannon fodder that Hitler was consuming. Some of its leaders were wavering in their belief in the ultimate victory of the Axis...In 1938 the first anti-Jewish law appeared, "for the restoration of social equilibrium." In 1941, on the establishment of a comradeship-in-arms with Germany, the Nuremberg legislation was introduced—in some

instances, especially where half-Jews were concerned, even more severely than in Germany itself.[23]

Sometime in 1940, a foreign businessman appeared in the upper-class scene of Budapest. He stayed in one of the most expensive hotels and charmed everyone with his sophisticated demeanor and convincing smooth talk. He approached wealthy Jewish aristocrats, offering his help taking their assets out of the country and saving them for after the war. My grandmother Vera was one of the wealthy victims he managed to deceive. Of course, the police knew about this swindler and kept an eye on his every move. Once they found enough evidence of Vera's involvement in this attempted smuggling case, they arrested her. My grandmother found herself in a notorious women's prison amid terrible circumstances and at the mercy of exceptionally cruel female prison guards. After spending a year behind bars, her final trial took place, where she was sentenced to another year and a half. Upon hearing the verdict, Vera was so devastated she swallowed nails. She had to undergo surgery to have them removed. Fortunately, her condition wasn't too serious, and she made a full recovery. As a result of a special clemency, my grandmother was released ten months early, in the summer of 1942. Very thin and with lots of newly earned gray hair for her young age of thirty-six, she was happy to be free again.

For those unfortunate Hungarian soldiers who were sent to fight in the eastern front, the misery of war started in the early 1940s. They endured the most unimaginable and indescribable horrors, as two survivors told me their stories in the 1970s. But for those remaining in Hungary, World War II did not fully show its teeth until the German occupation in March 1944.

My great uncle Bandi described his days in Budapest in a letter to his sister Lili in America: "Life goes on as before, people lunch, dine, dance, love, play bridge, opera and theatres are filled."

Following the air raids in September 1942, when the Soviets bombed Budapest, he assured his faraway sister that he and their mother Fanny were safe and comfortable in a good shelter that even had armchairs in it.

On the whole, Hungary was the only country within the German sphere of influence where great numbers of Jews lived in comparative safety. Obviously this was a situation that the Nazis could not tolerate for long. To placate them the Hungarian Government announced that it would remove Jews from all positions of influence and after the war deport all 800,000 of them.

Regent Horthy was summoned to meet Hitler and Ribbentrop in Klessheim Castle, and was treated to one of the Fuehrer's notorious harangues, which, while covering the entire political situation, gave special prominence to the Jewish question. Horthy retorted that he had virtually deprived the Jews of all means of livelihood and did not know what else to do with them. "It is impossible, after all, to liquidate them or beat them to death."…Two days after the conference, on April 19, 1943, the very day the Warsaw ghetto revolt started, Himmler was informed that the Hungarians hesitated to deliver the Jews and preferred to give them good treatment.[24]

The Germans decided to appoint Lieutenant Colonel Adolf Eichmann to handle what they called the "Jewish problem" in Hungary. By the spring of 1944, he had gained extensive experience in eliminating Europe's Jewry.

Eichmann was dispatched in great secrecy to Mauthausen to prepare a special commando. Himmler's order was: "Send down to Hungary the master in person." His directive to Eichmann was simple: "Comb the country from East to West; send all the Jews to Auschwitz as quickly as possible…See to it that nothing like the Warsaw ghetto revolt is repeated in any way"…Rudolf Hoess was ordered back to Auschwitz to prepare the camp for its great new task. Finally, when everything was ready, Horthy was again summoned to the Klessheim Castle, ostensibly "to discuss the withdrawal of Hungarian troops from Russia." Upon his arrival Hitler presented him point-blank with a choice between a complete German occupation and a German-appointed Cabinet. Horthy chose the second alternative and sped back to Budapest, where he arrived on March 19, 1944. On the same day, SS Standartenfuehrer Dr. Edmund Veesenmayer arrived to announce his appointment as

"Plenipotentiary of the Reich in Budapest in charge of forming a new Government." Also on the same day, "the master" and his whole outfit, a military column a mile long, now called Sondereinsatzkommando Eichmann (Special Operation Group Eichmann), reached the capital to solve "the life-and-death issue for the Third Reich."[25]

The first trains for Auschwitz left Hungary in May 1944. They were called transports, as if they carried cargo instead of human beings. It was the fastest and most efficient deportation of Jews during the entire war.

"The deportations were carried out with staggering speed; sometimes as many as five trains, loaded with fourteen thousand people, arrived in Auschwitz on a single day. Upon the 'advice' of Eichmann's representative, a hundred persons were loaded in a car."[26]

The Germans could not have been able to accomplish this without the help of extremely eager and willing Hungarian contributors. It was the Hungarian administration that offered a hand to the Germans. It was the Hungarian gendarmerie that often denied water or even a small window for air from the people jammed into freight cars like cattle. It was a sizable portion of the Hungarian population that cheered on as Jews were rounded up and taken away, and it was often a neighbor or a former classmate who led the police to those in hiding.

"The pace of the deportations was so rapid that it brought Hoess to Budapest to inquire what Eichmann meant sending him many more people than Auschwitz could destroy a day. Eichmann insisted he must work at high speed. They finally agreed on a schedule of two trains one day and three the next. On July 11, 1944, Veesenmayer summed up the final total figures: 437,402 Jews deported."[27]

Irén Hatvany and her husband, Albert Hirsch, were among them. They put their fate into the hands of someone who promised to help them escape from Hungary. But instead, they were betrayed. The very person they trusted with their lives handed them over to the Gestapo.

⁓

Irén was known for her kindness, empathy, and generosity, dedicating much of her time and money to charities in order to help the less fortunate. She was also known for her passion for gardening. It was she who transformed the neglected twenty-acre park of the family's castle in Hatvan into a picturesque English garden, complete with precisely trimmed hedges, marble columns, sculptures, and lavish fountains. She traveled throughout Europe to find the most beautiful orchids and palm trees to fill her green house with and created a beautiful rose garden, a pond full of water lilies and goldfish, and a vegetable garden supplying the castle's kitchen with fresh produce. Irén's fate paralleled the fate of the family's estate in Hatvan.

> After years of battling an illness, and with her daughter getting married, Irén Hatvany chose the Castle in Hatvan as an escape. She was already forty during a big renovation of the building's facade in 1927-28, and after it was finished, she decided to modernize the landscaping. She thought that the income generated by a well-organized commercial flower garden could cover the significant cost

of the Castle-park's upkeep…In fact, Irén Hatvany was infatuated with horticulture. For her, the garden meant fulfillment. It meant the purest form of esthetics, the easing of loneliness, and emancipation. For her, the garden was, what creating an ever-growing wealth was for her father [Sándor], what writing was for her brother Lajos and for Anna Lesznai, what painting was for Ferenc Hatvany, exploring the Orient for Bertalan Hatvany, theatre for Lili Hatvany: means of coping with life. Irén Hatvany's story was synonymous with the story of the Castle-park. Their lives blossomed into perfection together, and ended at the same time. The park was destroyed in the war. Irén Hatvany died in Auschwitz.[28]

Almost half of Hungary's Jewish population lived in Budapest. Most of them were spared by the first wave of mass deportations between May and July 1944, but not anymore.

> Plans for the great final knockout (eine entaegige Grossaktion) to round up the 400,000 Jews of the capital in one day had been laid down by Eichmann much earlier, to take place in the middle of July…When all was ready for the great round-up, a hitch occurred. Horthy suddenly got cold feet and called a halt to further deportations… The King of Sweden protested against the deportations. So had the Pope, the Swiss and Turkish governments, and

various personalities from Spain and from Hungary itself… Eichmann intended "to carry out the expected expulsion of the Jews from Budapest once it is proceeded with, with the utmost suddenness and with such speed that they will be driven out before anyone has had a chance to obtain a travel document of visa to a foreign country."…When his mission was near its successful completion, the news of Horthy's intervention to stop the deportations sent Eichmann into a thundering rage…"The master" was now moving heaven and earth to achieve to ends: to get all the Jews of Budapest to Auschwitz and to prevent Hungarians from letting any of them out…Eichmann meanwhile had successfully blocked any rescue of Jews by Hungarians.[29]

My great-grandmother and her oldest son owed their lives to a handful of kind and fearless non-Jewish Hungarians who were willing to offer them shelter during the German occupation. In the spring of 1944, Fanny was staying at the apartment of a pharmacist, but in June someone reported him to the police, suspecting he was hiding a Jew. This nice pharmacist found another place for my great-grandmother to hide, where she was in relative safety until September, when the same thing happened again. Fortunately, Fanny was able to join her son Bandi at a third location: the doorman's apartment at Hotel Pannonia. When the war was over, they moved back to their house in 7 Werbőczy Street in the Buda Castle District. As Bandi writes to Lili in November 1945, he found it astonishing how well his mother handled seeing all the damage.

The house was partly in ruins, and the Germans had taken most of their belongings. Despite the severe shortage of food and heating fuel, they managed to find enough to get by. He was worried but still quite optimistic about the future.

"We are strictly cut off from the World, and nobody can leave the country…so I am afraid it will be quite difficult for mother to go and see Berci [Bertalan] this winter…Communistic tendencies and plans to nationalise industry are rather strong. But if this does not happen and if private property remains untouched in this country, you will have enough to live on in a modest way. I am glad you will soon be an American citizen and I hope damages will be paid to you and for your losses."

History would prove my great uncle wrong. The family was not allowed to keep their property, as everything was eventually nationalized, and Lili had never returned to Hungary. Her daughter Mariella would write in her memoir fifty years later: "In 1944 Hatvany Palace became home to six SS officers. It was only after the War and many inquiries that we found out that Hatvany Palace still stands and is being used as the Institute of Musicology. We have received no reparations or restitution."[30]

⚭

Ferenc Hatvany was also hidden by a number of generous people, including some fellow painters, mostly in Szentendre, a small artist town in the Danube bend just north of the capital. His wife, Lucil, and their three daughters, Alexandra, Sonja, and Antoinette, were less fortunate. As Alexandra writes in a letter to Lili after the war:

Oh, Aunt Lili, you cannot imagine what horrors we had here! The entire Jewry from the countryside (those with Jewish ethnicity) was deported to Germany in closed cattle cars. Most of them were murdered (gassed), a small number of them were used for forced labor. Very few returned, they couldn't bear the terrible torture, starvation, etc.…. We, mama and my two younger sisters, were also interned. First we were all here in the amassing camp for Jews in Hatvan, at the Sugar Factory grounds, in the wooden barracks designed for storage. They constantly threatened to shoot us…In the last minute, before the entire camp was deported to Germany, we were taken to the internment camp in Kistarcsa. We were already standing in front of the wagons ready to get on, when we were ordered to march away. What can we thank our enormous luck, I will never know, since we had already been taken from Pest to Hatvan with the intention to be deported together with those in Hatvan. We were in Kistarcsa for four months, where it was bearable, but the constant threat of deportation was still there. In the end of September things eased up a little, and we were released. From that time forward, we were hiding, my sisters in Pest, in the house in Nádor Street (not the smartest place, but they survived, and that's what counts), and I in the country…The house in Nádor Street was bombed above my sister's head…There were many lives lost during the siege, and the entire last year was the year of the dead and of mourning. What a big fortune that Aunt Lili wasn't here. I wish we had also left, that was the only smart thing to do, away, just away from here. Unfortunately, the majority of Hungarians behaved very ugly last year, just like the Germans…Here in Hatvan, last year, the city castle was a hospital for Germans with venereal disease, now a hospital for Russians. Not one piece of furniture remained. A part of the roof of the castle is missing along with the windows and doorframes. The park is no more, only a neglected plot.

In the same letter, Alexandra also mentions that her poor young brother Sándor died in Budapest, as he couldn't cope with life in the basement, the cold, and the starvation during the siege. Lucil was severely beaten by both the Germans and the Hungarian Nazis, the Arrow Cross, during an interrogation about her husband's hiding place. She didn't give away Ferenc's whereabouts; neither did she reveal where they had hidden the family's treasures. Fortunately, Lucil and Ferenc survived along with their three daughters, but the majority of their valuable painting collection vanished. Some were destroyed in the war, but most of them were looted.

My grandmother Vera never talked about what happened to her during the German occupation in Hungary. It wasn't until 2014 that I found a document, a sworn declaration of persecution she made five years after the war that revealed details of her ordeal:

> As a person of purely Jewish decent, I was not at any time from September 1, 1939 until the repeal of the anti-Jewish

laws after the Armistice in enjoyment of full civic rights in Hungary…In April 1944 I was living alone at Nemetvolgyi Ut Budapest. At 5:30 one morning two armed members of the German Gestapo entered my flat and ordered me to go with them immediately to the Gestapo Headquarters at the Majestic Hotel. I had barely time to dress before I was roughly marched off without being allowed to leave word with anybody or make any arrangements whatsoever. At the Gestapo Headquarters after being made to stand on my feet for ten hours I was interrogated and cross-examined for several hours about my mother and sister and connections in England and abroad. Thereafter I was locked up in a cell without food or drink. At dawn the interrogations continued again for several hours and in conclusion I was whipped and beaten by Gestapo Guards. I was kept in prison for five days during which time I was tortured and beaten up several times at the conclusion of further interrogations. The food and drink was barely sufficient to keep me alive. Eventually I was released and thereafter lived in hiding under an assumed name until November 1944.

I heard vague anecdotes about Vera hiding at various places in Budapest during the spring and summer of 1944, either wearing a red wig or dying her hair blond. As there were many Nazi sympathizers, fortunately, there were also many selfless, incredibly brave Hungarians who were willing to risk their lives by hiding Jews in the basement or the attic of their own residence. My grandmother was among the lucky ones who were hidden by these compassionate Hungarians.

Raoul Wallenberg was a Swedish diplomat accredited to Budapest in July 1944. This exceptional humanitarian was determined to save as many Jews from the Holocaust as he possibly could. He issued protective passports and sheltered Jews in buildings designated as neutral Swedish territory. My grandmother received a *Schutz-Pass*, a protective passport signed by Wallenberg on September 22, 1944. This document declared her a subject of Sweden and exempted her from wearing the yellow star on her clothes, the distinguishing sign all Jews had to display on their lapels.

The Hungarian government's poorly planned attempt to break its ties with the Axis powers failed. In fact, it turned into a disaster. After the Red Army crossed the Hungarian border in September, Horthy tried to negotiate an armistice with the Soviets and hoped to pull out of the war. On October 15, he made a radio announcement informing his people that the Germans had already lost the war, and in order to avoid further bloodshed, he would enter into an armistice with his enemies. Of course, the Germans were well aware of Horthy's plans. They kidnapped his son in order to force the regent to resign. Ferenc Szálasi, head of the fascist Arrow Cross Party, became the new prime minister. The Arrow Cross Militia began to concentrate Jews into yellow-star houses and a single large ghetto. Buildings protected by the neutral diplomatic corps and the Red Cross became frequent targets of raids, looting, rape, and torture by the Arrow Cross. Deportations resumed, this time on foot. Thousands of Jews were forced to march toward Vienna with minimal food or water. Those too weak or falling behind were shot on the spot. Despite holding a protective passport from Wallenberg, my grandmother was not safe anymore, as I learned from her declaration:

On the 24th November 1944 the house I was hiding in was raided and after being identified as a Jewess I was marched off to the closed Ghetto of Budapest by armed guards. Upon entering the Ghetto through the Dohany utca gate I was searched—again by armed guards—in a most brutal and humiliating fashion and everything of the slightest value was seized including all my warm clothing and the little money I had with me. After great difficulty I found a small room without windows or heating which I was allowed to share with fourteen other persons. We had no warm things at all and were entirely dependant for our food on the starvation rations distributed by the Jewish Community...The gates were manned day and night by armed guards who had orders to shoot anybody attempting to escape. Severe beatings by the Arrow Cross Militia were daily occurrences. Until the beginning of December Jews were regularly being marched off from the Ghetto by armed Arrow Cross guards in the direction of Germany. As the Russians advanced our jailers became more than ever ferocious and the number of beatings and murders was increasing. In the end preferring even a slight chance of escape to what seemed the certainty of a brutal death on the 9th January 1945 I attempted to leave the Ghetto. I succeeded and for a few days hid in cellars until the Russian troops entered the Pest area of Budapest.

The siege of Budapest began right after Christmas 1944. The Soviet Red Army encircled the Hungarian capital, where it was met by Hungarian and German troops. Hitler declared Budapest a fortress city to be defended to the end. Stalin wanted to display his full strength to Churchill and Roosevelt. The battle of Budapest was one of the bloodiest in World War II. Food and water were in short supply. My mother often talked about having to eat beans, and only beans, for six weeks. Not surprisingly, she couldn't even look at them for the rest of her life. She also told me that between air raids, she and some of her neighbors left the relative safety of the basement that served as a bomb shelter, went to the top of their four-story apartment building, and climbed on the roof to collect snow for drinking and cooking. In those days Budapest still had horse-drawn carriages for transportation. It was a very cold winter, colder than usual, and the horses shot in the streets were preserved in the freezing temperatures. People desperate for food emerged from the basements with buckets and knives and cut up the rumps of those dead horses for meat. An estimated thirty-eight thousand civilians died during the siege of Budapest. About twenty-five thousand of them succumbed to starvation and disease.

During the months of December 1944 and January 1945, the reign of terror by the Hungarian far-right Arrow Cross Militia claimed further innocent lives. They rounded up several thousand of the remaining Jews of Budapest, lined them up on the Danube embankment, ordered them to take off their shoes, and shot them in the river. Since the spring of 2005, a beautiful and touching memorial graces the Danube bank on the Pest side of the city, close to the Parliament. Sixty pairs of 1940s-style shoes cast in iron and attached to the stone of the embankment, similar to the ones left behind by Jews whose lifeless bodies floated down the river between sheets of ice, serve as a painful reminder of these horrible atrocities.

On February 13, 1945, the Hungarian and German forces surrendered unconditionally. This was a strategic victory for the Allies, pushing toward Berlin. Budapest lay in ruins. The majority of the buildings suffered significant damage. About thirty thousand of them were completely destroyed. The Germans blew up all the bridges over the Danube that connected the two sides of the city, Buda and Pest. To add insult to injury, the Soviets entered into a rampage of large-scale theft and mass rape.

"The worst suffering of the Hungarian population is due to the rape of women. Rapes—affecting all age groups from ten to seventy are so common that very few women in Hungary have been spared."[31]

Credited with saving the lives of tens of thousands, Raoul Wallenberg himself met his tragic fate before the war was over. He was captured in Budapest by the Soviet Red Army in January 1945, detained for alleged espionage, and disappeared. Wallenberg was presumed dead in a Soviet prison in 1947, at the age of thirty-four. Decades later, he would receive worldwide recognition and numerous humanitarian honors including the Congressional Gold Medal by the United States Congress.

Chapter Ten
Ambition

FAR FROM THE HORRORS his fellow Hungarians had to endure at home, my father had his own encounters with the war in England. He too experienced severe food shortages and was among the many young civilians who were recruited to help the British army spot and shoot at German planes that were bombing London. While the war served as the backdrop to everything, compared to the world at large, daily life in Oundle was relatively peaceful.

Gone were the days of an extremely privileged boy chauffeured to school in Budapest only to bring home a report card with less-than-desirable grades. Once a nonchalant little baron, too lazy to live up to his potential, József Hatvany matured into a high-achieving young man coming of age in Oundle. He excelled in everything from science to humanities. On Speech Day in 1942, he was awarded prizes in English and French, and in 1944, for Spanish. He was a member of the Modern

Languages Society as well as the Debating Society. In 1944 he took part in the school play, *Much Ado About Nothing*, for which he was praised in the school magazine:

"Hatvany gave a very convincing study of villainy in black and gold, the effect of which was heightened by a sinister make-up. This was one of the outstanding performances of the play and only a minor point could have been improved. I think Don John might have shown more relish for the villainy. Most Shakespearean villains thoroughly enjoy their crimes."[32]

In the British school system, one could take high school final exams in several segments. My father started his at the age of sixteen with Latin and French, continued at seventeen with Greek and German, and finally finished at eighteen with Spanish. Toward the end of his high school years, he would have loved to add Russian to his repertoire but could not find a tutor in Oundle. Nonetheless, he managed to learn the Cyrillic alphabet and some basic Russian from books he found at the library. He graduated with honors in physics, mathematics, and engineering studies. Such academic excellence opened the doors for him to continue his education at Cambridge University.

$$\backsim$$

Just like Oundle School's, the history of Trinity College, Cambridge, goes back to the sixteenth century, founded by Henry VIII in 1546. Its famous Wren Library contains many treasures, such as an eighth-century copy of the Epistles of St. Paul and Milne's manuscript of *Winnie-the-Pooh*. Undergraduates of Trinity College in the sixteenth century included Francis Bacon, while one of the greatest minds of all times,

Isaac Newton, completed some of his most important mathematical and scientific work there in the late seventeenth century. Byron, Thackeray, and Tennyson were also Trinity undergraduates in the early nineteenth century. Life at Trinity has changed greatly over the centuries, but it maintained a very strong academic tradition. Trinity College has provided over thirty Nobel Prize winners in science and economics since they were first awarded in 1901.

Despite being exceptionally talented in languages and showing a keen interest in history, literature, and all forms of art, as everyone did in his family, my father chose a scientific career for himself. He decided to study physics, mathematics, chemistry, and electronics at Trinity College, Cambridge. Once I asked him why he chose this path instead of liberal arts. He said that one could learn languages and history solely from books—perhaps he was referring to his father, who educated himself completely on his own to become a recognized authority in Oriental studies—but in his opinion, in order to become a scientist or an engineer, one must enroll in classes and receive a formal education. Having an insatiable appetite for knowledge and an interest in topics reaching far beyond his chosen field of studies, he eagerly attended philosophy lectures by Bertrand Russell and logic by Ludwig Wittgenstein.

As a young adult studying at Cambridge University, József Hatvany showed little resemblance to the twelve-year-old baron who left his very wealthy, aristocratic life behind in 1938. Having a much clearer picture of the Hungarian political climate between the two world wars, one that resulted in his father's decision to leave before it was too late, filled him with resentment not for his country, but for its ideology. He turned against the unrestrained capitalism he grew up in. Although he enjoyed luxury, comfort, and a glamorous lifestyle, he resented the environment it created in his household. Raised mostly by his nannies and governesses, he lacked the emotional attachment, a loving bond most children have with their parents. All he had was an hour of rather formal discussion with his father every day, if that. As for his mother, their relationship was even colder and far more distant. My grandmother's personality could have been blamed for this in part, but mostly it was due to the etiquette a family of their socioeconomic standing was expected to follow.

My father also resented the semifeudalistic society that suppressed the majority of people into deep poverty while allowing only a handful, including his own family, to live in abundance. He strongly resented—in fact, remembered with utter disgust—the nationalistic slogans he and his classmates had to chant at school in 1930s Budapest during physical education class while performing militaristic jumping jacks and simulated punches. These slogans were to ingrain hatred in young Hungarians against some of the neighboring nations that were granted large portions of Hungary's former territories by the Treaty of Trianon after World War I, agitating for the restitution of Greater Hungary.

During World War II and immediately afterward, the idea of communism attracted many young, progressive intellectuals in England, presenting itself as the one and only logical answer to fascism. Seeing what fascism had done to his family and to his country, my father was more and more drawn toward what he considered the ultimate antidote. He diligently read all twelve volumes of Lenin's *Collected Works* as well as the *Capital* by Marx, and he soon became a very enthusiastic believer in a system that seemed to promise equality and a fair chance for everyone.

In the summer of 1946, Péter Nagy found him while visiting in England. Péter was the older brother of András Nagy, my father's former classmate in Hungary, at *Mintagimnázium*. This meeting led to a long-lasting friendship between my father and the two Nagy brothers. Soon my father started exchanging letters with András Nagy after an eight-year hiatus, picking up where they had left off in 1938. Fortunately, András kept my father's handwritten letters for the rest of his life, together with carbon copies of his own typewritten answers. To my great surprise and delight, these letters would find their way to my hands several decades later.

Nothing describes my father's political evolution better than the first letter he sent to András from Cambridge, in November 1946:

> My dear comrade András…As you see, I am taking advantage of your offer, and am writing in English—I can read and understand Hungarian perfectly, so do answer me in Hungarian, but I have not written a word since 1938…As you rightly point out, my outlook at that time was (in so far as I had one), very different to my present one. I am all the more glad to establish this contact with you, and hope that it will lead to a lasting friendship…As you know, I left Hungary in '38, and spent the next six years at school here. Towards the end of my time at Oundle (a public school), I became interested in socialism, from a philosophical point of view, and organised a small Marxist study circle. I then came up to the University, and immediately joined the Socialist Club, which at that time united all left-wing student opinion. After four months there, I became

editor of "Front",—the weekly organ of the Socialist Club
(C.U.S.C), and shortly afterwards I applied for admission
to the Party. Because of my national status, this was not,
at that time, granted, so I made up my mind to do such
outstanding work that they would be obliged to admit me,
despite my background, etc. I was elected to the executive of C.U.S.C., and in the summer, with the General
Election, I saw my chance. In Cambridge I organized the
backing of the students for the Labour candidate, and in
London, after the end of the term, I rose to the rank of
Polling District Organiser…We were defeated, but carried
straight on with the campaign, for the municipal elections,
in which I was election agent. It was at this stage that
someone noticed that I did not hold a party card. So the
London District Committee recommended my admission,
which was accepted by the Executive. I was overjoyed. At
Cambridge, I was elected on the political secretariat of the
University branch, and it was in the midst of this job that
Péter found me when he came this summer…So much for
my political past—you may think me egocentric for writing
all this—its object is to make clear that whatever you knew
of me in 1938 is not now operative.

As I would later learn from Alan Mackay, a former classmate and
good friend of his at Cambridge University, my father was obligated
to register at the local police once a month as an "enemy alien," which
explains why it must have been particularly hard for him to be admitted
to the British Communist Party.

It was in the summer of 1945 that my father met his future wife Doris, as he describes in his letter to András:

> While I was working in London during the General Election, the Organiser of the neighbouring District, was a charming young Scots girl, Doris Elrick, who at that time had just been released from her War Service in the Foreign Office (!), and was waiting to go back to Aberdeen University to finish her course in History. We have since got engaged, and she has now come to Cambridge to read for a doctorate, after getting an M.A. at Aberdeen.

In the rest of his letter, my father describes his peculiar relationship with his family to András:

> To make my position quite clear, I must tell you of my relations with my rather notorious family. I had, of course, been entirely out of touch with them throughout the war, and when I went to see my father in Geneva last Xmas, I did so with some trepidation. However, he was very nice to me, and though I quarreled with him on politics, his outlook appeared to me to be fundamentally progressive, in a liberal-bourgeois way. It was while under this illusion that I talked about him with Péter. But at the end of this summer I went to see him, plus my grandmother in Paris, and his real attitude and position as a reactionary was made bitterly clear to me. To my regret, we quarreled very badly—and it became clear to me that it was impossible to maintain any sort of relations with a man who, over the

bodies of the 7 million Soviet dead, of the antifascist war, is still able to say that communism is a sort of fascism. He has allied himself hopelessly with the 3rd way gang of the Churchill-De Gaulle type.

The rest of the letter to András, together with several more that followed, mainly dealt with my father's plans to return to Hungary. Péter and András regularly sent him *Szabad Nép* (*Free People*), the leading Hungarian communist newspaper of the time, occasionally accompanied by another publication: *Ifjuság* (*Youth*). My father read these papers cover to cover and was very eager to return to his native country. He was debating whether to go in 1947, right after finishing his undergraduate degree at Cambridge University, or stay until 1949, giving Doris a chance to finish her doctorate, while he would take advanced courses in physics or gain practical work experience in a modern British laboratory. He was weighing the arguments for and against both options while asking for András' advice and guidance. Meanwhile, Doris diligently studied Hungarian.

Upon receiving my father's first letter, András took some handwritten notes (in Hungarian) before answering it. He would meticulously keep them over the years together with the entire correspondence. Some of his observations read as follows:

"He writes in English. Friendship. Is it real? He is 'overjoyed' by his admission to the Party. Too bad, we don't have this here. While it seems unintentional, his tone is frigidly polite. Too English!"

Chapter Eleven

Outlook

In December 1945, my grandfather met his son for the first time in six years. In August 1939 József was a little boy, three months shy of his thirteenth birthday, when he visited Bertalan in Paris. Just days before World War II broke out, he was sent back to his boarding school in England, where he had already been studying for a year. At Christmas 1945, a nineteen-year-old greeted my grandfather in Geneva, a grown man with a strong and independent personality. Bertalan wrote letters to his sisters Antonia and Lili in America, describing his joyful reunion with his adult son:

> My greatest pleasure is now the visit of my son. He is bigger than I am, thin, but putting on weight rapidly with the good food here. He is quite good looking, resembling mainly his mother, but sometimes somehow reminding me of you [Antonia] and of Bandi. He has my eyes. As for his

mentality, he is an excellent debater—I love to argue with him—, he has a very good sense of humour, very English though—naif and idealist to an enormous degree. He is exceedingly good-natured, has lots of charm, and, in spite of his lamentably extremist political views, as reasonable and tolerant as one can be at his age. I do not doubt he will grow out of his present political creed and also of his very ardent love for a rather fierce young Scottish female "comrade." I think he should finish his studies in Cambridge (two more years) and then he ought to go and do some postgrad work in America. Unfortunately, he would not like to continue his studies after graduation, but wants to get married at 21 and go home to Hungary. I told him this would not be wise and then we shelved the problem for two years.

Bertalan also voiced his predictions and concerns about the future of Hungary in his letter to Antonia:

Sometime this spring, the Russians will certainly clear out except for some small garrisons, and life will begin again. What I am afraid of, is the recrudescence of fascism in the country…in spite of occasional feelings of some slight disgust, I cannot help thinking that one absolutely must help the present system to get on. People of all political creeds, socialists as well as conservatives, have very plainly told me it was my duty to go home and be useful. I can't share your hatred of the Russians. I dislike them, and wish them to hell, but all the hatred that was and still in me is used up for my feelings towards the Nazis, German and Hungarian. We shall have to find some way of understanding with the Russians—there is no other way.

In early 1946, when multiple attempts by various family members failed in an effort to bring Fanny out of Hungary, and seeing his son aligning himself with the communists, Bertalan's outlook became even more pessimistic as he wrote to Lili:

> Unfortunately, I am "bearish" on the World situation. War may come this spring—or in ten years. It will come, it's unfortunately inevitable. And to know Mother still in the middle of the prospective front, to know my son all for the wrong side, these two things make me pretty sick. This time, I won't be able to volunteer, I'm too old and can't walk much. It certainly does look rotten…Damn Stalin.

❧

Planning his return to Hungary, József asked András about the political climate, the economic situation, and possible job opportunities for himself and for his fiancée. As my father described in his letter, Doris applied for a position with the British Council in Hungary, but it was later refused. They had another hope. Doris was the recipient of a £250 per annum scholarship from Carnegie Trust, a charitable trust based in Scotland, and there was a good chance of her continuing to receive it if she carried on with her research. My father also asked his friend repeatedly about what they should bring back from England.

There was an undeniable feeling of renewal in Hungary, an

enthusiasm right after the war. People were hopeful and ready for a fresh start. However, most of Budapest was still in ruins, and people had to cope with a severe shortage of basic necessities. András tried to describe 1946 Hungary to my father as accurately as possible. In a very subtle way, he might have even suggested my father and Doris rethink their plans.

Although András didn't mention it in his letters, there was one thing that best characterized the economic turmoil of the time. Between the end of 1945 and July 1946, Hungary experienced the worst case of hyperinflation in history. While in 1944 the largest banknote was 1,000 pengő, by the end of 1945, it was 10,000,000. Prices doubled every fifteen hours. In July 1946, the 100 quintillion (10^{20}) pengő was introduced, the largest denomination bill ever printed. People received their pay twice a day and immediately rushed to shop for groceries before their cash became worthless. Banknotes were piling up on the pavement like garbage, swept up by street cleaners as if they were autumn leaves. Barter trade took over for useless money. Watches, gold rings, necklaces, and other valuables changed hands for sugar, lard, and flour. In August 1946, the pengő was replaced by the new Hungarian currency, the forint, at a rate of 10^{29} to one. A slow and painstaking recovery was underway in Hungary.

The British Communist Party first encouraged my father to maintain a relationship with his family but later suggested he cut all ties with them once and for all. Given my father's ambivalent relationship with my grandfather and a virtually nonexistent one with my grandmother, he promptly complied. As he mentioned in his letter to András, he had a painful breakup with his father in the summer of 1946 when he visited him in Paris. Although it pushed him to the verge of a nervous break-down, József felt it was completely justified to sever all ties with Bertalan.

Looking back on it several decades later, it is very difficult to under-stand the decisions my father made while at Cambridge University, just as it is very easy and tempting to judge and criticize his political views and the path he chose for himself as a result. Making excuses for him is not my intention. Finding explanations to his actions is. Trying to under-stand his motivation, attempting to look at it through his eyes, given his background and the circumstances, are indeed my intentions. It was right after the war. Considering his country's and his family's history, and taking into account his surroundings and the political atmosphere of the time in Cambridge and in London, one should step back and try to put it all in perspective.

My father never did anything half-heartedly. He always had an all-or-nothing mentality. The so-called third-way moderate, centrist approach that Winston Churchill and Charles de Gaulle stood for, the ideology my grandfather identified with, was not an acceptable path for him. He wanted more. Communism was his answer, he believed in it, and he was far from being alone with this view, especially given the place and time. Stalin was an ally during the war, and philosophically speaking, communism was viewed by many as the only logical answer to fascism.

At the age of twenty, even those much less hardheaded and stubborn tend to see the world in black and white. He certainly did. Everyone coming of age searches for a strong sense of belonging and acceptance. Parents may often provide a filter to a teenager trying to find his way and his voice negotiating the difficult labyrinth toward adulthood. They may guide their youngsters away from their emotional pendulum swinging too far. My father didn't have this built-in system of checks and balances during his most formative years, between the ages of twelve and twenty. He might have been very smart and very well educated, but emotionally he was raw and completely unrefined. There was no one to sit and reason with him and tone down his sharp, black-and-white views. Neither did he have a healthy adult relationship to model his upon, nor could he rely on his peers for an example, growing up in a boys-only school with very rigid, old-fashioned rules, and stiff upper lips surrounding him. He fell for the first girl he found "charming," as he characterized her in his letter to his friend, during his university years, and became engaged to her. Doris's humble, blue-collar background and her strong belief in communism, in addition to her sharp intellect, immediately appealed to him. So did the communist ideology of progressive student groups in postwar Cambridge.

József turned his back to his family and to the world it represented to him. Was it entirely his decision to denounce them, or was he obeying the British Communist Party? I tend to believe it was a combination of the two. He was definitely not forced to do so. Did Doris play a role in him taking this drastic step? József's family was convinced she had.

One thing is for certain. My father believed in a utopia. He had a dream of a brighter future, a future that looked just and fair for everyone. He had a dream of building a new world.

Chapter Twelve

Diaspora

FANNY FINALLY SUCCEEDED in leaving Hungary during the summer of 1946. As I would learn from my father's letter to András, she visited Bertalan in Paris on her way to America. To the best of my knowledge, it was then and there that my father saw her for the last time. My great-grandmother arrived in New York in November 1946 and took up a lavish lifestyle, living at the Stanhope Hotel on Fifth Avenue, opposite the Metropolitan Museum, a fitting address for an art lover. Times changed, but Fanny remained as intimidating a matriarch as ever. Her great-grandson, Anthony Sundstrom, remembered visiting her in New York when he was a child:

> Fanny was tough. When we visited, I waited to be summoned, stepped forward, kissed her hand, went and sat down, and did not make a peep, save please and thank you as needed. Mom [Mariella] was largely raised and educated

by Fanny, and she always tried to find the good in others, but even she said Fanny was "hell on wheels." Fanny never let anyone forget she was a baroness. Her upkeep cost Antonia thousands, almost paupering her. Odd, as Antonia left Hungary in the 1920s to get away from Fanny. Such is family.

Bandi arrived in New York in September 1947 but eventually settled down in Beverly Hills, California.

Antonia lived in New York until she bought a house in New Jersey, near Princeton, an estate she fittingly named Hatvan.

Mariella became an art history teacher at Solebury School in New Hope, Pennsylvania. Although she had never received any formal education in the subject, her upbringing in Hungary proved to be enough to make her qualified. Growing up with an art history enthusiast grandmother, Fanny, visiting Venice, Florence, Rome, and Naples with her as a child and having her uncle Bertalan, my grandfather, a very knowledgeable Asieologist, awakened her appetite for history, paved the road for her chosen career later in life.

Ferenc Hatvany left Budapest for Paris in 1947 and later moved to Lausanne, Switzerland, where he lived for the rest of his life. He never painted again. Unfortunately, his famous collection dispersed after World War II. Most of them were looted by the Germans and later by the Russians. Some are in Russian Museums, some in Germany, but the whereabouts of the majority remain unknown. Only a handful of paintings were returned to his heirs.

Gustave Courbet's *Nude reclining woman* witnessed more than its fair share of history. Ferenc Hatvany originally bought it at a Paris auction for 36,100 francs.

> The painting had one of the most adventurous fate among the myriad of masterpieces leaving Hungary following the chaotic years after 1945. From the great Russian "sink hole," it was saved by an acute venereal disease. Having been stored in a bank vault since 1942, the picture was obtained by the special corps of the "liberating" Russian army. They didn't reach the motherland with this expensive luggage, however. The looting soldiers gave the painting to a Slovakian doctor in exchange for treating one of their fellow officers. From the doctor's estate, the picture surfaced again in 2000, in the hands of a Slovakian art dealer. After multiple unsuccessful attempts to sell, in 2005 he reluctantly gave it back to its rightful owners, the descendants of Ferenc Hatvany. After yet another change of owners, the *Nude reclining woman* was sold in 2015 at an auction by Christie's in New York for more than $15 million.[33]

Yet the most controversial piece in his collection remains an explicitly erotic painting, Courbet's *L'Origine du monde*. Ferenc Hatvany bought it in 1910 and kept it in a box covered with another painting, as it was too risqué to display on the walls of his Budapest mansion. Toward the end of the war, the painting was looted by Soviet troops but ransomed by Ferenc. When he emigrated, he was allowed to take one piece with him. Luckily, the Soviets did not consider *L'Origine du monde* a serious work of art; hence, he was able to take it to Paris. Today it is displayed at the Musée D'Orsay.

⁓

Bertalan returned to Hungary in 1946, but he didn't stay. He could not identify with the strong communistic tendencies and the direction Hungary took after the war, nor was he welcome by the new leadership. For the second time in his life, he felt like a fish out of water in his own country. For the second time in his life, he made a decision to leave.

My grandfather spent the rest of his life in Paris. Although he never set foot in Hungary again, not even for a visit, he remained a Hungarian citizen, refusing to change his nationality. He lived very happily with his new wife Claire at Rue Chaillot in the 16th arrondissement in Paris, where one of Claire's two daughters, Marie-Françoise, joined them in 1954.

Bobette, as everyone in the family called Marie-Françoise, received the nickname little Bob after her father Robert Alexandre. As she would tell me in 2012, laughing, her parents were "both beautiful, charming and selfish like hell." Hence Bobette and her sister grew up in Nice, with their maternal grandparents. Although it was back in 1946 that Bobette first met my grandfather, she didn't see him often until 1950. Between the ages of fourteen and eighteen, she spent Easter vacations with Bertalan and Claire in Paris, and Claire would visit her two daughters in Nice every Christmas. Bobette was eighteen in 1954 when she moved to Paris and actually lived with her mother and my grandfather for a couple of years. She became very fond of Bertalan, treating him as her own father. He felt the same way, welcoming her as the daughter he never had. It is very likely that he also tried to make up for all those years he wasn't the father he should have been to his own son. Once he admitted to Bobette that he felt terrible about leaving my father in England all by himself at the age of twelve, letting him grow up without any parental guidance. In retrospect, he regretted his decision to stay in France in 1939 instead of joining József in England, but by the time he realized his mistake, the war broke out, and they were cut off from each other for six years. It eased his guilt to know that my father was safe in England.

Claire and Bertalan eventually divorced in 1958, remaining very good friends, sincerely caring about each other. Claire moved to New York in the mid-1960s and lived on Manhattan's Upper East Side, at the corner of Fifth Avenue and East 78th Street. She often returned to Paris, and always visited my grandfather on those occasions.

After his second divorce, Bertalan moved to a small apartment on Rue de l'Assomption, in the 16th district of Paris, where he lived alone for the rest of his life. He and Bobette remained very close. For many years, Bertalan was a regular contributor to a Hungarian periodical, *Látóhatár* (*Horizon*), based in Munich. They published his second book, his Hungarian translation of Lao Tze's *Tao Te King*, in 1957. A second, revised edition of the same book came out in 1977, with a new foreword that admittedly took my grandfather longer to finish than the time it took him to write the entire book itself.

Bobette remembered traveling to London with Bertalan two or three times in her twenties, already divorced from her first husband, working full time in an office. She told me that my grandfather had lived in a completely different world, far from reality, as if he were in the era of the French Revolution. Apparently, Bertalan was accustomed to having everything arranged for him by his staff in feudalistic prewar Hungary to such extent that he was still unable to buy a postage stamp or book an air ticket or a hotel room on his own during the 1960s. In London, Bertalan's main mission was to have a couple of new suits made by his tailor. He chose the fabrics, had his measurements taken, and then had to wait for several days until the first fittings. As Bobette recalled, my grandfather developed a routine, almost a ritual, to pass time. It was very similar to the lifestyle he adopted in Hungary in the 1930s. He would have breakfast quite late, then go to a museum, followed by a cocktail and a quick lunch at noon. Another museum was on his program for the early afternoon, after which he would retire at the hotel for a nap. In the evening, he would have a cocktail at the hotel's bar and go to an elegant restaurant for a late dinner. Bobette welcomed the opportunity to accompany my grandfather on these occasions, since they offered a vacation from the grind of her everyday life. She especially enjoyed visiting museums with Bertalan, a walking, talking encyclopedia, happy and eager to share his tremendous knowledge of art history.

Vera survived the war in Budapest, narrowly escaping the Holocaust, the wrath of the German and the Hungarian Nazis, and the atrocities committed against the civilian population by the Russian Red Army. I was able to recreate her subsequent international travels from her Hungarian passport. In the summer of 1946, she received a visitor's visa to England, along with all the necessary transit visas to travel across continental Europe. Vera arrived in Dover on July 30 and continued to London, where she was reunited with her mother, Erzsébet, and her sister Marutha.

During the war, Vera's mother and sister were supporting the Allied troops by knitting socks, helmet linings, gloves, and sweaters, as well as sewing camouflage outfits for the Red Cross in London. Members of the international air force were stationed close to where they lived, and Marutha enjoyed spending time in their company. She was particularly fond of a pilot from New Zealand. Much to her mother's delight, soon they were engaged. Unfortunately, he died when his plane was shot down. Later, Marutha met a member of the United States Air Force, William Wilson. Unlike the fellow from New Zealand, Bill was not a pilot. Erzsébet was against this relationship, since she didn't want her younger daughter to move to America. Despite her mother's wishes, Marutha followed Bill to the United States in 1947. The couple got married in New York and moved to the Washington, DC, area the same year.

Erzsébet remained in England. She believed life would go back to exactly the way it had been before the war in Hungary, and she would be paid restitution for all her losses. Nursing these hopes, she paid a brief visit to Budapest in 1948, only to realize she was wrong. Disappointed, she returned to England, where she soon became very ill. In 1950, she died penniless in London.

It remains a mystery whether Vera reunited with my father while in England in late 1946. Did she meet her son she hadn't seen since he was twelve? It appears she arrived in London after József's breakup with Bertalan, which would suggest he did not want to see his mother. There was a much bigger gap between Vera's and József's political views than there had ever been between those of Bertalan and his son. If my father indeed found it impossible to maintain any kind of relationship with my grandfather following their meet and quarrel in Paris in the summer of 1946, he certainly wouldn't have had the desire to resume one with my grandmother a couple months later. Had my father already severed all ties with his ancestors at this point, on the advice of the British Communist Party, or did he make that decision only later that year? I will never know with absolute certainty, but I assume they met in the fall of 1946 in England. I am inclined to believe they actually reunited, however briefly, and my grandmother had a chance to meet her son as a young adult before he denounced her. The entry and exit stamps in her passport suggest Vera returned to Hungary in December 1946.

My grandmother finally left Hungary in the end of 1948. Knowing she spent eighteen months behind bars in the beginning of the war; was arrested by the Gestapo during the German occupation in 1944; was locked up, beaten, and threatened with death in the ghetto by the Hungarian Arrow Cross; narrowly escaped deportation; and survived the siege of Budapest, only to be denounced by her son upon his return from England, I often wondered what took her so long. I found an affidavit signed by her American brother-in-law, William Wilson, dated April 1948, offering to be her sponsor in the United States. I also found a report of a house search conducted at Vera's residence by the Budapest Public Prosecutor's Office, Department of Foreign Currency, in September 1948. Did they look for Western currency upon suspecting she was planning to leave? As the report states, nothing that could have been used as proof of criminal activity was confiscated during the search.

In December 1948, shortly before the Iron Curtain sealed off the boarders, Vera arrived in Austria. She spent the next two years traveling between England and Switzerland, visiting her mother in London for the last time, and probably waiting for visas and transit permits. There were no further stamps in her Hungarian passport after May 1949. According to the passenger list, she arrived in New York on September 3, 1950, aboard a KLM flight from Amsterdam. Under citizenship, she was noted as "Stateless."

In New York, Vera took a small apartment at First Avenue and East 61st Street, next to the Queensboro Bridge. In contrast with the wealthy socialite she used to be in prewar Hungary, she lived a rather modest life, first working as a medical assistant and later as a trained x-ray technician at a New York hospital. It was there, sometime in the 1950s, that she cared for a famous patient, Eleanor Roosevelt. As I would learn from her nephew Andrew Wilson, Vera helped a lot of new immigrants, mostly Hungarian Jews, settling into their new lives, finding apartments and jobs. In 1953, she received a gift of $20,000 from her ex-mother-in-law, Fanny. As the accompanying letter states, she meant to express her gratitude and acknowledge Vera's "help in numerous vital situations." I wonder if Fanny was referring to something Vera might have done in Budapest during the war, possibly helping her hide from the Nazis. While this was a very generous sum of money in 1953, my grandmother would have to wait another decade before she received restitution from Germany in a considerably larger amount.

Chapter Thirteen

Contrast

LAJOS SWAM AGAINST THE STREAM. While everyone else in his generation settled abroad after the war, he returned to Hungary from Western immigration and stayed for the rest of his life.

I have never had the opportunity to meet Fanny, Lili, Antonia, Bandi, or Mariella. They lived in another world, both literally and figuratively, and my father had no connections with them. Lajos was the only one living in Budapest, but I never met him either, since he died when I was only three months old. I was fortunate enough to know his widow, however, Jolán Somogyi. *Loli néni* (Aunt Loli), as my parents and I called her, would occasionally invite us for Sunday lunch to her home in Pozsonyi Street. I remember we always took the elevator on the way up to her elaborate penthouse apartment, and the circular staircase on the way down. Growing up in a one-story house with small windows and low ceilings, I loved buildings with stairs, elevators, high ceilings, balconies, everything we didn't have at home. There was a huge living room with enormous windows and a large balcony overlooking the Danube and the Buda hills. The apartment was furnished with quaint elegance, unlike ours, a testimony to the 1960s.

Lunch was always served by Marcsa, the live-in maid, who herself was a relic from a long-gone era. She chose to ignore the fact that we were living under a communist regime and remained loyal to Loli néni for the rest of her life. She insisted addressing her *méltó*, short for *méltóságos asszony*, a feudalistic term used to address women of nobility in prewar Hungary. While it is almost impossible to translate to English, my closest attempts would be milady or distinguished lady, neither of which truly delivers the flavor of the original expression. Marcsa made the best celery cream soup I have ever had in my life. There was a painting hanging in the dining room by a very famous Hungarian painter, József Rippl-Rónai. My mother was mesmerized by the fact that Loli néni was able to keep such a painting in her home in communist Hungary. My young brain associated this beautiful piece of art with the taste of Marcsa's celery cream soup, one always reminding me of the other.

We would have coffee or tea in the living room, served in elegant blue-and-white porcelain cups complete with saucers, delicately chiseled silver spoons, and matching dessert plates. It was quite a departure from the most basic mismatched plates and cheap cutlery we had in our house. There were a couple of very deep, soft, oversized armchairs upholstered in dark green velour. My father and I found them too comfortable to get up from. We just called them the "sinking chairs." Lots of blue-and-white porcelain plates were displayed on the wall as artwork, and a bronze bust of Lajos Hatvany stared at us from the corner.

Loli néni always wore a simple black dress with white pearls. Her face was covered with an almost grotesquely thick layer of loose powder that she often reapplied during our stay. She had very pale skin, especially in contrast with her brown eyes and her hair, which was dyed ebony black. She was very kind and attentive toward me. This exquisite apartment with its rich decor, Loli néni's polished looks and dignified demeanor, her choice of archaic words, and her inexhaustible and fascinating anecdotes transported us back, as if by a time machine, to an entirely different era. Unfortunately, my father had a sudden falling out with Loli néni, putting an abrupt end to these luxurious luncheons. I never learned the reason behind their final breakup, but I missed her world, a rare and isolated island of old-fashioned charm, sophistication, culture, and splendor. It was a world my generation only heard of or read about. It was a world my father had experienced firsthand as a young child.

Lajos Hatvany would also make his mark on my life in an indirect way, many years later. Soon after the communist regime ended in Hungary in 1989, the new government decided to rename many of the streets in Budapest. The initial thought was understandable—nobody wanted to see streets named after Lenin and Marx and their comrades after the Berlin Wall came down. However, they went too far in their enthusiasm to wipe out the communist past, changing some of the street names that had nothing to do with the previous regime. There was a narrow street in the Buda Castle District named after Lajos Hatvany, and much to everyone's surprise, it was suddenly renamed Kard utca (Sword Street) in 1990, returning to its prewar name. *Népszabadság (Liberty of the People)*, the leading Hungarian daily newspaper, published an editorial about this illogical and unfortunate mishap of the newly elected government. The article pointed out the absurdity of associating Lajos Hatvany with the communists and commended him for his invaluable contribution to Hungarian literature.

I wrote a letter to the newspaper explaining that Lajos Hatvany had been my grandfather's cousin, and as far as I knew, I was the last member of the entire Hatvany family still living in Hungary at the time. I expressed my gratitude to the editor for voicing his opinion and bringing light to this issue. Much to my surprise, *Népszabadság* published my letter, word for word. A couple of days later, the phone rang. A very polite gentleman with immaculate and maybe a bit old-fashioned manners introduced himself as István Rozsics, a historian of literature specializing in my ancestors' role in Hungary's cultural life. As I learned soon after, István had developed a close friendship with Loli néni, paying her regular visits over several years, learning as much about Lajos and the entire family as he could soak up while enjoying her very entertaining company. As a result of these visits, they published a book together in 1985 titled *Hatvany Lajos levelei* (*Lajos Hatvany's Letters*), compiling his extensive correspondence with various famous literary figures. I cherish a copy with István's personal note in it: "To Helga Hatvany, the last, charming offspring of the Buddenbrooks of Pest, with compliments from the coauthor. Budapest, Easter 1991."

Thanks to an overenthusiastic Hungarian government, I met a fascinating person and gained a very good friend. István was working for Sotheby's at the time, as their only Hungarian representative, reporting to the company's office in Vienna. Later he opened a succession of shops for old and rare books in Budapest and established himself as a successful art dealer. I had the pleasure of attending many of his late-night parties with the most interesting mix of people—Budapest intellectuals, artists, foreign diplomats, and journalists accredited to Hungary right after the political changes in the early 1990s. István and I remained very good friends until his untimely death in 2008.

Chapter Fourteen
Leap

DURING HIS THIRD YEAR IN CAMBRIDGE (it takes three years to earn an undergraduate degree in England), my father was so wrapped up in politics and so eager to go back to Hungary that he completely neglected his studies. He turned his focus entirely toward his involvement in the Communist Party and his dream of building a new world in his native country. Despite having the talent, the brains, and an appetite for knowledge, all the necessary ingredients for academic success, his performance suffered. At the end of his last year at Trinity College, he failed his final exams. In August 1947, József Hatvany arguably made the worst decision, the biggest mistake of his life. He abruptly left Cambridge University only one set of exams short of receiving a degree, embarked on a ship to cross the English Channel, and took the Arlberg-Orient-Express toward Hungary.

József and Doris arrived in Budapest, a city still wearing numerous scars of the war. Despite aggressive rebuilding efforts, most of the bridges over the Danube and many of the buildings were still in ruins. Yet Hungarians were full of energy and hope, in an almost euphoric state, looking forward to a brighter future. My father and his Scottish bride were immediately swept off their feet by this fever. Doris immersed herself in an intensive language course. Despite the fact that Hungarian is completely different from any other major European language, quite unique in its grammar, vocabulary, word order, conjugation, and pronunciation, she mastered it to a high proficiency. This—and, of course, her impressive education in history—enabled her to become a research fellow at the Historical Institute of the Hungarian Academy of Sciences.

My father found it quite challenging to find a job as a physicist, but he was able to join the Trade Union of Engineers. Soon he was sent to the Communist Party School, in order to "adjust his political views to the Hungarian requirements," as he would later recall. That is where he met László Rudas, a member of the Hungarian Academy of Sciences, director of the Communist Party School, and soon to be rector of the newly established Karl Marx University of Economics. As the head of Faculty of Philosophy, László Rudas asked my father to join him at the University of Economy as a departmental university teacher. My father was honored and happily accepted the position, becoming the youngest university lecturer in the country. He plunged into work with the energy and enthusiasm only the very young can.

After finishing his course at the Communist Party School, other members of the Communist Party recommended that my father join the Foreign Special Services of the Hungarian News Agency, which prepared the Hungarian Radio's English-language broadcast. This was a politically sensitive position, and as such, it had to be discussed in several party forums whether my father was the right fit. Finally, they came to a consensus and deemed him suitable. For the next two years, József Hatvany's day job was to teach Marxist philosophy at the newly established Karl Marx University of Economics, and in the evening, he worked for the Foreign Language Department of the Hungarian Radio. The English-language broadcast aired at midnight, and my father was in charge of compiling and editing the news—and, of course, reading it on the air. It was more than a full schedule, an exhausting lifestyle, but he wouldn't have had it any other way.

In July 1948, József and Doris went to the registrar's office of the 6th district in Budapest and got married in front of two witnesses.

Chapter Fifteen

Injustice

WHILE THE FIRST COUPLE YEARS after the war were about transition, uncertainty, and great hopes for new beginnings, the political climate in Hungary soon took a turn. In the 1947 elections, the Hungarian Workers' Party became the largest single party. By 1948, the communists gained control of the government, and the Socialist Democratic Party ceased to exist as an independent organization. In August 1949, the Parliament passed a new constitution modeled after the constitution of the Soviet Union. It was also at this time that the name of the country became Hungarian People's Republic. Complete with barbed wire and land mines, the Iron Curtain appeared on the Austrian border, and the darkest night of the Stalinist era began.

The Soviet-style show trials that swept across the entire Eastern Bloc, especially after the Stalin-Tito split in 1948, reached Hungary. Staged and rehearsed as if they were theater performances, these show trials became powerful tools of propaganda in the hands of the overenthusiastic followers of the Soviet Union, the leaders of a newly established dictatorship. Accusations were based on trumped-up charges, witnesses were coached, evidence was forged, and in most cases, the verdict was decided well before anyone set foot in the courtroom.

The Rajk case in 1949 became one of the most talked-about examples of Stalin's infamous purges. Minister of the interior and later minister of foreign affairs, a popular communist before, László Rajk was a threat in the eyes of Mátyás Rákosi, general secretary of the Hungarian Communist Party and Stalinist leader of Hungary. Accused of being a Titoist spy and an agent of Western imperialism, Mr. Rajk was interrogated, tortured, and consequently executed.

György Pálóczi-Horváth was József Hatvany's boss at the Radio. He too spent the war years in immigration and returned to Hungary from England in 1947, voluntarily and full of hope. Just like my father, he truly believed in the new ideology that promised everyone equal opportunity and a better life. He was especially enthusiastic about the so-called people's colleges, where students with the most disadvantaged background could get a free college education. Eighteen years older than my father, with considerably more life experience, György Pálóczi-Horváth seriously weighed the arguments for and against returning to Hungary before he finally made his decision. For him, leaving his second home, London, was a harder, bittersweet experience:

In February 1947, Martin Horvát, the editor of the Hungarian party daily, came to London, and asked me whether I would like to be the managing editor of a popular front weekly in Budapest, a sort of Hungarian *New Statesman and Nation*. I agreed. In April the official invitation arrived. On a May morning I drove through London for the last time. My train was leaving from Victoria Station....In January 1948 I was made head of the Foreign Language Department of the radio and of the Hungarian Broadcasting and News Agency. My department was responsible for broadcasts in French, English, German, Russian, Esperanto and later in some other languages. This was a most responsible position, because for Communists exact wording has a supreme importance. My department was busy from early morning till well past midnight.[34]

However, Mr. Pálóczi-Horváth couldn't enjoy leading the Foreign Language Department of the Hungarian Radio for too long.

Sudden shocks momentarily revealed the true face of the party. Such a shock came to me in March, 1949, when I was called to the party headquarters and was simply informed that next week I was to be transferred from my present position to the "cultural front", and made literary director of one of the nationalized publishing houses. Nobody consulted me about this. But what's more, I knew that this abrupt transfer was a demotion, since my work at the Broadcasting and News Agency was politically far more important. My job there was taken by a former Security

Police colonel. His transfer was also a demotion. Both of us pretended to be enthusiastic about the transfer...I was transferred in the beginning of March, 1949. Early in June László Rajk, a member of the Politbureau, Minister of Foreign Affairs, was suddenly arrested. His arrest caused tremendous shock and bewilderment...It was next to impossible to believe that he was an imperialist agent and a spy...During July and August many of my friends, mostly Communists who had returned from the West, but also members of the illegal old guard, were also arrested... At the end of August, 1949, Rákosi gave a reception in the Gellért Hotel in Budapest...He came to our table too, and stood next to me and asked: "How are you unruly characters, you artists and intellectuals?"[35]

Mr. Pálóczi-Horváth was soon arrested and sentenced to fifteen years in prison for spying. He was interrogated by the ÁVH—Államvédelmi Hatóság (State Protection Authority)—the dreaded and feared secret police, similar to the Soviet KGB and the East German Stasi, at their headquarters, Andrássy út 60. One episode stood out for its absurdity:

The first occasion would have been comical if it had not been the beginning of torture. One morning Tommyrot asked me where I met Professor Szentgyörgyi, the Nobel Prize winner Hungarian scientist during the war. I told him truthfully that I met him in Istanbul..."This will teach you, you fascist swine, that it is no use to lie to us. We knew all the time—we have it here in writing—that you met Professor Szentgyörgyi not in Istanbul but in Constantinople."[36]

The interrogator made sure his subject was well aware of his position and accepted the fact that he had no chance arguing with the authorities: "We don't like innocent people here. Anyone we pull in is guilty. We never make mistakes."[37]

∽

Standard Electric was one of the last companies still in foreign ownership, not yet nationalized by the Hungarian government.

> Established in 1928…most of its stock, and from 1935 all
> of them were owned by ITT (International Telephone and
> Telegraph Company)…Standard Electric's products: tele-
> phones, switchboards, radio and transmission equipment,
> were popular around Europe. During World War II, the
> factory was primarily engaged in war production, and after
> 1945, it was responsible for rebuilding and expanding the
> Hungarian telephone network as well as for handling resti-
> tution shipments to Yugoslavia. Deadlines were slipping,
> mostly for economic reasons. The factory's management
> was in regular contact with the American owners, and their
> representatives in Hungary, thus arousing the curiosity
> of the ÁVH from 1947. They soon started monitoring
> Standard Electric's activities using their embedded
> personnel, phone tapping, etc.…On 29 December 1949,
> a government decree was issued on the nationalization of

factories employing more than 10 persons and the ones still in foreign ownership. Speaking at a mass rally, Ernő Gerő, second only to Rákosi in the Communist Party leadership, said—and these words could indeed be taken as draft indictment for the Standard show trial—"We are talking about huge companies, such as Standard, the Telephone Company, Shell, Vacuum, First Hungarian Thread Works, and the Budakalász Textile Mill. Through the owners and management of these companies, foreign imperialists used them mostly as front organizations for building up a spy network and carrying out actions of sabotage. We have seen this in the MAORT - Magyar Amerikai Olajipari Rt. (Hungarian American Oil Company) case and more recently in the case of Standard, which is now being nationalized."[38]

"The Hungarian government wanted to nationalize Standard Electric without paying compensation to its foreign owners, and the only way they could do this was by fabricating a case against them, accusing them of spying. The indictment was clearly just a façade. This case was to be the first one to include foreign defendants. Meticulously planned and staged, this public show trial was to slander and vilify not just any foreigners, but citizens of two leading powers, the United States and Great Britain. Robert Vogeler and Edgar Sanders were both arrested in November 1949 along with numerous Hungarians.

All in all, 24 persons were arrested and another 80 interrogated as witnesses or experts during the trial…During the war, Sanders was an officer in the British army and was stationed in Budapest as a member of the Allied Control Commission afterward. He joined the company after demobilization. As his CV revealed, Vogeler had attended the US Naval Academy at Annapolis for three years. These were reasons enough to take them for professional spies… Vogeler's and Sanders' detention and court trial received great publicity in the American and British press. A leader in the 20 February issue of *The New York Times* said that it was a theatrical production taking place in Budapest with coached players.[39]

∾

Robert Vogeler, an American engineer, was assistant vice president of Standard Electric, assigned to Austria right after the war. Based in Vienna with his wife and two children, he traveled to Prague and Budapest on numerous occasions between 1945 and 1949. His confession was coerced out of him in a typical ÁVH fashion, as he details his ordeal in the book *I Was Stalin's Prisoner*:

> "Under prevailing conditions," I had written, "it was impossible for Standard Budapest to operate at a profit, which is why we wanted to modify the unfair penalties that were being imposed by the Hungarian government."
>
> This statement, as distorted by No. 1, was read back to me as follows: "We were eager to sign an agreement in order to charge exorbitant prices and thus destroy the popular benefits of the Three-Year Plan."

I pointed out that all we wanted to do was to make a profit, or at least break even, so as not to be forced into bankruptcy and thus provide the government with an excuse for confiscating Standard Budapest.

"Aha," said No. 1. "What you mean to say is that you wanted corrupt government officials…to play your game and thus give us a legal excuse for sabotage. You wanted to make the Hungarian people pay for your inefficiency. We fixed fair prices, but you wanted to increase them in order to form an imperialist monopoly"…

On the seventy-first day I surrendered to despair. This was on January 27, 1950. For seventy days, in spite of growing doubts, I had nourished the hope that the American Legation would somehow be able to procure my release. No. 2, however, insisted that I had been abandoned. In the beginning I knew that he was lying, but toward the end I began to wonder.

No. 2, with my help, now prepared a superconfession that ran to more than sixty pages. This time, instead of attempting to minimize my "crimes," I attempted to multiply them to such an extent that no one but a Communist or a fellow-traveler could possibly believe that I was guilty. In this endeavor I was apparently successful, for as my friends were able to demonstrate, I confessed at my subsequent trial to more than 200 acts that I couldn't possibly have committed.[40]

Just to make sure he wouldn't ruin the master plan, his ÁVH officer gave Mr. Vogeler some advice before the trial:

"Your entire future," he said, "will be determined by your behavior at the trial. If you fail to answer the president's questions in the proper spirit, you will be removed from the courtroom and taken to a special hospital. There you will be given treatment that will make you happy to come back and answer the president's questions. But it will also make you a cripple for life."[41]

Meticulously scripted and rehearsed to the last dot, the trial itself was indeed like theater, but this drama could ruin or end the lives of its performers, as a documentary film reveals:

Once the script was complete, it was time to find the right actors. They went through several versions before agreeing on the final casting:

Imre Geiger	bourgeois engineer
Vogeler and Sanders	imperialist spies
Zoltán Radó	Trotskyite spy
Kelemen Domokos	bookkeeper with fascist sentiments
Edina Dőry	has-been aristocrat, bartender at the Hotel Astoria
István Justh	representative of the clerical reactionary forces[42]

The cast was not yet complete, however. They needed two interpreters with flawless English. The authorities identified József Hatvany as one of best English speakers in Hungary and chose him to interpret for Robert Vogeler.

Since they had too much information about the trial, the interpreters themselves had to be followed and observed by the ÁVH:

> Subject: József Hatvany, "Jóska," resides at 3rd district, Hunor utca 20.
>
> Report: Budapest, February 13, 1950. I report that we started observing above subject at 19:00 hours in front of our headquarters. Monitored individual left the building at 19:50 hours, got in a vehicle provided by our authorities, license number AK 207, and was driven to the studio located at Bródy Sándor utca [the building of the Hungarian Radio] at 20:05 hours. We stopped his observation at 24:00 hours.[43]

Naturally, there were ÁVH agents assigned to the two interpreters during the rehearsals and the trial itself, to ensure their full cooperation. Furthermore, even the judge himself was constantly monitored and supervised. Years later, my father would write in a report that during the dress rehearsal, one of the ÁVH agents reprimanded the judge for slightly deviating from the original script while questioning Vogeler.

> The trial began on the 17th…The audience was admitted by personal tickets made out for numbered seats. Of the 106 seats, 40 were given out to ÁVH members, 20 to journalists, 2 each to the American and British legations, and the

rest were distributed among trusted ministry and factory employees. ÁVH agents kept an eye on the audience at the trial and made a summary of the remarks they heard and also of the "criticism" that appeared in the foreign press, and these were attached to the documents of the case... On 21 February 1950, the Budapest Criminal Court sentenced Imre Geiger and Zoltán Radó to death and Robert Vogeler and Edgar Sanders to 15 and 13 years of imprisonment respectively. The others in detention, both the accused and witnesses, were sentenced in camera to several years in prison...On 8 May, Imre Geiger and Zoltán Radó were hanged.[44]

With the help of the American government and especially due to his wife's relentless efforts, Robert Vogeler was released from prison in April 1951, and he left Hungary. Edgar Sanders was only released in 1953. The twenty-four people sentenced in the Standard trial were not formally acquitted until November 1989. Only four of them would live to see it.

Chapter Sixteen

Collapse

My father had never been one to hold back his opinion. *Reserved* and *diplomatic* are not exactly the most fitting words to describe him. One can only imagine how his uncensored, straightforward way of expressing himself combined with his rather stubborn personality might have sabotaged his efforts to fit in. While engaging in heated arguments about politics with Professor Bertrand Russell at Trinity College, Cambridge must have been an exhilarating and stimulating experience, questioning the views and actions of a rigid and extremely insecure establishment in Hungary was not at all advisable. Whether he voiced his opinion about the Standard trial or kept his thoughts to himself, we will never know for sure. It almost doesn't matter, however, since he was already on the radar of the authorities.

Trouble started when he refused to submit his university lectures in writing. An exceptionally gifted public speaker, József preferred giving talks without a script. This was not welcome in a world of ever-tightening censorship. But it was just the first sign of more hurdles to come. His Communist Party membership card was stolen out of his pocket together with his wallet. Losing one's party membership card was considered a cardinal sin. He was accused of exposing it to the enemy. My father was immediately expelled from the party and simultaneously fired from the University of Economy. Upon the suggestion of Mrs. Hárs, an overzealous ÁVH investigator, he was soon kicked out of the Radio, despite the protest of his colleagues. Fortunately, the Hungarian Academy of Sciences took him in as deputy head of department. My father appealed against his exclusion from the party immediately, but it took two years for the Central Control Commission to respond, suggesting they postpone the hearing to a more appropriate time. Simultaneously, they ordered my father's supervisors, the president and the secretary general of the Hungarian Academy of Sciences, to make sure he wouldn't suffer any disadvantage for being excluded from the party.

During the time he worked at the Academy of Sciences, my father wrote a book about the life of a very famous Hungarian physicist, Loránd Eötvös, best known for his work on gravitation and surface tension. Following in the footsteps of his father, József Eötvös, Baron Loránd Eötvös also served as minister of education and theology for a while, though he dedicated most of his life to scientific research and teaching. At the turn of the century, he became president of the Hungarian Academy of Sciences. In 1950, Hungary's biggest and most prestigious university was named after him. József Hatvany's book about Loránd Eötvös was published in 1951 as part of an educational series introducing Hungarian scientists to the general public. Being a physicist himself, my father had a thorough understanding of the work of Loránd Eötvös, and he must have been happy to undertake this task. Yet when I read it, I was completely taken aback by the exaggerated political comments and conclusions, as well as the enthusiastic quotes from Engels and references to Lenin. They heavily coated this otherwise very informative book about a brilliant scientist in a nauseatingly thick layer of communist propaganda. His style of writing—the entire tone of the book—was a departure from anything and everything he had ever written before or after this publication. It was completely uncharacteristic of him. Even for the dedicated communist he was those days, it seemed so over the top, I cannot help but wonder if he wrote it in an attempt to protect himself from further scrutiny. At this point, he had already been expelled from the party and fired from the university and the Radio for no apparent reason. He was by all means smart enough to know that his heritage and upbringing were thorns in the administration's eyes. As one of the interpreters, my father had a front-row seat to the infamous Standard case. The rehearsed and staged nature of these show trials became painfully clear to him. By 1951, he must have realized that his hopes and dreams for a just and fair society, a bright future for his country, something he full-heartedly believed in, had begun to slip away.

Show trials were loud and public displays of power by the dictatorship, but one didn't have to be involved in such a high-profile case in order to be arrested. Individuals quietly disappeared one by one. Intellectuals were especially considered serious threats to the newly established totalitarian regime. Highly educated Hungarians who voluntarily returned from the West after the war became prime target. It was ironic, since they included some of the most honest communists, the true believers, yet they were deemed imperialist spies. "Why else would they have returned to Hungary?" argued the government. In order to avoid naming their actual acquaintances as Western spy connections, many of them came up with creative answers when questioned by the ÁVH after their arrests:

"The architects who studied in France confessed that they spied for Le Corbusier, those in Britain had a spy chief of the Intelligence Service, called Sir Patrick Abercrombie. People in Italy spied for Ignazio Silone. Many in France spied for Voltaire or Arouet…George Faludy, the poet, spied for two Office of Strategic Services officers—Edgar Allan Poe and Walt Whitman."[45]

$$\backsim$$

In August 1952 my father was suddenly drafted into the army for reserve duty. He applied for the skydiving division, partly for the adventure, partly because members of this special branch of the military could enjoy privileges such as oranges and fine chocolates. These delicacies were completely unavailable for the general public of Hungary those days. He could only indulge in these rare treats for two weeks. One night, abruptly awakened from his sleep, József Hatvany was arrested. He was driven directly to the ÁVH headquarters, where an officer addressed him in a very condescending way: "Well, my dear Baron," he said, "it's time for the final showdown."[46]

During the first night, the interrogation officer told him that the authorities had proof of his spying activities, and when my father dared to ask for an explanation, his request was dismissed as provocation. The authorities listed the following accusations against him: his bourgeois decent; the fact that he wasn't arrested in Cambridge, let alone expelled from England despite his active work in the British Communist Party; and that he "exposed his Party membership card to the enemy" when, in fact, it was stolen from him. Details of József Hatvany's experience in the hands of the ÁVH can be found in his court documents, as he described them in his own words:

> From this time forward, with just a few exceptions, my interrogation always took place at night, conducted by a lieutenant. He began by saying he was authorized to tell me that the party gave an order to the authorities to convict me. He ordered me to mention occasions when I was in contact with foreign citizens, or people who have since been convicted for spying. "It is possible," he said, "that these contacts don't qualify as spying, according to your opinion, but it is up to the party and the authorities to decide."
>
> Based on the material discussed in this manner, my interrogation officer drafted statements that were distorting the facts, portraying them in false light. When I hesitated signing these documents, he threatened repeatedly, and in an increasingly serious way, with my wife being arrested, convicted and beaten. He even drafted an alleged proposal for the implementation of all these threats in my presence. Further sanctions against me included repeated hits in the face, kicks in the ankle, while I always had to stand in attention during my interrogations that lasted several hours. The lieutenant also gave orders to the guards not to let me sleep.[47]

Sleep deprivation was a preferred interrogation method of the ÁVH. After being forcefully kept awake for several days, most people experience confusion, impaired judgment, and hallucinations. Interrogations would either continue in this state of mind, until the subject is ready to confess virtually anything, or he would be allowed to sleep for a very short time, only to be abruptly awakened and immediately questioned again. Almost everyone arrested in those days was subject to this interrogation technique. György Pálóczi-Horváth recalled his ordeal during his lengthy stay at the ÁVH headquarters as follows:

> When one dozed off, the guard kicked the iron door of the cell with his heavy boot. This terrific bang woke one up scores of times a day. It was as if something exploded in one's head. One awoke with a pounding heart. Six weeks of this kind of life produced a headachy, hungry state in which one had constant hallucinations.[48]

Arrested in the middle of the night and interrogated in this manner for weeks, my father would never recover from the trauma. For the rest of his life, every time he was suddenly awakened, he would jump out of bed, shaking, drenched in sweat. I learned this the hard way as a child. Once I accidentally woke him up from his deepest sleep. The sight of him in such a vulnerable state of mind was both shocking and frightening. After that, I was extremely careful not to put him, or myself for that matter, in that situation ever again.

As part of the interrogation process, my father had to endure systematic beatings, constant humiliation, and sleep deprivation while being confined to a tiny, windowless space equipped with only a small opening for air. If these circumstances weren't enough to break him, the lieutenant came up with various other ways to coerce a "confession" out of him:

> My judgment was also severely impaired by the statements of my interrogation officer, whom I considered a representative of the party. He declared some people spies, whom I respected as communists. He made very derogatory comments of people who enjoyed the respect ¬f the Hungarian and international worker's movement. The lieutenant declared the British Communist Party a gathering place for spies. He repeatedly stated that everyone who came back to Hungary from British immigration was a spy, without exception. Every time a new name came up, the first thing the lieutenant wanted to know whether the person in question was a Jew. He had a terribly beaten and tortured detainee placed in my cell, and repeatedly threatened me with being beaten until crippled. Every time he interrogated me, he started with the same question: "What will happen to you?" and he always demanded that I answered, "I will be hanged."
>
> Hearing these statements, I more and more succumbed to my inevitable fate of having to die, and all I cared about, was to do everything in my power to keep my wife out of harm's way.
>
> Using the above methods, and based on distorted records, my interrogating officer fabricated the following case against me: The Communist Party of the Countries of the British Empire held a conference in the summer of 1947, where I reported to Marton Horváth, head of

the Hungarian delegation, on the order of the Head of Department of Foreign Affairs of the British Communist Party. The British comrades informed Mr. Horváth about my activities in England, and I had to discuss with him the details of my return to Hungary. Marton Horváth authorized Imre Patkó, a fellow delegate, who at the time was an employee of *Szabad Nép* [*Free People*, a Hungarian newspaper], to discuss these issues with me, and so we did. Meanwhile, Imre Patkó had a meeting with an immigrant communist journalist, György Pálóczi-Horváth, in the London underground, at the ticketing platform of the Piccadilly Station. I accompanied Mr. Patkó to this meeting, where he introduced me to Mr. Pálóczi-Horváth. After this, I exchanged a couple words with Mr. Pálóczi-Horváth, telling him that I had read two of his books, and I was glad to meet him. According to my interrogation officer, this is when György Pálóczi-Horváth recruited me into the English Intelligence Service. In order to make this statement plausible, my interrogation officer made me admit to a further meeting with Mr. Pálóczi-Horváth in London, by threatening with my wife's arrest. In fact, there was no such meeting.

Even at that point, I denied having been recruited into the English Intelligence Service by György Pálóczi-Horváth, and had never signed any record containing this statement under any threat.[49]

While working at the Hungarian News Agency, part of my father's job was to keep contact with a reporter from Reuters. According to the agreement between the two news agencies, he was supposed to inform his colleague at Reuters about the material that was used for compiling the text of the English broadcast to be aired at midnight on Hungarian Radio. All his colleagues working in other languages did the same with their relevant news agencies.

> According to my interrogation officer, communication with foreign news agencies constituted the criminal offense of spying, seriously jeopardizing the national interest of the Hungarian People's Republic, and I committed these actions of espionage within the framework of an organized criminal conspiracy with György Pálóczi-Horváth... Though I, of course, admitted that I shared news material with foreign reporters, neither then, nor later did I admit to the spying nature of this communication. I have never signed any record admitting it, nor did I make such statement at court. My interrogation officer tried to make the existence of the organized criminal conspiracy plausible by showing me records, in which György Pálóczi-Horváth stated he had been in favor of me joining the Radio because he thought I could be a helpful accomplice in his spying activities. When I asked for a face-to-face meeting with Mr. Pálóczi-Horváth, the officer said, he had already been hanged.[50]

Of course, this couldn't have been further from the truth. György Pálóczi-Horváth was alive, serving his fifteen-year prison sentence. At one point, he too was interrogated about my father's alleged spying activities, but neither he nor my father could be pressured into confessing that the other one was an imperialist spy.

⁓

John Desmond Bernal was an internationally known scientist, considered to be a pioneer in x-ray crystallography and molecular biology. Born in Ireland and educated in England, he became a fellow of the Royal Society.

In the late 1940s, he became vice president of the World Peace Council, and in 1959 he took over its presidency from Frederic Joliot-Curie. In 1953 the Soviet Union awarded J. D. Bernal with the Stalin Peace Prize.

My father met Professor J. D. Bernal on two occasions in 1950. First, they visited Szob, a small town in northern Hungary, with my father's boss, the secretary general of the Hungarian Academy of Sciences. On another occasion, the three of them traveled together to Sztálinváros (Stalin Town), a newly emerging industrial town along the Danube, a place showcased by communist leaders as one of their achievements in the early 1950s. Based on this information, the interrogation officer concluded that my father must have shared unauthorized information with Professor Bernal, thus putting the Hungarian People's Republic in jeopardy. He stated that Bernal was an imperialist spy and an agent of the British Intelligence.

My interrogation officer also compiled records about my correspondence with my English friends, which correspondence, in his view, also constituted the criminal offense of spying. In these letters, that I only happened to exchange with the members of the British Communist Party, I shared the economic and political achievements of our people's democracy, because I thought it would help the comrades with their propaganda. My interrogation officer considered these spying, because, in his opinion, the British Communist Party was a gathering place for spies, and I did not receive specific permission to share the data (that I copied from *Szabad Nép*) with foreigners. I did not admit to spying at this point either.

He was extremely dissatisfied with me for not admitting to any criminal activity in any of my records. He repeatedly emphasized that if I continued this behavior, he would implement the threats mentioned earlier. He reasoned that the Party had already made a decision to convict me, and since I considered myself a communist, I should feel obligated to admit to at least one criminal act entirely, based on which I could be sentenced. He suggested I admit to disclosing official secrets, since according to him, everyone committed it anyway. He also explained to me that parting with any insignificant work related information, such as an event, a name or any personal opinion without specific, written permission, is considered disclosure of official secrets. Based on these, I admitted that in this sense, I did, in fact, disclose official secrets, and had been doing so continuously. During my work, I had discussions with members of various offices and Party organizations, with whom I shared, or refused to share pieces of information using my own judgment, without having been given specific and written permission in advance. My interrogation officer acknowledged this with great satisfaction, and included it in the records.[51]

⁂

Political trials in 1950s Hungary had nothing to do with justice or reason. My father's trial was no exception. He was assigned a defense attorney who only received the indictment in the courtroom when the hearing was already underway. Prior to that, my father was not allowed to talk to him. During the trial, instead of making the slightest attempt to defend his client, the defense attorney actually delivered a second speech of prosecution. Not a single witness requested by my father was summoned to appear.

Even under such circumstances, the court threw out all charges based on the data submitted by Mrs. Hárs, the ÁVH investigator, who had my father fired from the Radio and expelled from the party, since all her accusations were deemed completely ungrounded.

At his trial, my father denied all spying activities he was accused of, yet he admitted to the disclosure of official secrets as previously defined by his interrogation officer, due to the threats he faced. Regardless, the court found him guilty of the following:

1. Espionage committed for the duration of some three weeks, on the order and under the leadership of György Pálóczi-Horváth;

2. Disclosure of official secrets to official personnel and an English professor without specific authorization;[52]

József Hatvany was sentenced to eleven years in prison. Despite his request, he was not escorted to his hearing of appeal and had no knowledge of what happened there.

Chapter Seventeen
Walls

IT WAS OCTOBER 1952. After two months of brutal interrogation at the ÁVH headquarters and a swift sentencing by the court, my father began his prison sentence. Márianosztra, a town of less than a thousand residents in northern Hungary, is synonymous with its prison. Originally built in the fourteenth century as a monastery, it was turned into a woman's penitentiary in the nineteenth century. Ironically, it was the very prison where my grandmother Vera was locked up for about eighteen months for trying to have some of her assets smuggled out of the country in the early years of World War II. After 1949, the building was taken over by the ÁVH, and its cells were filled with political prisoners. The conditions at Márianosztra were dreadful. Very cold cells in the winter, severe malnourishment, and regular beatings by some sadistic prison guards took a toll on my father's health and psyche.

As a supplementary punishment, in addition to the eleven-year prison term, my father was also sentenced to complete confiscation of his property. He and his wife, Doris, had a comfortable one-bedroom service apartment that the Hungarian Academy of Sciences assigned to them. It was furnished in a basic but functional manner, complete with central heating and hot water, modern conveniences that could not be taken for granted in Hungary those days. He and Doris managed to bring back a sizable private library when they arrived from England in 1947. All of that was taken away. Doris was evicted and forced to move to a much less comfortable studio apartment. My father's carefully selected collection of several thousand books was confiscated, along with his scientific notes, manuscripts, technical drawings, personal documents, and clothes. Almost all their furniture was taken together with other home goods, such as the radio, area rug, and so on, leaving Doris with just the bare necessities. The modest amount of savings they had in the bank, in the form of Peace Bonds that everyone was encouraged to buy as a contribution to the government's postwar rebuilding efforts, was also confiscated.

One day, in the spring of 1954, a prison guard entered my father's cell. It wasn't his scheduled round. It wasn't mealtime either. The guard looked at my father, who was surprised by the unexpected visit, and asked him, "Are you married?"

My father replied, "Yes."

After a short silence, the guard said, "Not anymore. Your wife divorced you." And with that, he was gone.

Many of the wives of political prisoners were told by the authorities that their husbands were hanged. There were some who filed for divorce and eventually remarried, only to find themselves in an impossible situation when their husbands were released from prison years later.

Others held on to their hopes, suspecting they were given false information, and waited for their loved ones to return. Some were pressured into divorcing their imprisoned husbands in order to keep their jobs or escape harassment or even internment. Whether Doris belonged to one or more of these categories or just couldn't bear the thought of waiting for nine more years, facing uncertainty, we will never know. Given the circumstances and the spine-grinding atmosphere of the times, any of the above choices seems as plausible and justified as the next one.

When I read the official divorce papers that I found in a folder together with some of my father's prison documents, the language and the tone used to describe the reasons Doris would divorce her husband made me wonder if the whole thing was staged just like the trials in those days. It doesn't read like a divorce ruling in one particular couple's case. It reads more like a form letter fitting all similar cases, names and dates being the only variables.

After three years in Márianosztra, my father was transferred to another prison in Budapest. Circumstances were slightly better there, but what really set this place apart was the opportunity to work. Highly educated, creative professionals represented a significant percentage of political prisoners. The authorities realized they had tremendous brain capacity at their disposal and decided to use it to the country's advantage. They divided the professional prison population into two groups: engineers and scholars of philology. The latter included historians, journalists, writers, poets, and so on. Among other highly respected and well-known intellectuals, the writer and publicist Pál Ignotus worked in this group. Back in 1936 he, my grandfather Bertalan Hatvany, and their mutual friend, the poet Attila József, founded *Szép Szó* (*Beautiful Word*), a progressive literary periodical. György Pálóczi-Horváth also worked in this group as a translator. In fact, he even shared a cell with Mr. Ignotus for a while.

My father joined the group of engineers. The fact that he was not an engineer but a physicist by training didn't pose as an obstacle. All engineers and scientists were glad they were finally allowed to put their brains to good use instead of spending further years staring at the walls of their prison cells, desperately trying to hang on to their sanity. This group included some of the greatest minds in Hungary, for example László Kozma, a former director of Bell Telephone in Antwerp, Belgium, university professor, and cofounder of the electrical engineering faculty at the Budapest Technical University. After the war Mr. Kozma acted as technical director of Standard Electric until 1949, when he was arrested along with the company's entire management and sentenced to prison on trumped-up charges during the Standard show trial. Neither Mr. Kozma nor Mr. Pálóczi-Horváth crossed paths with my father, however, since both of them had been released from prison prior to my father's transfer.

Members of this elite group of engineers were given all the Hungarian and international publications the ÁVH could obtain for them. Thus, ironically, they had access to the latest results of scientific research taking place in the West, information otherwise censored, not readily available to scientists outside, in the greater prison called Hungary.

It was then and there, during his fourth year in confinement, that József Hatvany laid down the foundation of his future scientific career. In the first few months alone, he submitted seventeen innovations, three of which were accepted. Together with a couple of his fellow prisoners, he started working on the development of numerical control, and designs for digital machine tool automation. Some of their work from prison even received patents.

❧

For years, my father tried everything in his power to have his case reexamined. His first letter to the court in 1954 fell on deaf ears. At the end of 1955, when he learned that Mr. Pálóczi-Horváth had been out of prison for over a year and since been acquitted and fully rehabilitated, my father sent a second letter to the Public Prosecutor's Office with a new request. This time he argued that the false charges on which he was sentenced to eleven years in prison were entirely based on the equally false charges made against György Pálóczi-Horváth. It was no surprise that this too was left without response. His third letter to the court, in May 1956, was also unanswered, and it is hard to say whether these requests had anything to do with what happened next.

Two months later, in July 1956, József Hatvany was released on parole, and on August 24 the Supreme Court acquitted him from all charges in the absence of criminal activity. The Hungarian Academy of Sciences immediately took him back as deputy head of the Presidential Secretariat. However, his newly acquired freedom was far from smooth sailing. A world apart from the tremendous wealth and privilege he experienced during his early childhood as an offspring of a powerful industrial dynasty, a family of fame and nobility, he found himself with absolutely nothing. Not a change of clothes, not an extra pair of shoes. One can only imagine how extremely humiliating it must have been for him to write a letter to the Ministry of Justice, explaining his case and asking for immediate financial aid.

In September 1956 he was rewarded rehabilitation. It was supposed to compensate him for his arrest, his missed income during the four years he spent in prison, and for the loss of all his personal property. The amount of money he actually received was just shy of his forty-seven months' worth of lost salary.

My father also made attempts to recover the bonds that were taken from him, as well as trying to plead with the Academy of Sciences to provide him with a service apartment similar in type and comfort level to the one Doris and he had before his arrest. Neither of these attempts proved successful, nor did his intent to start a criminal investigation against the prison in Márianosztra.

The wristwatch he had deposited there as a personal item of value was stolen by one of the prison guards, and the relevant ticket was forged. Apart from the principle, of course, it is highly debatable whether it was a smart move to send a very harsh letter to a prison those days, threatening a criminal procedure. On the other hand, valuable or not, that wristwatch would have served as the one and only material link to his life before prison.

In the fall of 1956, what started as a peaceful demonstration by university students in Budapest turned into a massive revolution soon to be talked about all over the world. On October 23, people took to the streets demanding free speech, free press, and the withdrawal of Soviet troops from Hungary. Things soon turned violent when police forces started using teargas and handguns against the crowds, but it paled in comparison to what happened two days later.

On October 25 Soviet tanks appeared in the streets, and the city turned into a war zone once again. Hungarians were desperately pleading for help on the waves of Radio Free Europe, but help never came. Without the West behind it, Hungary was no match for the mighty Soviet army. Shocked and disappointed, Hungarians had to face the cold fact that their country was not big enough and important enough for Western Europe and the United States to risk a military conflict with Khrushchev. Left to fend for themselves, Hungarians saw the revolution promptly suppressed with extreme force and brutality. The death toll approached three thousand, while twelve thousand were arrested and imprisoned and hundreds executed by the government. Amid the chaos that followed the bloody retaliations, more than two hundred thousand Hungarians succeeded in crossing the Austrian border and fled to the West.

Time magazine named the Hungarian Freedom Fighter man of the year in its January 1957 issue, but it took more than thirty years for Hungarians to freely celebrate the date of the uprising. I grew up learning very little about it in school under the communist regime, where it was only marginally mentioned as a counterrevolution. It wasn't until 1989 that October 23 became a national holiday.

My father did not participate in the 1956 revolution, despite some of his colleagues urging him to do so. Rather, he decided to stay under the radar and "save the building and the documents of the Academy of Sciences for future generations," as he would put it decades later in an interview. His car was caught in a crossfire when he was trying to deliver medicine to a coworker in need across town, and he narrowly escaped injury or death.

Although he didn't play an active role in the uprising itself, József fiercely opposed the intervention by the Soviet troops, not to mention the terrible retaliations that followed. He welcomed some of the changes that took place in Hungary since his release from prison, but after the revolution was suppressed, he feared the return of the previous regime that had senselessly robbed him of four years of his youth. Sadly, it wouldn't be long before my father learned just how valid his fears were.

Chapter Eighteen
Doris

WHETHER JÓZSEF'S RELATIONSHIP with Doris ended at the time of their official divorce in 1954 while he was in prison or in the weeks or months after his release in 1956 will remain unanswered. I always wondered if Doris really turned her back to him when he was in dire straits, or was it a much more complex question, as in the cases of so many other wives of political prisoners at that time. Regardless, my father did close this chapter of his life soon after regaining his freedom.

In August 1957, exactly ten years after her arrival in Hungary, Doris returned to Scotland. As far as I was aware, they never had any further contact with each other.

I always wanted to know more about her but couldn't bring myself to ask. My father rarely mentioned anything about his prison years, nor did he ever talk about Doris with me. I sensed an invisible barrier, an unsaid rule that made it obvious to me that Doris was not be mentioned, and that part of my father's life was not be discussed. Had I tried harder, maybe I could have pried something out of him, but I didn't want to cause pain by reopening old wounds. Nevertheless, Doris had been in the back of my mind over the years. From time to time, I even entertained the thought of trying to look for her, hoping she would hold the key to some of my father's personality traits, especially regarding his subsequent, often peculiar relations with women.

Fifty-five years later, on a cold, foggy day in February 2012, I arrived in Sanquhar, a tiny little town in the Dumfries and Galloway region of Scotland. Doris turned eighty-nine that day. As I entered her room at the Queensberry Care Home for the Elderly, I saw a very small, fragile lady almost completely swallowed by the large armchair she was sitting in. When she lifted her eyes, an intelligent, lively person was revealed behind the curtain of an extremely frail physical appearance. She looked at me and said in a soft, barely audible voice, "It is lovely to finally meet you." I don't know how I managed to keep my composure and reserve the flood of tears for later that night. My initial worries about her having a strong Scottish accent, hard for me to understand, disappeared the minute the first words left her lips, and so did my fear of not being welcome. After exchanging some pleasantries, I asked her if I could use a voice recorder. She agreed without reservation. While I tried to ask many questions and steer her toward certain topics, I didn't mind when she took care of the conversation, telling her story as she remembered it.

Doris said she was quite happy to accompany my father to Hungary in 1947. "It was a different life, quite a change from the small coastal town [Forres] in the north of Scotland where I grew up," she said. She was the only child, "an oddly only child," as she put it, of a gardener of a county estate, and a housewife, living in a beautiful but remote country-side, in a household where money was very tight. Luckily, Doris excelled at school and received a scholarship to Aberdeen University, a rare honor at that time, especially for a woman.

At the end of the war, she was sent to London for war service. "There weren't many opportunities besides this one other than getting into the forces and so on...and they were taking women at that time, since I was a student...and that's when I learned to love London. I was at the place where the decoding arrangement was," she told me. As I learned, Doris worked for the Foreign Office at Bletchley Park, about an hour northwest of London. At this extremely secretive code-breaking center, they used a number of increasingly sophisticated computing machines, the predecessors of the modern computers, to break the encrypted mes-sages sent by the German Enigma machines. In addition to dedicated code-breaking teams, there were thousands of wireless radio operators at Bletchley and around the country, intercepting and transcribing mes-sages, as well as a large group of clerks, mostly women, who handled the resulting decoded messages. Doris was one of the clerks.

"There were lots of American boys there [in London]," she said, laughing. "It was quite interesting, as I remember. I was running for the air raid shelter, but I didn't run from the American soldiers. I almost married one, but I am glad I didn't. I don't think I would have been happy living in America, especially in the southern part of the United States."

It was also in London where Doris met my father. They were both district organizers during the general elections in the summer of 1945. "He was very politically active, very left wing, and so was I," she recalled.

After receiving her master's degree in history from Aberdeen University, Doris was given another scholarship to attend Cambridge University, where she started working on her doctorate. Almost four years her junior, my father was still in his undergraduate years. The following summer the two of them went on a cycling tour from Cambridge to the North of England. They stayed overnight at my father's alma mater, Oundle School. That's where he told her about his horrible ear infection and how nobody helped him despite his excruciating pain until it was too late and he lost his hearing in one ear as a result. I told her I could never remember which ear it was. Apparently, Doris herself couldn't keep it straight either. Most people never knew he was deaf on one side, as we both remembered, unless someone stood on his deaf side and he didn't expect to be spoken to. He was able to disguise it most of the time. Interestingly enough, Doris's father also happened to be deaf in one ear, and she couldn't recall which side it was.

Upon arriving in Budapest in August 1947, Doris went to university to study Hungarian. "My scholarship [from Carnegie Trust] continued for a year or two after we arrived in Hungary. I had a hard time settling in. People were very suspicious those days of someone who came from the outside." She said she learned some Hungarian in Cambridge, but there wasn't anybody who could teach her, and she couldn't speak it with my father. Once in Hungary, she read a lot of poetry, which I found quite amazing and impressive, since reading poetry requires a deeper understanding of the fine layers and nuances of a language. "At that time they published seven volumes of Hungarian poets, and we bought some of these volumes. I would take them with me everywhere. I had some very good friends at the Historical Institute. On the other hand, at the Academy where Józsi worked, they were not friendly to me. They thought I was an impostor and I shouldn't be there. They also thought Józsi was too good looking for me. And he was indeed good looking as a young man, very handsome," she told me with a smile.

It surprised me to hear her referring to my father as Józsi, a nickname for József, mostly used when addressing a child. Until I met Doris, the only people I had ever heard calling my father Józsi were his parents and his stepsister Bobette. Understandably, they all stuck to his childhood nickname. However, by the time I was born, everyone in Hungary called my father Jóska, another nickname for József, used for adults. To complicate things even further, later in his life, many people in Hungary adopted the English nickname Joe, by which he was known to his classmates in England, and later on to his foreign friends and colleagues. However, nobody in Hungary called him Józsi anymore. I was actually pleased to hear Doris remembering him by this nickname, since I never liked the sound of Jóska.

"We had a flat that was at the time very good for Budapest, and we were comfortable. Your father was very eager to go back to Hungary, and he fit right in from the first minute as if he had never left. It was very difficult for me before I learned the language. All I knew was to say *átszállójegyet kérek* [I would like a transfer ticket, please], and every head on the bus turned around and looked at me. I was very embarrassed and hated to travel by myself," Doris said.

"I got married in Hungary. I wish I didn't get divorced in Hungary as well. I could really tell you that! We had some very good friends. One knew Józsi as a child. What was his name? Nagy Péter," said Doris in the Hungarian order, family name first, given name second. She recalled the two siblings as follows: "There was Nagy Péter and his younger brother…András. And these two were friends with him. We went a lot to András's for Sunday meal. It was very good. On the day we were married, there was no wedding, not even a bouquet of flowers. Józsi went off and got some very, very tacky-looking roses. They were terrible. I didn't say anything, but András came in with this great big bouquet, so I had a bouquet after all. He was a very good friend. It was awkward. I forget how I handled it, but I managed to get through," she said, laughing. I mentioned my father's correspondence with András while he was still in Cambridge, but she didn't remember it. I pointed out that in one of those letters, my father referred to her as a "charming young Scots girl," to which Doris replied, smiling, "I thought he was charming as well."

She had quite vivid memories of my father's disappearance in August 1952:

> We went on a picnic somewhere south of Budapest. Some colleagues I was working with and Józsi came along. He was supposed to be coming home with me, but the army was there and told me that he had been called up [to reserve duty], so I had to walk home, for miles and miles along the railway track. I didn't know what happened to him. People just disappeared then. A young lad from the ÁVO [Állam-védelmi Osztály (State Protection Department), the old name of ÁVH Államvédelmi Hatóság (State Protection

Authority), the secret police] said to me that he's been up to some mischief, but he said, "Don't worry!" Of course, I worried.

Andrássy út was the place to fear. I spent hours and hours there when Hatvany disappeared, trying to find out what happened to him. That was the headquarters of the secret police. So I had the courage, but one time they told me, "Oh, but you will be next to be arrested." I was determined to find out what happened to my husband. I was lucky, in a way. They [the ÁVH] made a very careful selection of what was mine and what was his and so on [referring to the complete confiscation of my father's property after his sentencing in October 1952].

The next thing I got was a letter just before Christmas. I could send a three-kilogram package to Márianosztra [the prison]. And then I got a pass to see him. When I went there, he was wearing wooden-soled boots, and the towel I sent him was wrapped around his neck as a scarf because it was so cold there. The conditions were dreadful, really dreadful. He said his interrogator told him every single day: "This is your last day, Hatvany. This is your last day. You will have to die."

Doris repeated this Márianosztra story over and over again during my two-day visit. This was the one and only story she told me several times. It must have been burned into her memory deeper than anything else she saw or experienced during the ten years she lived in Hungary. Sixty years later it still haunted her. She said her colleagues at the

Historical Institute didn't believe her when she described Márianosztra to them. She remembered them saying, "Nonsense. We don't treat our fellow Hungarians that way."

⚬⚬⚬

More than anything, I was truly hoping to shed some light on the details, reasons, and circumstances of their divorce. Unfortunately, it turned out to be the very thing left in a haze forever. The official divorce papers indicate the marriage ended in the spring of 1954, while my father was in prison. However, the tone of the document and the pressure most spouses of political prisoners faced that time suggest it might have been a formality rather than a real divorce. When I asked Doris, she didn't seem to remember the details. There is nothing unusual about having memory lapses at the age of eighty-nine. Yet, I was somewhat disappointed and sad not to have been able to unlock this particular door to my father's life. Doris didn't remember exactly when and how they got divorced, but she kept suggesting it most likely happened after my father was released from prison, sometime toward the end of 1956 rather than in 1954. When I mentioned the divorce papers and the prison guard who casually informed my father about Doris divorcing my father without his knowledge or consent, she said her friends advised her to do so, since it was supposed to be safer for her under the circumstances.

"I can't remember," she said. "I saw a very flimsy piece of paper that said I was divorced. I think I divorced when I came back here, but I just can't remember the sequence." Apparently, they still lived together for a short while after my father's release, but something broke between them. "Those were very difficult times," she continued. "He had a terrible time in prison, but it was also quite a struggle outside. When he came out, he was a different person, a very bitter one. But of course, I changed too. I went from someone who barely knew how to ask for a bus ticket in Hungarian to a very independent person."

∽

While working at the Historical Institute of the Hungarian Academy of Sciences, Doris wrote a three-hundred-page book about the life of the Hungarian working class and peasantry in the early twentieth century. It took her three years to finish this ambitious undertaking—in Hungarian, of course—and she was very much looking forward to having it published. To her utter disappointment, the higher-ups in the Communist Party did not find it appropriate for a foreigner to write about Hungarian history, or at least that's what they told her. Thus, it never went to print. Doris was so upset about this that shortly after returning to Scotland, she destroyed the manuscript.

I read in George Pálóczi-Horváth's book, *The Undefeated*, that after his release from prison in 1954, he worked at the Historical Institute of the Hungarian Academy of Sciences for a while, even though he wasn't a historian himself. When I asked Doris, not only did she remember him, she told me they had actually shared an office for a year. "He was very nice, a true gentleman," she said.

I asked if she had ever met any of my father's relatives, and she didn't remember for sure, but it seemed she might have met my great-grandmother Erzsébet Wolfner, who lived in London with my grandmother's younger sister, Marutha, during the war. While Erzsébet Wolfner didn't leave lasting impressions on Doris, she mentioned meeting Lajos

Hatvany, my grandfather's cousin, in Budapest. "We used to go to Lajos a lot. He was brilliant and a very charming person. I was very fond of him," she reminisced.

Doris also remembered walking the streets of Budapest in the beginning of the 1956 uprising: "I still treasure that time. I was walking the streets all day, and I was so tired. The next day, it was back to fighting. It was suppressed very badly. Before I came back to Scotland, I was sorry to see things like that. I had to walk home for about an hour and a half at night, through the streets full of blood."

She also recalled experiencing an earthquake in Budapest. Everyone ran out of the building except for her. A magnitude 5.6 earthquake that shook Hungary in January 1956 was one of the strongest recorded in that region. My mother used to talk about it. My father never mentioned it, I wonder if he even noticed it while he was in prison.

When I asked Doris whether she had any contact with my father after she returned to Scotland, she said, "No, except for one letter the year you were born. He just wrote to me that he had a baby daughter. I had great pleasure hearing that. He adored children. He was wonderful with them, very kind and very patient. It was good. I was pleased to hear that. He had a hard time. We both had."

She said she would have loved to stay in Hungary but had to return to Scotland in 1957 to take care of her "ailing father and ill-tempered mother," as she put it. Doris was able to leave the country legally, without any difficulty, due to her dual citizenship. She settled in the small town of Methlick, in Aberdeenshire, where she taught history at a secondary school. This was not the career of her choice, but she had to earn a living. First she hated it, thinking it was dry and boring, but she slowly made her peace with it.

I told her that I found some of her publications on the internet while searching for her. One of them was an article on Budapest, published by the Urban Society of Cambridge University in the 1970s. She said she met a very friendly professor who encouraged her to work with him for a while. She focused on the history of the working class and women's history, as well as reviewing articles about the architectural history of Budapest. "I didn't really know about architecture, but I would pretend," she said, laughing.

Later, she moved to Thornhill in the Dumfries and Galloway region in Southern Scotland. It was there that she started teaching students with special needs. She found it much more rewarding than teaching history. "I liked those kids," she said, "There was something genuine about them. There was one boy who had to ride his bicycle six or eight miles before school to deliver the morning paper, so I let him sleep. Who cared? He was better off sleeping. I really liked them."

The biggest surprise I encountered while searching for her on the internet was to find her under the name Doris Hatvany. She didn't return to her maiden name, nor did she ever get married again. When I asked her about it, she said she considered using Elrick again, but she earned more respect as a teacher in rural Scotland by keeping her married name. "Otherwise, they would have thought I lived in sin for all those years in Hungary," she said with a smile.

Not only did she keep the name Hatvany, she also lived completely alone after returning to her native Scotland, her dog being her only companion. When I asked why she never married again, she said, she didn't find anyone suitable. I sensed a great measure of sadness in her voice. Throughout our conversation, she seemed quite nostalgic for Hungary, even though the years she spent there were not among the country's best and proudest. She lived through the dark Stalinist era that destroyed her marriage, yet she remembered it as the most vibrant and interesting period of her life. She spoke about her work at the Historic Institute of the Hungarian Academy of Sciences as the height of her professional career, despite the disappointment of her book being swept under the carpet. She loved Budapest with its history, culture, and architecture; she loved Hungarian literature, especially its rich poetry; and she made very good friends for life.

After moving back to Scotland, she felt she was torn away from everything and everyone meaningful. She said she would love to go back and see Hungary again but doubted it would ever happen. "I am too old to travel too far. After all, I am eighty-nine today," she said with resignation in her voice.

"Yes, but you are young in spirit, and that's what really counts," I replied, in an attempt to soften the edges.

She smiled and said, "I can't travel very far on spirit, I am afraid."

I told her I had always been curious about my father staying in Hungary after everything that happened to him in the 1950s. "Yes, I wondered that too," she said. "When I came away myself, I wondered whether he would come after…but he didn't. He was given all the books he needed, which was rare in Hungary those days. The Academy of Sciences regarded him as a talent that should be fostered. I think that was probably the main reason he stayed. He was a very clever person, much more so than I ever was. I could never keep pace with him."

Upon telling her how I had searched for her using the internet and how happy I was to finally locate her, she said, "I am glad you did that." She was quick to add that she had never used a computer, never learned to drive a car, and never traveled by air.

It was a former colleague and a very good friend of Doris who made it possible for me to meet her. When I first found her after an extensive search on the internet and the consequent help of a British attorney, whom my husband knew through his line of work, I sent a letter to her home address in Thornhill. As the weeks went by, my hope for an answer started to fade. One day I received an email with *Doris Hatvany* in the subject line. My heart was racing faster than I could click to open it. The sender introduced himself as Raymond Budd, a friend of Doris, and informed me that she had just moved into a care home in Sanquhar, about twelve miles north of Thornhill. Raymond explained that Doris was "crippled with arthritis," as he put it, finding it very difficult to write, but she had asked him to correspond with me on her behalf after he delivered my letter to her. Much to my relief, he also added the following: "To say that she was thrilled to hear from you is an understatement—she was more delighted than I have ever seen her in the thirty-seven years of our acquaintance."

Raymond used to teach German and French at the school where Doris worked. Many years her junior, he continued teaching long after Doris retired, and he kept very active after his own retirement giving private piano lessons, playing at concerts given at St John's Episcopal Church in Dumfries, and working with charitable organizations benefiting less fortunate children in developing countries, as well as being an advocate for Greenpeace. He also remained a very loyal and caring friend to Doris, visiting her regularly at the care home and arranging occasional outings for her.

About six months after I first met Doris, Raymond told me he had finally managed to persuade her to make the care home her permanent residence, since she wouldn't be able to fend for herself alone anymore. Giving up her home in Thornhill and returning it to the local authorities she rented it from was not an easy decision, but she finally agreed. There were no noteworthy possessions in her house except for a vast library she had accumulated over several decades. Since she didn't have any relatives anymore, Raymond was nice enough to ask me if I was interested in taking some of her Hungarian books before he would donate the rest to the Edinburgh Library. Thus, in July 2012, I returned to Scotland. I was absolutely overwhelmed by the library I found in her very modest house.

A strange sense of guilt came over me by the mere thought of touching, let alone taking, anything, but both Doris and Raymond assured me there weren't anyone else who would appreciate those Hungarian books. I only selected a fragment of her enormous collection. To my delight, I stumbled on some books written by my great uncle Lajos Hatvany, some of which I had never seen before. There were also several volumes of collected poems and prose by Endre Ady, one of the most prominent figures of early twentieth-century Hungarian literature, a close personal friend of Lajos's.

As I opened a volume of Ady's books, I saw Doris' handwriting on almost every page, commenting his work, some of the most difficult and complex poems ever written in Hungarian. Her notes exhibited such depth and sophistication they could put a native Hungarian speaker, even a university student of literature, to shame.

I also found a picture book of Budapest published in 1956 with her dedication on the inside front cover: "With love from Doris & Joe. Xmas 1956." This made me wonder whether they were indeed still together after my father's release from prison. It is safe to assume that Doris had sent this book to her parents as a gift from Hungary.

A big box arrived at my home in California the following month. I was surprised to find several old photographs and some of Doris's diaries in it, items I did not come across while in Thornhill. Raymond thought I might be interested and decided to send them along with the books I had selected. I was also surprised to see that Doris had written her personal diaries in Hungarian until 2004, when her arthritis must have become so severe that she had to abandon handwriting. I faced a difficult moral dilemma whether to read them or not, let alone use their contents. Upon my request, Raymond asked Doris during his next visit, and she granted me permission to do anything and everything I wished.

It was a very emotional experience for me to read some of Doris's diaries. I was moved to tears by her description of her loneliness. She felt terribly alone and abandoned for several years after returning to Scotland. Indeed, she fell into a serious depression. No doctor and medication could ease her pain. She exchanged letters with her Hungarian friends, only to be reminded of her isolation: "A postcard came from Bözsi: a person who loves me—and how very far she is," Doris writes in her diary in 1964.

She didn't find satisfaction in teaching history in secondary school and tried to force herself to continue her work toward a doctorate she put on hold when she left Cambridge in 1947. She dove into various Hungarian topics such as Ady's poetry and Széchényi's life, only to end up in a seemingly endless state of procrastination. Thirty years after leaving Hungary, she wrote in her diary that she couldn't work because she felt panic whenever she thought about work: "I think I have been nervous and tense constantly, ever since I turned 29." Upon reading this entry, I came to realize that she was twenty-nine years old in 1952, when my father was arrested.

Doris also had to support her rather demanding mother over several years from her very modest teacher's salary. Right around her retirement in the late 1980s, she was so poor that she lived on rice and beans, gathered firewood in the nearby forest, and heated her house only during the day in order to make ends meet. Yet this was the time she finally reconciled with her life and was able to move forward, as she notes in her diary in 1988:

> I decided that I have in fact accomplished something. I wasted a lot of time in Hungary, but at least I better understand the political sufferings of other nations. I had two articles published in *Századvég* [*End of the Century*, a political periodical in Hungary], perhaps I helped the students at Eötvös Kollégium [Eötvös College—an institution that provided free higher education for exceptionally talented youth with limited financial means], and I delivered some useful presentations, one of them in Debrecen, the other at a conference about the workers' movement. The years of "emptiness" may not have been so completely useless either. Some children might have learned something

about history…When I worked with "slow" children, I made many of them happy. So even if I die tomorrow— or today!—I haven't lived in vain. Therefore, regarding the future, I will have to work with optimism. First, I will have to finish my thesis.

It wasn't until November 1992, three months shy of her seventieth birthday, that Doris received her doctorate from the University of Strathclyde in Glasgow. The title of her thesis was *The History of Trade Union Movement in Scotland in the 1920s*.

According to her diaries, Doris would only learn about my father's death several years after it had happened: "A letter came today from Irén, that me made sad. Among others, she says Hatvany died a long time ago. I mourn him…I also felt, that I would never find such love again— and my prediction came true. Since August 1957, without my friends in Hungary, without Józsi, I haven't lived. I have only had a boring, idle existence. It was only after 1980 that I started working again: doing some research and writing, although very slowly due to illnesses. 'He that dies pays all debts' [in English]—(*The Tempest*)."

∽

Two months after my second visit with Doris, I learned something that shook me to my core. In September 2012, I traveled to Paris to see my father's stepsister Bobette and interview her for my book. It was then and there that I heard for the first time about Fanny's and Bertalan's conspiracy theory regarding Doris. According to Bobette, my great-grandmother and my grandfather were both convinced it had not been by accident but by deliberate planning that József and Doris had met at a political event in London during the summer of 1945. In fact, they firmly believed Doris had been a spy working for the British Communist Party, used as a decoy to lure my father into the communist movement and to subsequently persuade him to return to Hungary. Fanny and Bertalan both found it rather strange that József would engage in a relationship with a woman coming from the exact opposite end of the socioeconomic spectrum. They also found it suspicious that Doris had never been arrested or harmed by the Hungarian authorities, nor had she lost her job at the Historical Institute of the Hungarian Academy of Sciences in the early 1950s, while my father was in prison.

More than two years later, in November 2014, I went to visit my cousin Andrew in Washington, DC, where I was in for another surprise. Apparently, Andrew's mother, Marutha, and my other great-grandmother, Erzsébet, also blamed Doris for my father's drastic change of views and for denouncing his family at the age of twenty. Similarly to the Hatvanys, they believed it was indeed Doris's doing that he became a communist and severed all ties with his rich, capitalist ancestors. They argued that the young József they knew and occasionally met during his school vacations in London was a pleasant, charming gentleman with immaculate manners and perfect behavior, someone they found very easy to get along with. Once he met Doris, they felt he became hostile toward his family, showing no resemblance to the once nice, kind boy they remembered. Just like Fanny, Erzsébet also found it feasible—in fact, logical—that my father would have been recruited into the Communist Party in such fashion specifically because of his bourgeois, noble heritage.

I was completely taken aback on both occasions, hearing a similar story from Bobette and Andrew respectively. To add fuel to the fire, they were both surprised to see my reaction. My father's stepsister and my grandmother's nephew both presented the "Doris conspiracy theory" to me with utter confidence, implying the question "How else could it have happened?"

As the dust settled, I tried to line up arguments for and against this conspiracy theory. While I certainly understand why they might have come to this conclusion, trying to look at it from their perspective, I still remain skeptical. From his letters to András, it seems more likely to me that my father had already formed his political views well before meeting Doris—in fact, when he was still studying in Oundle. I also think it was indeed Doris's humble, blue-collar background that he found attractive, given his political leaning at the time, as opposed to choosing someone with his own socioeconomic background. It may very well be that Doris helped tip the scale in certain aspects, but I tend to believe József mostly followed his own convictions.

In early 2020 when I talked to Alan Mackay, my father's former schoolmate in Oundle and good friend at Cambridge University, he immediately dismissed this conspiracy theory, finding it very unlikely.

Nevertheless, without a single piece of evidence supporting either scenario, I will have to leave the door ever slightly open to both possibilities. I can't help wondering, however, had I heard about this conspiracy theory prior to meeting Doris in February and in July 2012, would I have asked her about it? I doubt that I would have, and I especially doubt that I could have. This, along with many other unanswered questions, will remain a mystery.

Doris died in June 2014, at the age of ninety-one. She took her secrets, if she had any, to her grave. During my two visits in Scotland in 2012, I learned fascinating details about her life, her youth, and my father's youth set against the background of 1940s Cambridge and 1950s Budapest. Despite the terrible times they both had to endure and despite the very unfortunate circumstances that tore them apart, Doris never had a single bad thing to say about my father. She spoke of him only with the utmost respect and kindness. I want to believe it was love. I want to believe they had a few years of happiness together. Why would she keep her married name for the rest of her life otherwise? Why would she follow my father's career, keeping track of his achievements and awards several decades after they ceased all communication with each other? Why would she keep carefully arranged newspaper clippings about him, complete with her handwritten notes on the margin? Had she been a spy, was it merely out of guilt that she felt terribly depressed for so many years after her return to Scotland, or was it extreme loneliness, a void, the memory of a love she would never experience again, as she writes in her diaries? Was it just bad luck that she never found a suitable partner during the next six decades, or was it, rather, her belief that nobody could fill my father's shoes?

I will never have answers to these questions, but what I know with absolute certainty is that meeting her was a pivotal point in my life. It was one of the most dramatic, most emotional, and most important things I have ever done. Not only did I learn things about my father that nobody else could have told me, I also became richer and wiser by opening a window to her life, as small as that window might be.

Chapter Nineteen

Dismay

Soon after his release from prison and cutting all ties with Doris, my father fell in love. It was a brief relationship, which is why I found it rather strange that he referred to Zsuzsi as his fiancée. In retrospect, considering his understandable and justifiable insecurities toward women, it is quite feasible that he was longing for a commitment at first sight, as much as it may sound like an oxymoron.

To his great sorrow, József found himself abandoned again. Along with nearly quarter of a million fellow Hungarians, Zsuzsi took advantage of the temporary cracks in the Iron Curtain amid the chaos after the 1956 Revolution. Seeking freedom and a better life, she fled to the West, thinking it would only be a question of time before my father followed in her footsteps.

In August 1956 the Supreme Court acquitted József of all charges and a month later rehabilitated him for the four years spent in prison, yet the authorities failed to remove his criminal status from their records.

In January 1957 my father was shocked to receive a letter from the National Prison in Budapest informing him that his parole had been extended until July. Despite his repeated requests to honor the Supreme Court's decision, his official status in the books remained parolee. Another letter followed in July, extending his parole till January 1, 1958. The third and final letter, dated December 31, 1957, informed him that his parole would expire on January 31, 1958, at which date he was to report to prison in order to serve the remaining seven years of his sentence.

Desperate enough to risk everything, even his life, my father made an attempt to cross the Austrian border with the help of a smuggler. He didn't succeed. By the summer of 1958, the window of opportunity had closed. The Iron Curtain was virtually impermeable again. József was captured at the border and locked behind bars for the second time.

⟋⟍

Exactly a year later, on August 15, 1959, my father was released from prison, but he did not regain his freedom. The National Headquarters of Detention for Public Safety ordered him to report to the police headquarters within forty-eight hours. He was put under police observation "to supervise his behavior, necessary for public order and safety."[53] Obligated to report to the police every Sunday morning, he was not allowed to leave the city limits of Budapest without special permission from the authorities and was banned from leaving his registered residence between

10:00 p.m. and 5:00 a.m. He couldn't attend meetings or gatherings or go to bars or other places of public entertainment. Neither was he allowed to operate a telephone at his apartment. My father tried to appeal this decision without success.

During his house arrest, József turned to his excellent language skills to make a living. He translated everything from newspaper articles to speeches of political leaders, from books on politics and economy to literature, including plays and poetry. He didn't use a dictionary. He just read the original Hungarian text, and flawless English sentences appeared on the paper by the stroke of his fountain pen.

Some of his work appeared in an English-language periodical, the *Hungarian Quarterly*, but the books he translated did not reveal his name, probably because of his "undesirable" status at the time. Nevertheless, he received an Award of Excellence for his outstanding translations and two letters of praise, one from the editor in chief of the *Economic Review* and the other from the Foreign Language Book Publishing Company.

While the authorities insisted on continuing his police observation due to his "political orientation,"[54] in the spring of 1960 he was allowed to join a scientific research group as a part-time employee. It wasn't until late September 1960 that my father finally gained back his freedom, as fragile as it might have been. It was a rather hesitant decision on behalf of the Ministry of Interior. The police major who reexamined his case and consequently overturned the previous ruling made sure to voice his reluctance:

"I made my decision according to the relevant rules. Although the subject's behavior would justify further measures of constraint, I am taking his time spent in detention and under police observation, as well as his achievements in his scientific work into consideration."[55]

Chapter Twenty
Zsófia

OCTOBER 1960 marked another major milestone in József Hatvany's life. He became a father. Six months later, he married my mother. For the first twelve years of my life, I wasn't aware of the reverse order of these two events, nor did I know that my parents' marriage was deeply troubled from the beginning. As a small child, I thought I was growing up in the happiest family, the most harmonious household anyone could wish for.

Zsófia Matild Erzsébet Dományi was born in Budapest, November 11, 1924. Her father, Gyula, was of Transylvanian origin, and so was my grandmother, Alojzia Denz. Unlike my paternal ancestors, they were neither Jewish nor wealthy. Both of them were Saxons, which explains my mother's very basic knowledge of German. She recalled her parents switching to this language when they didn't want their daughters to understand their conversation. Needless to say, *Nicht für den Kindern* (not for the children) was the first German sentence Zsófia and her sisters mastered very early on. I remember my mother always using the German term *Fleisch Nudeln* (meat noodles) for one of her staple dishes, a pork ragout cooked with a generous amount of marjoram, served over fettuccine and topped with sour cream. She also called her signature Christmas cookie *Ausgestochen* (cut out), a fabulous treat enriched with walnuts, filling the entire house with the scent of nutmeg and cinnamon during the holidays.

I learned very little about my maternal ancestors growing up, as my mother rarely talked about their background. Having been considerably older than my paternal grandparents, they were rather frail by the time I was mature enough to interact with them, but I do remember both of them being kinder, warmer, incomparably easier to talk to, and far less intimidating than my father's parents.

Gyula studied industrial mold making, spending a year in Switzerland as a young apprentice. Soon he became a master craftsman of his trade. He was twenty-six when World War I—or, as it was called at the time, the Great War—broke out. I have a photograph showing him in uniform with a group of soldiers, but I have never learned whether he was actually deployed to the front lines or just drafted and trained. He was fortunate enough to avoid injury or capture if he was sent to war.

In 1922, Gyula married my grandmother Alojzia, and a year later, they welcomed their twin daughters, Emilia and Katalin. My mother, Zsófia, arrived just fourteen months after her sisters. My grandmother had her hands full with three children. She didn't have an expansive domestic staff at her disposal that all my paternal ancestors were accustomed to in the 1920s. In fact, she didn't have any help.

Grandmother Helen, as we called her, was a true homemaker in the most original sense of the word. Not only did she take care of three children by herself, cooking and baking everything from scratch, she also grew her own vegetables and fruits in her tiny backyard and made legendary stews and preserves that she bottled and stored for the winter. My mother remembered with longing how she would devour a whole jar of her heavenly plum jam in one sitting. My grandmother sewed many of her children's clothes with her Singer sewing machine, which she eventually passed down to my mother. It was indeed a true museum piece with its chiseled cast-iron body and mechanical pedal by the time I learned to use it. Helen also made dolls, complete with their little wardrobe from scrap material, so her three daughters would each have their own to play with. Of course, there was no washing machine or refrigerator in her house. Once a week, a horse-drawn carriage appeared in the neighborhood with its driver loudly announcing his presence as *jeges* (iceman), and all the women ran out to the street and stocked their icebox to keep perishables fresh for a couple of days.

My mother was very nostalgic about their little house on the outskirts of Pest. She was a tomboy, a complete opposite of her twin sisters. While they sat quietly inside, Zsófia climbed trees, made her own swing by tying an old pot on a tree branch with some strings, and did not shy away from a fistfight with the boys in her neighborhood. She told me she had cried for weeks when they moved to a multistory apartment building in Buda, especially after learning she wasn't allowed to bring her pet squirrel with her.

It probably stemmed from her early childhood enjoying the outdoors and then suddenly being confined within four walls that she developed a fondness toward anything and everything athletic. Zsófia competed in gymnastics and track and field throughout her school years. She was very proud to have been only two centimeters shy of the high-jumping record held by Hungary's national champion at the time. In her twenties, she played table tennis competitively as a member of a sports club and was also captain of a women's amateur soccer team.

An avid player herself, my mother loved to attend professional soccer matches. She had very vivid memories of one particular event at the largest stadium in Budapest, where she, along with some ninety thousand screaming fans, witnessed the proudest moment of Hungarian soccer history in May 1954: Hungary beat England 7–1. Later in her life, probably after I was born and she married my father, she stopped going to the stadium, but she would never miss the broadcast of a major soccer match on the radio and eventually on television.

All three sisters attended a vocational school of trade where they would learn practical skills such as typing, shorthand, and bookkeeping. This was a safe path for a girl in order to secure an administrative position at any office after graduating at the age of eighteen. My mother did not excel at academic skills, but she demonstrated raw talent toward the arts. She was very creative throughout her childhood, learning to sew and knit at an early age and making dresses for her dolls, but most of all, she loved drawing and painting. At sixteen, she single-handedly designed and painted the entire stage decoration for a theater performance at her school. She hoped to continue her education in an arts school, but when she finally gathered her courage to bring it up with her father, she was met with instant resistance. My grandfather Gyula strongly advised against it. In his opinion, choosing fine arts as a career path was not something one would call a stable, reliable future. He recognized my mother's talent but worried his daughter would not be able to make a living in the unforgiving and unpredictable world of struggling artists. Therefore, my mother had to give up her dreams, finish vocational school for trade, and start working as a secretary. There is no telling what could have become of her had she had the opportunity to pursue her dreams, but it is well within the realm of possibility that she could have succeeded.

Zsófia proved herself as an extremely fast and accurate typist with outstanding multitasking and organizational skills, making an excellent secretary. Her twin sisters didn't even contemplate anything else than the safe path they were destined to follow. They both became financial administrators, looking at spreadsheets all day long, adding up numbers on desk calculators with long rolls of paper crawling out of them like a snake. Katalin spent most of her career working for the Office of Social Security, while Emilia worked for the Hungarian Film Laboratory.

My mother often mentioned with some satisfaction and relief in her voice that relative to her siblings, she was lucky. As a secretary at the Presidential Office of the Hungarian Academy of Sciences and later at one of its institutes, the Central Research Institute for Chemistry, she worked for highly educated scientists and performed a wider range of tasks, often taking the initiative into her own hands. She was also able to interact with a variety of interesting personalities on a daily basis. Nevertheless, it always remained just a job for her, a way to make a living, not a truly satisfying and fulfilling career she would have chosen for herself.

It wasn't until several decades later that Zsófia finally had a chance to explore her artistic talent again. Our neighbor Éva was a well-known graphic artist. She gave my mother the opportunity to help her paint beautiful, intricate designs for postal stamps, but only as a ghost artist. Without the required credentials, Zsófia was not eligible to become a member of the Hungarian Artist Foundation. In the late 1980s, well after her retirement from office work, my mother finally got her foot in the door at this exclusive organization, and had a brief stint as an artist in her own right. For a couple of years, she painted hundreds of greeting cards for Christmas and Easter, as well as various beautiful designs with flowers and butterflies for every other occasion, printed and sold with her name on them. It was a short-lived fame, however. In 1990, shortly after the regime change in Hungary, the new leadership at the Artist Foundation noticed that Zsófia had been working without proper credentials and stopped giving her further assignments.

Chapter Twenty-One
Oasis

OUR HOUSE IN THE BUDA HILLS was unique in many ways. Although it was situated well within the city limits, halfway up János-hegy, the tallest hill in Budapest, it seemed so remote and secluded in the dense woods that it felt like living in the countryside. It was a U-shaped house surrounded by a very large, completely private yard, under the shade of ancient chestnut trees. My father used to entertain our guests, especially foreign visitors, with its unusual history, and once I was old enough to recite it in English, I took pride in taking on the role of storyteller.

Built around 1780, it was originally a press house for wine. Phylloxera, a pest for grape vines, spread across Europe about hundred years later, destroying most of the vineyards, including the ones on the slopes of the Buda hills. Since it lost its original function, the house was converted into a weekend retreat for Baron Manfred Weiss (1857–1922), a Jewish industrialist who gained fame and fortune with Manfred Weiss

Steel and Metal Works in Csepel, an island on the Danube in Budapest. His industrial complex, later known as Csepel Works, became one of the biggest in Hungary. During World War II, Manfred Weiss's descendants were allowed to immigrate to Portugal, thus escaping the Holocaust, but they had to surrender their entire industrial complex together with the family's considerable art collection to the Germans in exchange for their freedom.

One side of the house was converted into a residence, and the other side became the servants' quarters and a big laundry room. The walls were made of adobe and fieldstone. They were at least two or three feet thick, with deep windowsills. On winter days, I loved to curl up in one of them and watch the snowflakes gently land on the bare tree branches. The outside of the house was almost completely covered with ivy. At the turn of the century, it must have been the perfect place to enjoy quiet, relaxing summer weekends in the lush green forest, so close yet so far from the city center.

∞

In 1960 there was virtually no privately held real estate in Hungary. Most people lived in government-owned apartments. Rents were heavily subsidized in order to make housing affordable for everyone, but it wasn't easy to qualify for a nicer apartment at a desirable location, equipped with central heating, and with a decent bathroom and at least one dedicated bedroom. One had to meet certain requirements. People with a blue-collar background had an advantage as well as those with notable achievements and good standing in the Communist Party. Larger families with children also stood a better chance of receiving an entire apartment with multiple rooms without having to share with another family. My father failed to meet any of these requirements. Nevertheless, he was lucky.

Péter Nagy, the older brother of my father's childhood classmate András, was renting the bigger and nicer part of this house from the government, the part that used to be Manfred Weiss's weekend retreat. Both Nagy brothers reconnected with my father right after the war, while he was in England. Péter visited Cambridge in the summer of 1945, where he met my father, and it was upon his suggestion that József started exchanging letters with András. The three remained friends after my father's return to Hungary in 1947. Although there is no evidence or document to support this anecdote, I heard a story suggesting that András might have played a role in my father's release from prison in 1956.

This time it was Péter who helped my father find housing in late 1960. The whole house was too big for him and his wife, and he had to find another tenant in order to be able to keep his part. My father had a very small apartment, probably a studio, and so did my mother. Once I was born, neither of those apartments seemed sufficient for a family of three. It was perfect timing, but there was a catch. The part that used to be the servants' quarters and the laundry for the residence needed a complete renovation. The government was happy to find someone desperate enough to take on such a big project.

The house was considered rather remote that time. Living so far from the city center was not as desirable as it became later on, but my father was both adventurous and a visionary. My mother, on the other hand, told me she cried when she learned we were going to live there. It was quite a long walk from the bus stop on a narrow, unpaved road lit by a lonely streetlight that only worked occasionally. The trees lining both sides of this dirt road formed an arch, making it even more eerie, like a tunnel. My mother recalled walking home one winter night from work and literally bumping into somebody in pitch darkness. From this road, one had to walk up about a hundred yards on a steep driveway covered with scattered remains of cobblestones. Although there was running water and electricity, our part of the house only had a toilet and a sink with cold water.

Despite my mother's understandable apprehension, my father took on this challenge. The fact that he was not a trained engineer had not stopped him from joining the elite engineering group in prison, and it certainly didn't stop him from drawing up a blueprint for central heating and electric wiring for the house, as well as a plan for adding and moving internal walls. He found a plumber named Béla, who lived nearby, and hired him to handle the entire construction. The laundry area was converted into a kitchen and a bathroom, a water heater and further plumbing were installed, and central heating was introduced with a large cast-iron radiator in each room circulating warm water. There was a furnace in the back of the house and a small room next to it for coal storage. Once a year, a truck dumped coal in this room through a small window in the back, facing the hillside. My parents shoveled the coal into the furnace from this room.

The renovation itself was an enormous challenge. My father had to take out a loan from the bank since he didn't have any savings to speak of. Building materials were very hard to come by, and Béla was not even qualified to do most of the work. He also turned out to be a serious alcoholic. Sometimes he disappeared for days or showed up so drunk that he could barely stand up straight, and on occasion, he was found lying unconscious in the ditch along the road.

It was the middle of the winter and my father was under a lot of pressure to provide a livable place for us, so he came up with an incentive for Béla. They originally agreed on a fixed amount of money for the entire job, but when my father saw it was getting out of hand, he would change the terms of payment to a sliding scale. He threatened to progressively increase the amount he would deduct from Béla's fee for each day past the deadline. Miraculously, everything was finished on time.

I have no recollection of any of these events, as I was about three months old when we moved in. But I do remember spending much of my childhood playing outside in our secluded, private garden, under the canopy of giant trees, enjoying the peaceful, green surroundings. In fact, it was so quiet that one could sleep with the windows open on warm summer nights, awakened only by an orchestra of birds before sunrise. This ruined me for all other places I have called home ever since. I was so spoiled by such a deep silence in this house that any and every noise bothers me at night.

There was a funny story my father would tell me years later. During our first summer there, in 1961, Péter Nagy and his first wife, Ilse (Isi), used to stand around in the courtyard just in front of our bedroom window, engaging in loud conversations and rolling laughter with their friends late at night. My father asked his neighbors to kindly consider saying goodbye to their guests inside the house so they wouldn't wake me up. Péter apparently brushed it off, arguing that a baby didn't have to be treated as delicately as a Fabergé egg. The following Sunday my father set his alarm clock to four in the morning, went outside the courtyard, and started hammering on a piece of tin pipe. Within minutes, Péter and Isi appeared at the door, bewildered. My father looked at them with a poker face and said, "This piece of pipe needs to be straightened." After that, there were no more loud goodbyes to party guests in front of our open window on warm summer nights. Only the birds broke the silence.

⟨∽⟩

It took my parents several more years to make our part of the house into the cozy, comfortable place all three of us proudly called our home. Switching to electric heating, they were able to convert the coal storage into a bedroom and add a tiny shower next to it. By 1960s–'70s Hungarian standards, it was indeed a very nice apartment with three bedrooms, two bathrooms, a living room, a hallway with built-in closet space and shoe storage, a decent-size kitchen with a little walk-in pantry, and a separate dining room with access to the backyard. How on earth all this could fit in a space of merely 860 square feet still boggles my mind.

I think the house reached its peak in the early '70s when my mother painted every interior wall a different color she dreamed up and mixed herself, mostly pastels except for the dining room, where she chose a bold magenta. She also took pride in grooming the backyard to perfection. The quality of our lawn was nothing short of an English golf course, surrounded by neatly trimmed hedges and accented by beautiful roses, the crown jewels of our green sanctuary. They received individual attention, as if my mother knew each and every one by name. She probably did.

Chapter Twenty-Two
Climb

EARLY CHILDHOOD MEMORIES often blur the lines between flashes of pictures we store somewhere deep in our brain as snapshots and events we don't actually remember, only heard from our parents much later. It is hopeless to even speculate which of these two sources we rely on each time we recall a specific event from the first three or four years of our lives.

My father and I had a weekend hiking routine that falls into this category. I am not certain how much I actually remember and how much I was told later on, but one way or the other, I do recall these outings with great fondness. We would hike up Tündér Szikla (Fairy Rocks) to enjoy the view and walk on wooded trails with autumn leaves or fresh snow crunching under our boots. On the way back, as I got tired, my father would lift me up on his shoulders. I loved taking in the world from that high seat, as it gave me a different perspective on everything, let alone enjoying the comfortable ride. We played a game where he agreed to carry me to the next lamppost, and then to the next. Needless to say, I always managed to push him several lampposts past his original plan.

I clearly remember from subsequent years—in fact, from my entire childhood—how much he enjoyed everything our quiet house and its secluded surroundings offered. From late spring to early fall he spent most of his Sundays sitting and reading in the backyard. He would adjust his lounge chair throughout the day, always seeking the perfect, half-shaded spot where he could soak up some sun and read without squinting at the same time. He never wore sunglasses. In fact, I don't think he ever owned a pair. He cherished every minute he could spend outdoors, and if I showed even the slightest reluctance leaving my room on a pleasant Sunday morning, it was met with his instant disapproval. He would promptly remind me how lucky we were to live in a green neighborhood with our beautiful, private backyard. In his eyes, it would have been a shame to stay inside, a complete waste of a nice day.

Unaware of the problems and hardships my parents had at the time, marital or otherwise, I can confidently call my early childhood idyllic. Both my mother and my father made tremendous efforts to shield me from every unpleasant and stressful aspect of their lives. As far as I could tell, our home and our family represented a perfect little island of love and harmony. I was convinced our life was indeed idyllic. My father's professional journey was anything but. At the time unbeknownst to me, he had to navigate a long and rocky road before finding stable footing.

In August 1956, when József Hatvany was released from prison and cleared of all charges falsely brought against him, the Hungarian Academy of Sciences immediately reinstated him in his former position, as deputy head of department at its presidential office. In December, following the violent suppression of the 1956 Revolution, my father disapproved of the policies adopted by the government, refused to rejoin the Communist Party, and resigned his post at the Hungarian Academy of Sciences. He decided to leave politics behind and fully devote himself to scientific research work.

When the Academy of Sciences established the Research Group of Cybernetics in 1957, he joined them as a fellow, along with some of his former engineer colleagues he had met back in prison. They worked on the development of numerical computer control systems, already patented when he and two of his colleagues had come up with the initial idea behind bars. Unfortunately, at the end of the same year, József Hatvany's career path was interrupted when he was ordered to return to prison in order to resume his eleven-year sentence. Consequently, he attempted an illegal border crossing and was captured and imprisoned for the second time. After his release in 1959, he made a living as a freelance translator while under house arrest.

Still under police surveillance, and with very limited freedom and mobility, in March 1960 he was granted permission to work twenty hours a week at the Institute of Machine Tool Development. At the end of 1961, he had to quit his job due to a serious illness. I vaguely remember him telling me years later that he had been bedridden for months with kidney disease. My mother was convinced it was a result of what he had gone through in prison.

In September 1962 my father accepted another part-time position at the Research Institute for Measurement Techniques, but it was his subsequent job that defined his future career and shaped the rest of his life in more ways than one.

The Research Institute for Automation was established by the Hungarian Academy of Sciences in 1964. József Hatvany was still deemed politically undesirable and untrustworthy by the authorities. As a result, the Academy of Sciences did not welcome him back with open arms. He could only be hired as a part-time scientific research fellow, receiving his paycheck from another organization, the Committee of National Technical Development, not directly from the Academy of Sciences. It wasn't until September 1965 that he was able to join the Research Institute of Automation officially as a full-time employee. This created a lot of friction, leaving a bad taste in his mouth, as he felt a second-class citizen. To say he didn't exactly start on the right foot would be an understatement.

Another source of tension was the fact that he didn't have a university degree. When he left Cambridge in 1947, he was one final exam shy of receiving a diploma. During his last year in prison in the mid-1950s, he studied extensively in order to bridge the gaps in his education while working with a select group of engineers and submitting numerous inventions, several of which won acclaim. It was also then and there that he and his colleagues started working on numerical control of machine tools, a groundbreaking technology at the time. Some of their work received patents. In the mid-1960s, his new boss at the Research Institute for Automation made sure his professional achievements were recognized as the equivalent of a university degree, but one can imagine how my father might have been reluctant, even apprehensive, to accept such favors. Probably this was the reason why for the rest of his life he had a disdain for people who flaunted their degrees and measured themselves strictly by official titles. I remember him mocking German business cards with a long list of every imaginable title in front of someone's name.

Interestingly enough, József Hatvany wasn't the only one in his family achieving professional excellence without a formal university diploma. His father, Bertalan Hatvany, a self-taught Orientalist, was widely recognized by his peers, and was awarded an honorary doctorate from the University of Pécs for his book *Ázsia lelke* (*Asia's Soul*) in 1935. Lili Hatvany's daughter, Mariella, built a very successful career as a teacher of art history at a high school in Pennsylvania without any formal training. She tapped into her childhood experiences traveling around Europe with her art-lover grandmother Fanny and, of course, supplemented her knowledge with extensive reading. Not only did she become a beloved teacher for almost two decades, Solebury School also appointed her director of studies.

My father's situation was different, however. As he once told me, he chose to study physics, chemistry, and electronics in Cambridge because he believed one could learn a great deal of liberal arts at the library, but a structured, formal education was necessary in order to build a foundation for a scientific career. As opposed to his father Bertalan and cousin Mariella, he indeed attended university classes and successfully passed his exams, except for the final ones at the end of his last year.

As much as he made up for the last missing piece of his education by diligently studying on his own and proving himself more than capable of standing his ground among his peers, he must have encountered some measure of resentment. There were those who liked him from the very beginning, and there were those who despised him at the Research Institute of Automation. Behind his back, he was often called "Mr. Baron" with an obvious pejorative overtone, suggesting he felt entitled, having been born with a silver spoon in his mouth. It was ironic, since as a young adult, he took extreme measures to distance himself from his bourgeois ancestors. Thankfully, the institute's management recognized his talent and considered him an asset rather than a liability. They gave my father a chance to spread his wings, an opportunity to thrive.

Chapter Twenty-Three

Innovation

JÓZSEF HATVANY'S RESEARCH and development work was highly vision-ary, and together with his team of talented colleagues, he produced groundbreaking results. He started his scientific work by exploring how digital computers could interact with tools to improve production. As early as 1958, he patented a system for controlling the movement and operation of a factory machine tool by a computer directly instead of via a limited set of controls preset on a punched tape or similar medium. His vision was of a computer—despite processing information as discrete 1s and 0s in digital form—that could directly control a machine's cutting, shaping, welding, and other motions in a smooth, continuous, and precise manner. In the early 1960s his work focused on critical enabling details for this vision, such as accurately sensing the starting position and status of a machine tool, measuring feedback from the machine's movements as it responded to computer commands, and converting the digital computer language into continuous signals that would directly actuate machine movement. That early research allowed the team to advance beyond existing numerical control (NC) of machines to a more flexible and easily programmed system of direct digital computer control, leading to the first successful such unit in Eastern Europe. The work was described in Hungarian-language patents and periodicals at the time but was not well known in other countries.

In the next phase of their work, József Hatvany and his team explored how a human could interact with the computer, which in turn controlled machines. This meant creating an entire software structure for the computer to facilitate engineering design work and translate design data into manufacturing commands, known as computer-aided design and computer-aided manufacturing software, or CAD/CAM. For creative engineers to readily translate their visions from idea into computer-processed data, a new means of human-computer interaction had to be created: the graphical display unit.

This extraordinary vision was brought to life in the late 1960s in a workstation known as GD71 (graphical display 1971), the first of its kind in Eastern Europe and one of the first in Europe overall.

At the time my father began this work in the 1960s, almost no one interacted directly with computers. "Screen time" was many years, even decades, in the future for most. Computers consisted of electronics housed in giant banks of cabinets, locked in a secure and air-conditioned room where a cadre of acolytes tended to them. Problems and data were left with the attendants, and some hours or days later, a paper report was returned with completed calculations. The Hatvany team imagined a radical departure, a computer with a cathode ray tube (CRT) display able to project both text and images (a graphical display), operated by creative engineers directly, showing visual representations of designs that the engineers could manipulate virtually, using a keyboard and pointing devices such as a light pen and a track ball to draw and interact, all supported with sophisticated software.

Likely for the first time anywhere, the Hatvany team successfully combined computer-aided design data developed by creative engineers using the new graphical display with direct digital control of machine tools, to put into practice a complete end-to-end digital system from design to manufacturing. The group installed four major computerized design and manufacturing systems in Hungary in the late 1960s and early 1970s.

Equally, and in parallel to these scientific achievements, my father was drawn to the bigger picture of how society at large would be affected by these technical developments. He was generally optimistic, but also concerned about how the nature of work could change, and about the possible negative effects on people and society from increasingly pervasive computer automation. His ruminations and papers, which he published in the late 1960s and throughout the 1970s, earned József Hatvany nearly as much international scientific acclaim as his purely technical contributions to science and engineering.

In the late '60s, he had the sheer scope of imagination to ask—at a time when almost nobody outside specialized technical circles had even seen or used a computer—how interacting with computers in every aspect of life would affect us all. He postulated a world of ubiquitous computing, a paper-free world where people used all their senses to interact with computers: tactile, verbal, auditory, and visual. Would this render work obsolete or free up human creativity? How could a nation's education system prepare students of all ages for a fast-changing world of continuous learning and retraining to keep up with a new era of knowledge work? Would computing even take a physical toll on people by dramatically altering our daily movements as well as our office and home environment?

In May 1969, József Hatvany gave a talk at a symposium in the United States, raising the question whether computers were good for us:

> Displays are destined to play a vital role in displacing paper from its dominance in our lives. By examining and carefully evaluating the stress components of display systems, we must devise a means for keeping them below a tolerable threshold value. At the same time the next generation, the men and women of the display era, must be educated to value creative thought as the highest form of human activity. It is only by placing man at the center of our endeavours, that we can make sure displays in the environment of a modern industrial society will be a blessing, and not a curse.[56]

In the same year, a Hungarian weekly periodical, *Élet és Irodalom* (*Life and Literature*), published another one of his papers, in which he asked how people could remain the masters of our creations and not the other way around:

> One part of resolving the conflict is up to the designers of automation. We have to make equipment without vibrating letters and drawings, screens with pleasant colors,

keyboards that are comfortable to type on, and machines that are easy to use. We have to write programs that make the computer's messages adequately polite without seemingly mocking the user, ones that don't order their human partners around, ones that kindly bring it to their attention if they make a mistake. They should also flexibly adapt to their user's speed of thinking and responding. This, although a difficult task, is the easier part of the problem.

The adaptation however, needs to be mutual. The rapid spread of equipment that free man from performing tasks that machines can do better, makes it necessary to develop a new approach from humans...In a decade and a half, the number of direct users of computer increased from a couple hundred to more than a million. In the next decade or two, this trend will significantly accelerate, and our country won't escape this current either. Children who start school now, will live in this milieu. In order to harmoniously fit into this environment, we must come up with a new direction of education now. Perhaps art will play a much bigger role than it does now in developing a type of human who delights in the challenge of intense intellectual effort, who is creative, has a rich fantasy, and is ready to make decisions. Perhaps thinking, as such, has to be developed more with the help of classic disciplines: science and humanities.

The man of the future has to be the master of his machine slaves that perform routine tasks. For this, we have to provide the superiority he needs, by developing his full human potential.[57]

József Hatvany had the vision to explore these topics and more, at a time when few could even imagine the possibilities—issues that have only become more relevant with each passing year. In the second decade of the twenty-first century, people mindlessly walk into traffic while entranced, looking down at their mobile, networked, handheld supercomputer, also known as the smart phone. We have artificial intelligence systems, or AI, that drive automobiles and learn to recognize the difference between an image of a stop sign and a pedestrian. This AI is capable of anticipating the pedestrian will step into traffic without caution because he is entranced looking down at his smart phone. We face massive displacement of manufacturing workers in areas where computerized systems can direct machine tools with vastly greater efficiency, and even the machine tools are replaced by computerized robotics. How can our society and our education system respond to this real displacement and harm? My father postulated these types of issues could arise, warned of this sort of challenge decades ago, and even discussed possible ways society could collectively respond. Ultimately, he was hopeful human ingenuity could overcome the nightmarish unintended effects of the technology he was helping to create.

During the 1960s, József Hatvany authored or coauthored nearly thirty scientific papers, and as the decade progressed, his work was increasingly featured in international scientific publications and symposia, overcoming the considerable logistical and social-acceptance challenges of coming from a socialist country behind the Iron Curtain.

At the height of the Cold War, scientific research and development in Hungary were directed and controlled by the government. Like all other aspects of the country's economy, project assignments and research funds were centrally allocated based on a five-year plan. Cutting-edge computer technology was under strict embargo, making it extremely hard for Eastern European scientists to learn about Western advancements in their field, let alone cooperate with their peers in the capitalist world. Under these circumstances it was rather challenging for my father and a handful of his colleagues to be able to travel to Western Europe, Japan, and the United States of America, give presentations at prestigious international conferences, and have their papers published in their proceedings. But at the same time, it proved to be an invaluable aspect of their work in research and development.

In the early 1970s, the research and development efforts of József Hatvany and his team, especially the GD71, which was said to "break through the wall of the embargo," caught the attention of the Hungarian media as well as the scientific community. He made multiple appearances on various Hungarian television programs that brought the results of the latest scientific research from around the world to the general public.

⚭

It was also in 1970 that my father earned his PhD. As a culmination of his original research throughout the second half of the 1960s, he submitted and successfully defended his thesis, *Digital Interpolator for Continuous Path Control of Machines*, at the end of 1969 and was rewarded a degree of doctor of philosophy in the technical sciences in January 1970.

As enthusiastic as he was about the research and the work itself, I clearly remember a very intense discussion between him and my mother just before he was to appear in front of the committee to defend his thesis. If it weren't for my mother's persistence and downright pleading, he might have walked away from it in the last minute. Five decades later, I can still hear his voice arguing against degrees and titles, disrespecting those who measured themselves by such. Maybe my mother managed to convince him that it was helpful and necessary for his future career to go through with it, or maybe he knew it deep down in his heart but wanted to show his stubborn side and vent his emotions. I keep wondering what tipped the scale toward taking the next rational step, reluctantly conforming. I suspect he rejected the stamp of approval by anyone, whether it was his parents, his university, or the Hungarian scientific community. He didn't like the idea of giving the official authorities power to determine his worth.

Chapter Twenty-Four

Window

THE MID-1960s represented another turning point in József Hatvany's life. He reconnected with his parents, whom he had denounced nearly two decades earlier. The last time he had seen Bertalan was in Paris in the summer of 1946. The last time he had met Vera was a couple months later in London. As a hotheaded twenty-year-old with a black-and-white outlook right after the war, he followed his own convictions as well as obeying the British Communist Party and severed all contacts with his family. At that time, he thought his decision would be final. Eighteen years later, however hesitantly, it was time for a change of heart.

❧

I believe it was in 1964 when my grandmother Vera and her sister Marutha received restitution from Germany. The descendants of the

Wolfner side of the family were able to recover a substantial amount based on the value of the equipment and inventory the German army took from the Gyula Wolfner & Co. Leather factory during the siege of Budapest at the end of World War II. Vera and Marutha each received their proportionate share.

As far as I know, my grandfather Bertalan also received some compensation during the 1950s, mostly after the sugar factory in Nagysurány, but on a much smaller scale than my grandmother. I heard vague anecdotes about him refusing to go to Germany to testify, hence giving up his chances for a somewhat more substantial amount.

Whether there was any correlation between Vera receiving compensation for her ancestors' loss during the war and her attempt to reconnect with her son remains a matter of speculation. I think it might have played a role, if not in the decision itself, then in its timing. My grandmother's newfound financial security gave her the means to cross the Atlantic and the potential to invite all three of us for a visit in Western Europe. Back then, we needed an invitation letter from a relative in the West, promising to cover all expenses of our travel and lodging, in order to start the tedious process of applying for passports and visas. I know with certainty, and remember from later years, that my father had a very difficult time accepting anything from my grandmother. Looking at photos of our trips to Western Europe in the 1960s, I noticed how distinctly different his wardrobe was from ours. While he reluctantly let Vera shower me and my mother with beautiful outfits, he didn't don a single piece of Western clothing until a couple years later, when he started traveling on business and was able to afford them on his own.

The exact circumstances of the reunion will remain obscure. I assume my grandfather Bertalan had heard about my father's imprisonment and subsequent release and rehabilitation from his fiancée Zsuzsi when she defected from Hungary in 1957 and sought his support in Paris. Since my grandparents maintained a rather cordial, almost friendly relationship after their divorce, Vera must have contacted Bertalan and joined forces with him in an effort to reconnect with their estranged son. Who made the first step? When and how did it happen? Were they aware of József having a new wife and a daughter?

My mother told me it was her, who persuaded my father to rekindle his relationship with his parents. She argued they had the right to meet their only granddaughter as much as I should be given the chance to know my paternal grandparents. Since Bertalan and Vera both refused to set foot in communist Hungary, my mother thought I would benefit from visiting them in Western Europe from time to time, a rare and very attractive opportunity those days.

For Hungarians, traveling abroad in 1965 was not a right, but a privilege. Visiting a "friendly country" was considerably easier than going to an "imperialist" one, to use the official terminology of the leadership, distinguishing between the Soviet Bloc and the capitalist West. Apart from the obvious temptation of defecting, the government was afraid of travelers gaining a good impression of the Western world, especially when exposed to the abundance of merchandise. In the early 1960s, the number of people allowed to travel from Hungary to Western Europe was in the hundreds, and while restrictions relaxed in 1965, it remained a rare privilege. Those who were allowed to travel could expect to be observed and were often asked to cooperate with the authorities, sharing their experiences with them.

Making travel arrangements was anything but trivial. First, the Ministry of Interior had to give us permission to leave the country. Once approved, each of us received a coveted stamp in our passport, the so-called "window." It was extremely rare for an entire family to be granted permission to travel at the same time, since there would be no hostage left behind, no reason to return to Hungary should they decide to defect. In retrospect, I find it intriguing that all three of us received this stamp, a window of opportunity indeed. I wonder if the authorities meant to test my father and see whether he would return, or if they deliberately wished he would not.

Passport in hand, stamped with a "window," one could start the lengthy process of applying for a visa at the appropriate embassy. The Hungarian forint was not freely convertible at the time. Travelers were allowed to exchange a very limited amount of forint to "hard currency," barely enough to make ends meet while abroad. Hungarian citizens could only travel to the West once every three years unless they were able to provide a letter of invitation from a relative living in the West who would cover all expenses. With such an invitation letter, one could travel as often as once every year.

Budapest Ferihegy Airport was nothing more than a small building with only two doors inside the main hall, one for departures and one for arrivals. Hungarians were obligated to fly MALÉV Hungarian Airlines except in cases when the national carrier didn't provide service to a certain destination. Humbled, curious, and full of excitement, we boarded an Ilyushin 18 Soviet-made propeller plane.

I have flashes of memories mixed with stories my parents would later tell me about my first flight. Upon noticing the aircraft's asymmetrical layout, two seats on one side of the aisle and three on the other, I wondered whether it would tip to one side during our flight. I don't remember the explanation he offered, but I am certain my father dissipated my worries in a matter of seconds. As I would learn from my parents, I enjoyed every minute of the flight, singing nursery rhymes most of the way and walking up and down the aisle with my long hair bouncing in a high ponytail. Apparently, I barely noticed the thunderstorm sending most of the adult passengers into panic, holding on to their armrests with white knuckles and reaching for their sick bags.

I was even more oblivious to something else, and so were my parents and most likely every other passenger traveling with us. As I would learn only after the fall of communism, all commercial airplanes flying to the West doubled as military reconnaissance aircraft, equipped with a camera under the cockpit, behind a glass window. That particular day, given the cloudy weather, it is very unlikely that Hungary's intelligence service had any success locating strategic features in Austria, Germany, and France. I doubt they found anything noteworthy on sunny days, for that matter.

⌒

Paris was love at first sight. I felt as if I were stepping from a black-and-white movie into a color one. The minute we left Orly Airport, everything seemed overwhelmingly bright, shiny, and luxurious. I didn't recognize any of the cars in the streets. Until then, I had seen only Eastern European models such as Trabant, Wartburg, Moskvitch, and

Pobeda, all in sad, matte colors, mostly grayish-white, baby blue, or black. Suddenly I found myself surrounded by a variety of beautiful cars in all colors of the rainbow. I specifically remember sitting in a taxi on the way to my grandfather's apartment and deciding then and there it was the most beautiful car I have ever seen: a Citrôen Pallas.

The boulevards and avenues were lined with clean and well-maintained buildings, unlike the ones in Budapest, covered in thick, black dirt and bullet holes from the 1956 revolution. There was an abundance of beautiful shops with glamorous window displays and inviting outdoor cafés with rattan chairs and colorful umbrellas.

The French language was music to my ears, even though I didn't understand any of it except for *bonjour* and *merci*. My father made sure I knew these essential phrases before our plane touched down in Paris.

∾

Berci, as we all called my grandfather Bertalan, was a kind, jovial man, looking much older than his actual age of sixty-five, with his white hair and white beard. Despite having an undeniable aura about him that commanded instant respect, I found him very approachable. He smoked a pipe, holding it in his hand as an accessory long after it burned out. Berci enjoyed telling me long stories and anecdotes, speaking remarkably slowly and eloquently. He was eager to answer all my questions. There was a quality of wisdom in everything he said. One thing stuck with me for life. He taught me I should never be hesitant or embarrassed to ask questions, no matter how trivial they may sound. Only by asking questions are we able to learn new things and widen our horizons. I took his advice to heart and still live by it. My only regret is not asking him more questions during my subsequent visits.

My grandfather's apartment in the 16th arrondissement was full of old books and a handful of his vast, long-gone collection of Asian artwork, the few pieces he managed to bring with him when he left Hungary in 1938. There was a delicate, odd-shaped chair in the corner of his living room, much higher than all other chairs. I think its sole purpose was to serve as decoration, but I loved climbing up there and claiming it to myself, as if conquering it. I might have been the only person allowed to sit in it.

Despite living away from his homeland for several decades and rarely having the opportunity to speak Hungarian with anyone, Berci did not have a foreign accent, not even the slightest, nor did he search for Hungarian words. In fact, he was so meticulous about his mother tongue, he corrected my Hungarian every chance he had. He was disappointed by my inability to distinguish between the so-called open and closed "eh" sounds, a nuance in our language I didn't know back then and will probably never master.

After his divorce from his second wife, Claire, in 1958, my grandfather lived alone. But there was someone very close to him, a frequent visitor, a part of his immediate family, even if not a relative by blood. Marie-Françoise, Claire's daughter from her first marriage, joined us. Bobette, as all of us called her, was in her late twenties. Pretty and svelte, she embodied the ultimate French woman, radiating elegance, style, and confidence. I loved listening to her speaking French. It made her appear even more sophisticated. She also spoke fluent English, which I appreciated very much during my later visits, once I learned it myself. In 1965, however, it didn't really matter which language she used. József and Berci understood both, while my mother and I spoke neither.

My grandmother Vera flew in from New York to meet us, and we continued our vacation with her on the French Riviera. As beautiful as Paris was, I was too young to truly appreciate what it had to offer, with the exception of the Eiffel Tower. The Riviera however, proved to be an age-appropriate playground for me. I didn't know how to swim yet, but I could splash in the shallow waves and build castles in the soft, white sand. My father rented a water bicycle, and the two of us enjoyed pedaling in the sea. While I had the time of my life with him, my mother and my grandmother were sitting under an umbrella on the beach. They never learned to like each other. I would find it quite ironic later, once I became more aware of their incredibly tense relationship. It was my mother who initiated rebuilding the ties between my father and my grandmother, which had been fragile and completely nonexistent for almost two decades, yet she was barely tolerated by Vera. Was it because she hadn't come from a family my grandmother would have approved of, or was it simply her personality?

Vera was quite the opposite of Berci. To say she was intimidating, cold, and unapproachable would be an understatement. There was no place for arguing with her. She seemed to believe she knew everything better than anyone else, a trait neither my grandfather nor my parents shared, and of course, something I myself quickly learned to resent. One thing that distinguished her from all other members of my family was her lack of showing affection. At least that was how I perceived her. Maybe she was unable to express her emotions, maybe she was unwilling to show them, or perhaps she considered it inappropriate to wear them on her sleeves.

Despite the tense relationship she had with Vera, my mother truly appreciated the opportunity to see many beautiful places in the South of France and would talk about Antibes and Èze in particular, her two favorites, for decades to come. Cartier's shop window near the famous Monte Carlo Casino also made a lasting impression on her. As she would tell me years later, she was fascinated by its simplicity and elegance. There was only one solitary necklace on display, sitting on a red velvet cushion. Nothing else. Cartier did not feel the need to show its entire inventory in order to lure customers inside, a sharp contrast to most Hungarian retail stores in those days, as a result of severe shortage and limited selection of merchandise.

One of my mother's biggest regrets also stemmed from this trip. The Beatles were playing in Nice during our visit to the French Riviera. It could have been her one and only chance to see them live in concert. My father was quite indifferent toward them, not a particularly big fan of their music, but he possibly could have been convinced. My grandmother, on the other hand, found them downright scandalous. She said, "One does not attend a performance by longhaired hooligans screaming 'yeah, yeah, yeah.'" As I would learn from my mother many years later, she was within arm's reach of The Beatles in June 1965 but couldn't go see them. I rarely sided with her, but this is a notable exception. Had I been at least ten years older at the time, I certainly would have tried to tip the scale by winning my father over. With him on our side, we could have overruled Vera's decision.

⌒

Manners were of utmost importance in the Hatvany family, a heritage my father was eager to pass on to me. Although my mother was raised under very different circumstances than my father, she also thought it was crucial to ingrain the basics of good behavior in her daughter as early as possible. "Please" and "thank you" were two expressions in our household without which one could not get by. Using these phrases became second nature to me by the age of three. "Want" was a word I completely had to erase from my vocabulary very early on. My parents expected me to say, "May I, please?" or "I would like" instead.

Teaching me proper table manners at such early age was a very ambitious undertaking, but my father was determined to prepare me for meeting my grandmother. In fact, I think he wanted to show off. Thus, I learned how to eat properly with a knife and fork at four. Of course, my father did not resort to such extreme measures as his grandmother Fanny did with him, making him hold a book under each armpit and balance a third one on his head for proper posture. His methods included gentle persuasion, endless repetition, and, most of all, a healthy dose of positive reinforcement. Above all, he taught me by good example. By the time we arrived in the French Riviera in June 1965, I had impeccable table manners.

Of course, I don't remember this, but my mother would repeatedly tell me later how extremely proud she had been in those very upscale restaurants where we dined with my grandmother in Cannes and Nice. Several other guests came over to our table and asked my parents how old I was. Upon hearing my age, they expressed their disbelief. Apparently, I nicely sat through the entire multicourse meal, using a knife and fork properly, without ever playing with my food, touching it with my hands, chewing with an open mouth, putting my elbows on the table, or getting up before everyone else did. Being exposed to foods that were previously unknown to me, I had to learn new things in France, such as using a fish knife, handling escargot with utensils specially designed for this French delicacy, and rolling spaghetti the proper way, without a spoon.

Not for a moment did I feel deprived of a real childhood or forced to perform against my will. On the contrary, I was bursting with pride and felt privileged to be able to sit with the adults, eat what they ate, and do as they did. In fact, back in Hungary, I was deeply offended at day care, where the only piece of cutlery deemed safe for children my age was an aluminum spoon.

My first visit to France was full of culinary discoveries. I was introduced to a great variety of fresh seafood, artichokes, olives, and croissants with marmalade, to mention a few delicacies not available in Hungary in the '60s. Just like my father, I was happy and willing to try anything new without the slightest reservation. My mother drew the line at escargot.

It was also in France where I had my first lessons in politics. My grandmother put us up in five-star hotels and invited us to dine in the most elegant restaurants. She took my mother and me shopping for fabulous clothes and shoes, the kind we wouldn't even dream of, let alone find, in 1960s Hungary. It was me she really wanted to impress. At four and a half, I was too young to speculate that she might have been motivated by something else, beyond her obvious generosity. In the coming years, however, during my subsequent visits with her in Italy, Austria, and England, it would become clear to me that she indeed had an agenda.

Vera wanted me to get a taste of the glamorous life in the West, a life I could have called my own had I chosen to leave Hungary for a free country.

In stark contrast, my father was eager to point out the gap between the haves and have-nots. He wanted me to understand that not everybody in the capitalist world was fortunate enough to live the lifestyle we experienced during our visit. I believe it was in Cannes that we went to a beautifully manicured playground. I have always loved swings, and I saw this unusual one, shaped like a boat. I persuaded my parents to let me use it, and it turned out we had to put some coins in a machine, then go through a revolving gate in order to sit in the swings. We paid, and I enjoyed swinging in the yellow boat.

My father thought this was the perfect opportunity to explain the dark side of capitalism to his four-and-a-half-year-old daughter. He said it was indeed a beautiful playground, with much nicer swings than those in public playgrounds in Budapest. Having to pay at the gate, however, would unjustly exclude children whose parents could not afford it. I probably didn't fully understand this argument at the time, nor was I aware of my grandmother's intentions to lure me into freedom. As with table manners, I certainly started my political education at a very early age.

Two years after our first vacation in France, my parents and I traveled to Western Europe again, this time to Italy. Berci joined us from Paris. Venice simultaneously impressed and saddened me. I was fascinated by the mosaics of St. Mark's Basilica and captivated by the Bridge of Sighs. I enjoyed the unusual local transportation, navigating the canals of this unique city by vaporetto and gondola. Upon learning that Venice was sinking, my eyes filled with tears. I asked my parents, practically begging them to do something about it. As a young child, I was convinced they had it in their power to intervene and save it for the future.

Vera arrived from New York, and my parents and I continued our journey of Northern Italy with her. While sitting in an outdoor café in Milan, enjoying none other than spaghetti Milanese, my father offered an interesting explanation to how our pasta was made. "First they make the pasta in a thick cylinder shape," he said with a completely straight face, "and then they put it through another piece of equipment that pushes out the middle. This process results in a tubular type of pasta: the macaroni, and a thinner version: the spaghetti." As ridiculous as it sounds, his story made perfect sense to me at the age of six and a half.

Isola d'Elba just off the Tuscan coastline of Italy became one of my favorite places I visited in my entire childhood. After admiring the leaning tower of Pisa, my father and I boarded a very small plane. It seated four passengers, but we found ourselves alone with the pilot. Our journey to this beautiful island, a true gem in the Mediterranean, was an adventure itself. I was so excited to share the picturesque views with my father, let alone having an airplane to ourselves, that I was somewhat disappointed when we landed, wishing it would last longer. My mother and Vera arrived by boat. We stayed at a beautiful villa in Portoferraio just steps away from a secluded beach nestled in a cove. It was breathtaking. For the first time in my life, I was allowed to swim far enough from the shore, into the deep water, where my feet couldn't reach the seafloor. I had never swum in such crystal-clear water before and was mesmerized as my father pointed out the various types of fish and sea plants underneath us. I told him I was glad our plane landed after all.

Apart from a rather unremarkable vacation at Wörtersee in Pörtschach, Austria, the following summer, my grandmother never saw the three of us together again. Come to think of it, that was the last time she and my mother met each other. The tension between Zsófia and Vera must have reached a point where they decided it was better to keep their distance. My father visited with my grandmother during some of his numerous business trips to the West, while I was sent all by myself to spend month-long summer vacations with her, mostly in Italy, throughout the 1970s.

Chapter Twenty-Five

Compromise

I HAVE ALWAYS WONDERED why my father returned to Hungary in the summer of 1965. I never understood the reasons behind his decision to go back to a country where he had to endure mental and physical abuse and experience tremendous injustice and humiliation, where he had been robbed of five years of his youth, where he was treated as a threat well after regaining his fragile freedom, where he was still facing a steep uphill battle in pursuit of acceptance. He was among the very few people who were given the opportunity to travel to the West with their family, no strings attached, no hostage left behind. He had parents in the West with sufficient funds to help him, to help all three of us find our footing and build a new life in a free country. His command of English rivaled that of a highly educated, well-read native speaker. He was also fluent in French and German. Not only were his field of interest and expertise highly sought after, his line of scientific research was considered groundbreaking on both sides of the Iron Curtain. What motivated him to return?

For many years, I entertained one, and only one possible explanation: he identified with Hungary's political direction, led by a government that supposedly distanced itself from the mistakes of the overreaching Stalinist regime of the 1950s and promised to "build socialism" in the post-1956 era. Throughout my entire childhood and well into my adulthood, everything I heard and experienced unanimously supported this explanation. That was until I read a three-page document. It made me reevaluate the storyline I had created and believed in for decades. However, it raised more questions than it answered.

◦◦◦

At the end of 2014, my cousin Andrew invited me to Washington, DC, after the death of his mother, Marutha, to help sort through her papers and photos. Next to her own memorabilia, there were boxes of documents and pictures left behind by her older sister Vera. Among stacks of papers, there was a plain envelope with a copy of my father's curriculum vitae in it.

It is a carbon copy of a typewritten document in English. There is no name or address on it and no signature either, only József Hatvany's handwritten initials at the bottom. Nevertheless, it is undoubtedly my father's. His style and word usage are as easily recognizable as his handwriting. Why no date and address? I wondered. There could be only one explanation. Since this resume was intended for Western audience, he had to protect himself as much as possible should it somehow end up in the hands of the Hungarian authorities. Dating the document was quite easy for me, as it mentions my age. He must have written it in the summer of 1965, while in France. That way, he wouldn't have risked trusting someone to hand carry it out of the country and being caught. Mailing such a document those days was out of the question, since almost all letters were opened, read, and resealed by the Hungarian authorities. The last paragraph of the CV surprised me and made me rethink my perception of his views and intentions:

> I have a daughter, aged four and a half. My concern for her future in a country where the future is always uncertain and I have myself so badly burnt my fingers, has led me to consider the possibility of leaving Hungary and settling in the West, provided that a suitably remunerated job is forthcoming where I feel that I can make use of my experience in the application of digital operational techniques to measurement or control problems.

Upon reading this document, my mind was racing as much as my heart did. According to my cousin Andrew, my grandparents were adamant about helping their son defect from Hungary. More than anything, they wanted to see their only grandchild grow up in the West instead of a communist country they themselves refused to set foot in. I contemplated whether my father wrote this resume solely to please and silence his parents while being their guest in France, without the slightest intention of following through. As quickly as this hypothesis entered my brain, it dispersed. My father was far too stubborn to give in to such pressure. No, it had to stem from his will and his sincere belief. He must have considered leaving Hungary again, as he had attempted and failed once in 1958.

In the summer of 1965 he was still treated as a threat and an outsider at the Academy of Sciences, despite his notable professional achievements. Upon reading his CV, and knowing how much of a priority I enjoyed in his life, I truly believed he indeed considered defecting.

Why didn't he do it? Was it because he left Cambridge University without receiving a degree? At the Hungarian Academy of Sciences, they were willing to overlook that fact and recognize his professional achievements in lieu of a formal diploma. In the West, he probably would have been required to go back to school and finish his education. If so, was it a deal breaker?

In his CV, he mentioned that he had become an enthusiastic communist in his late teens. He disclosed his unjust imprisonment. He pointed out his consequent decision to turn away from politics and devote himself wholly to research work. Could it have been his honesty that sealed his fate?

Had he written this resume just a couple years later, once he earned a certain level of respect and recognition at the Hungarian Academy of Sciences, it would be easy to assume he preferred to be a bigger fish in a smaller pond, a pond not as poisoned as it used to be. But in the summer of 1965, at a time when he wasn't even allowed to be an official employee of the Research Institute of Automation, he didn't seem to have too much to lose by leaving.

Was my mother the reason he couldn't leave Hungary? After all, apart from her minimal knowledge of German, she didn't speak foreign languages and would have had a much tougher time trying to fit in and start a new life in another country. More importantly, she would have been separated from her family for a long time, if not forever. Her parents were already quite old and ailing at the time. Had she defected from Hungary in 1965, she might have never seen them again. It would have been several years before a possible reunion with her sisters. Was this the main obstacle, and in that case, could this have been the cause of friction between my mother and my paternal grandparents?

∽

As the Hungarian saying goes, "He was involved in the coat stealing." It refers to a situation when people can't recall whether the person in question stole someone's coat or it was his coat that was stolen. Nobody remembers whether he was the victim or the perpetrator, but most certainly there was a coat stealing, and he was involved in it one way or the other. It is a slippery slope, a dangerous way of trying to fill in the gaps between pieces of factual information available to us. This exact thing happened when someone I know blurred the lines between two distinctly different things, telling me that my father had been on the wrong side of the coat-stealing story, so to speak. His assumptions were based on fragments of questionable hearsay mingled with, and tainted by, his own perception.

Between 1962 and 1990, there was a special intelligence agency in Hungary, similar to those under the umbrella of the Soviet KGB or the East German Stasi, the so-called III/III Division. It was designed to monitor people's private lives, relying on a vast network of informants. Whether these internal spies were overzealous volunteers in hopes of personal advancement or recruited against their will, they had the potential to cause serious harm to their fellow citizens. Reports submitted by these informants could easily jeopardize careers, friendships, marriages, one's chance of receiving a passport or a government-assigned apartment, and, in some cases, even one's personal freedom. My father had nothing to do with the infamous "Three per Three" Division. He had never been recruited, nor did he ever act as an informant.

There was another part of the intelligence agency, however, a considerably smaller and much lesser-known division, that focused on gathering information about the latest technological achievements of other countries, primarily those in the West. A representative of this secret department of the intelligence agency approached my father sometime in the midsixties. Based on my father's own recollections, along with the unanimous and conclusive recollections of those very close to him, some of whom bore direct witness to it, I know for a fact that he was involved with this particular part of the agency. What I do not know is the exact date when he was first recruited. All logic and a clear chain of reasoning make me assume it must have been sometime after his trip to France and after he was finally hired by the Hungarian Academy of Sciences as a full-time employee. At that point, it was clear to the authorities that he would not be a flight risk, since he didn't attempt to defect from Hungary. But more importantly, by then, he indeed had a great deal to lose. For the first time in years, József Hatvany had a stable job, a reasonable level of acceptance and respect by his peers, and a chance to spread his wings and engage in scientific research of his choosing. He also got a taste of traveling to the West with his family, visiting his parents, and giving me an opportunity to know my grandparents and experience other cultures throughout my childhood.

As I understand from firsthand recollections, not only did the agency threaten to take all this away from him, should he refuse to cooperate, they also made it clear that they had in their power to jeopardize his personal freedom and throw him back to jail.

We may gasp in disbelief, perhaps even labeling my father an industrial spy, or we may step back and look at what was considered normal practice in the scientific world. Either way, my intention is not to diminish the past in an effort to defend him, but to put it in perspective.

Under the communist regime, most everyone in Hungary was required to submit a detailed travel report after returning from a business trip, regardless of their line of work or the country visited. In some cases, several copies of these travel reports gathered dust in a file cabinet without ever being read. In other cases, especially those concerned with new, cutting-edge scientific research, carbon copies made it to the hands of the highest authorities, catching the eyes of the aforementioned secret division of the intelligence agency. In cases involving highly educated scientific researchers fluent in Western languages, attending conferences and visiting research facilities abroad, the agency would often go one step further by conducting interviews. József Hatvany was required to meet with one of their representatives after each business trip and have a face-to-face discussion in hopes of gaining an insight into the latest achievements of a Western research institute, university, or factory.

My father never talked about this with me when I was a child, probably for my own protection, but I remember a mysterious man visiting us at our house once in the 1970s. He wore a beige trench coat, a black fedora, and sunglasses, reminding me of Columbo, the title character of the popular American TV series everyone watched in our country, dubbed in Hungarian. This quiet and polite gentleman accompanied my father to the back room, the room that had evolved from coal storage to my father's bedroom and study. Behind closed doors, they had a discussion for about an hour, but for me it seemed much longer. When I asked what it was all about, my parents were hesitant to give me an explanation other than his name was Lajos and that they had some important official business to discuss. As I would learn several years later, Lajos, a very common Hungarian first name, was only his cover. Apparently, my father continued with these meetings for as long as he lived. "Lajos" would even pay him a visit at the hospital, immediately after my father's last trip to the United States and just weeks before his death.

Some of my friends cautioned against revealing József Hatvany's involvement with this secret division of the intelligence agency, arguing it could strip away all the respect his Western colleagues and friends had for him, destroying the positive image they held on to throughout all these years. Taking their advice to heart, I considered shoving it under the carpet, pretending it had never happened, until I had lengthy discussions about this matter with two very respectable, highly educated Americans. Both came to the same conclusion, completely independent from each other, convincing me that it was a much lesser issue than I imagined. One of them was even smiling when I expressed my serious concerns about unveiling this information. He told me that he himself had been questioned multiple times by representatives of the American Intelligence after returning from various business trips to communist countries, and he didn't think it would make him an industrial spy.

Knowing my father as a private person and knowing how much he cherished the strong bond he had with his Western counterparts, I am confident in assuming he made every possible effort to protect their interests. He treasured his professional relationships abroad, but more than anything, he truly valued the personal friendships he developed in the 1970s and 1980s with some of his colleagues in Western Europe, the United States, and Japan. I clearly recall him considering them the closest friends he ever had. By all means, József Hatvany had enough wit and integrity to walk the fine line between the two sides of the fence. I have absolutely no doubt he managed to reveal just enough information to satisfy the agency but stopped short of disclosing too much, making sure he wouldn't hurt the interests of his foreign colleagues.

As far as the "coat stealing" is concerned, there isn't much difference between sharing industrial applications of technology and scientific research that might benefit your countrymen, and sharing newfound knowledge of technical and scientific advances that can improve the state of the art globally. All sides did this and continue to do so. However, both are radically different from giving in to pressures to share indiscretions, real or imagined, of a friend, neighbor, or family member, willing yourself to overlook the personal harm it can do to those individuals.

Chapter Twenty-Six

Trabant

It was East Germany's answer to the Volkswagen Beetle and one of the most recognizable symbols of the communist era. Trabant, often nicknamed Trabi, was a small two-door car populating the streets of most Eastern European countries. It was relatively affordable despite the fact that owning a car in the 1960s was still borderline luxury. The Trabant had a two-stroke engine, similar to a lawnmower, making it an extremely loud and polluting vehicle. Its body was made of plastic, a material quite practical in the winter, since it didn't rust from the salt spread on roads to melt the ice. As a very lightweight, front-wheel drive vehicle, it was able to negotiate roads covered with snow, even our steep driveway, with much more success than most other cars, especially in reverse gear. In case of a minor fender-bender, one could easily replace damaged parts of the frame using a little glue. The shift was in the middle of the dashboard, and it looked like a door handle, a feature

shared by some French cars of the time. Despite its unusual characteristics and a signature white cloud of exhaust fumes, this car was quite
reliable.

My father became the proud owner of a Trabant 601 model in 1967.
In those days, buying a car was not an easy undertaking. Hungary didn't
have its own car manufacturing, and the selection of strictly Eastern
European cars was rather limited. One could sign up for a particular
make and model, select his first two or three choices of color, pay half of
the purchase price in cash, and then patiently wait, wait, and wait some
more. Approximately three years later, depending on inventory and the
efficiency of the central distribution system, a letter arrived in the mail
stating the exact date and location where the lucky owner of a brand-
new car was to appear with the other half of the purchase price, also in
cash. After several hours of waiting in a crowded and chaotic room, one
would receive the keys, the papers, and the car. If all stars lined up, it
could even be the buyer's first choice of color. There weren't many colors
to choose from, nor were they very appealing. As far as I remember, the
Trabant mostly came in a grayish dirty white or a pale blue that everyone mocked as "panty blue." I vaguely recall a third color somewhere
between sad beige and diluted mustard. We were delighted to receive a
white one, our first choice of color.

The Trabant had another unique feature. There was no fuel gauge to
show the level of gasoline in the engine. Instead, it was equipped with a
clever backup plan. Once the main tank ran empty, it could be switched
to reserve. In order to know how much fuel was in the tank, one had
to use a measuring stick. Throughout Eastern Europe, where cars with
two-stroke engines were sold, every gas station offered a ready-made
blend of gas and oil, called "mixture," but crossing the Austrian border

driving a Trabant or a Wartburg posed a challenge. One had to carry oil in a can and mix it with the gasoline, calculating the right proportion at every fueling. My father mastered this to perfection on our road trip to Austria in 1968.

∽

One of my most vivid memories involving our Trabant was a strange incident that happened while we were traveling from Budapest to Lake Balaton. Hungary's first freeway hadn't been finished yet, so we took a two-lane country road to my favorite vacation destination, the summer resort of the Hungarian Academy of Sciences in Balatonvilágos. Approaching the main road from a small side street, my father slowed down in the intersection. As there was no car coming from the left, he turned right onto the main road. As soon as he did, a policeman jumped out from behind the bush and flagged him down.

My father pulled over and rolled down the window, and the officer said, "Didn't you see the stop sign? You were supposed to come to a complete halt instead of just slowing down. Give me your license and registration!"

Instead of admitting to a minor traffic violation, my father decided to teach the policeman a lesson in basic manners. "Good morning!" he said in a very calm voice.

The policeman seemed annoyed by being disciplined, so he raised his voice and repeated, "License and registration!"

My father said "Good morning!" again, hoping for some kind of a greeting before the "license and registration" demand, and possibly even a "please" afterward.

Of course, it didn't happen. The policeman became more and more agitated every time they went back and forth with their stubborn exchange, but my father was relentless.

Upon watching this seemingly endless standoff between her husband and a representative of an authority never to be disputed, my mother became extremely nervous. She was literally shaking in the passenger seat, begging him not to argue with the police, fearing we would all get in much bigger trouble should he persist. Finally, when my father realized I was crying in the back seat, he decided to give up and give in. This was the first time I witnessed such a behavior from him, something many of his colleagues were very familiar with, as I would learn several years later.

Chapter Twenty-Seven
Impact

JÓZSEF HATVANY's WEAPON of choice was his fountain pen. At the Automation Research Institute of the Hungarian Academy of Sciences, he often wrote fierce letters to his boss, the director, expressing his discontent or opposing views. He fought tooth and nail against a great number of decisions that unfavorably affected his department, whether it was the allocation of research and development funds, the approval of his next project, or the choice of companies he would work with as his clients and contractors. Internal politics also played a significant part in his frequent quarrels with his boss. There was a great rivalry between József and the head of another department within the institute. The ideas of two brilliant minds, two headstrong personalities, often clashed. To add fuel to the fire, the director played one off against the other so they wouldn't challenge his authority. Throw in a pinch of pride, vanity, and stubbornness, and you have a perfect storm.

When a ten-page handwritten letter didn't produce results, my father found alternative ways to make his point. Sometime in the late 1960s, following an argument with his boss, József took extreme measures even for his standards. He refused to set foot in the building unless the director apologized. Of course, he wouldn't miss a minute of work, so he asked his secretary to bring down the electric typewriter and the phone along with two extension cords from his office on the fourth floor. With the equipment plugged into outlets in the lobby, they conducted business as usual, sitting in my father's Trabant parked right in front of the institute.

László (Laci) Nemes joined my father's department at the Automation Research Institute in the early 1970s. Drafting his memoir almost fifty years later, he would reflect on the challenges and benefits of working with József as follows:

> I was given free hand at my new workplace to design a brand-new control architecture. I enjoyed the scientific atmosphere that surrounded me...Hatvany read through an enormous amount of scientific and industrial publications every weekend, and had the library make copies of the important ones for the research fellows. He read everything his colleagues wrote, whether in Hungarian or English. He was extremely particular, demanding a beautiful and clear style from everyone. Despite having been educated in England, nobody knew Hungarian grammar better than him.

I proudly handed him my first paper. At the next department meeting, he praised my innovative technical solution before reading some excerpts out loud, mocking my bad Hungarian and sloppy expressions. Oh, how I hated him then as he humiliated me in front of the entire department. At the end of the meeting, with a victorious smile, he handed me the paper full of red lines.

On my way home, I went to a bookstore and bought *Kis Magyar Nyelvtan* (*Concise Hungarian Grammar*), and started studying it that very night. Sometime later, I happened to stumble on a document he had hastily written. I corrected it in red ink. He took it laughing, and was visibly happy, having achieved his goal.

It was in 1972 when Laci and my father coauthored and submitted a paper for the 5th World Congress of IFAC (International Federation of Automatic Control) in Paris. My father thought it would be the perfect opportunity for Laci to get used to speaking in front of a large audience and practice his English skills, which were rather modest at the time.

I was petrified, thinking nobody would understand me. I said, I would read it. "That's completely out of the question," Jóska said, "only small children should be read to, so they go to sleep. Do you want your audience to fall asleep?" We came to an agreement. I would write a speech in simple English, Jóska would correct it, then read it to a cassette tape recorder, so I could memorize it like a parrot. Every night, I listened to his recording and repeated it sentence by sentence until I learned it perfectly. Even if someone woke me from my deepest sleep, I wouldn't have made a mistake. At the conference, when the moderator announced the next presentation, I went to the podium with confidence, and presented what I had rehearsed without a glitch. Upon hearing my pronunciation, they may have thought I actually knew English, as people from the audience stood up one after the other to ask questions in long monologues. While listening to the first one, I felt the podium sinking under my feet. I recognized a word here and there, but I had no idea what the question was. Jóska saved me. He stood up, introduced himself as the coauthor, which was true, and answered all the questions…

As we were flying home from Paris, I told Hatvany how much the conference made me realize I had a lot more to learn. I asked him if I could possibly go to America to study. Jóska enjoyed tremendous international respect, and I thought he might be able to make some arrangements. "The USA is out of the question," was his answer. "They won't let you in as someone involved in computer control. You must put your field of research on the application form, and won't be granted a visa if your project is under embargo. There is no use of going to Western Europe, as they themselves lag behind." After taking a minute to think, he said he would soon travel to Japan with a delegation where he would look around for me. That time, Japanese industrial research experienced a huge upward momentum, and it seemed easier to receive a fellowship at one of their universities.

When my father said he would look around and see what he could do, he didn't pay lip service. He went out of his way to give his colleagues opportunities to study abroad during the Cold War, when it was far from trivial. Upon his return from Japan, he was delighted to report that the research efforts he saw in industrial robotics were on par with those in America. He was also delighted to share the great news that Japan welcomed the idea of hosting a scientist from Hungary. As a result of his inquiries and encouragement, Laci applied for and received a fellowship at Tokyo University.

József Hatvany was highly esteemed by his peers abroad. Apart from his cutting-edge innovations, up-to-date knowledge of the latest technical developments in CAD/CAM, and being a true visionary, foreseeing the effects of automation on human life long before it became a concern, József had a unique combination of characteristics that made him very popular in the international arena. His eloquent Cambridge English certainly helped break down barriers, and so did his fluent French and German. He had an ability to move seamlessly across various cultures. József took pride in studying the history, culture, and traditions of every country he had ever visited. He always made an effort to learn at least a few sentences in languages he didn't speak already and to familiarize himself with the basic rules of conduct in his host nations. Of course, being the connoisseur he was, sampling local delicacies was a must. He didn't ask for a fork in Japan, but he asked for salt with his porridge in Edinburgh in a flawless Scottish accent. He knew when to wear a suit and tie, when to wear a polo shirt with khakis, when to speak, and when to listen. He had an appetite for expanding his horizons with an open mind for views and cultures different from his own.

Maybe the embargo regulations eased as the decade progressed, maybe József simply found a way to work around them. One way or the other, he successfully secured several fellowships at top American universities for young Hungarian researchers working for him. He opened doors that needed a special key to unlock.

My father also attracted Western scientists to join his department in Hungary. He invited Malcolm Sabin, a pioneer of computer-aided design from England, to complete his doctoral dissertation under his guidance in Budapest, while providing valuable on-the-job training for the entire group. Steven Coons, professor at the Massachusetts Institute of Technology, an early pioneer in the field of computer graphics, also spent time in Hungary. He created a school of his own at my father's department.

It was also in the early 1970s when Andries (Andy) van Dam, professor of computer science at Brown University, first visited Budapest. "I consider my time in Hungary the highlight of my non-Brown career. I had a lovely relationship with your dad, I just loved him," he told me over lunch in California in 2012. "He was a great man, and his flaws, they were great too. He wasn't just good professionally. He was top notch. He bootstrapped Hungary into the modern age of computers. He also had a gift for storytelling and teaching. He had a commanding presence. He was so much larger than life, easily the most remarkable person I have ever been friends with," said Andy.

Professor Hiroyuki Yoshikawa, president of the University of Tokyo, delivered a speech at the General Assembly of CIRP (The International Academy for Production Engineering), held in Budapest in 2011. "This is my tenth visit to Budapest," he said as he recalled meeting my father for the first time at a conference in Scotland in 1976.

> It was in 1982…in Norway, when I agreed with Prof. Hatvany to organize a Joint Japanese-Hungarian Project…I learned many things from Prof. Joe Hatvany. His ripe culture and deep knowledge on philosophy and history opened our eyes wider from our own narrow research area to the space of intelligence. I learned that engineering is not a simple discipline but integrated knowledge which must be grounded on ethics and humanism, and always be linked to society and history.

In an email in 2013, Professor Yoshikawa wrote to me: "I visited his house in Hungary and tasted Hungarian liqueur in front of many classical books on philosophy." Attached was a picture of my father's handwritten dinner invitation from 1985, which he framed and still keeps in his office.

Chapter Twenty-Eight

Divide

THE FIRST TIME József set foot on American soil was in the spring of 1969, when he attended the 10th Annual Symposium on Information Display in Arlington, Virginia, presenting his paper *Are Displays Good for Us?* As I would learn almost fifty years later, he was hoping to use this opportunity to reconnect with family members he hadn't seen since his childhood. Fanny died in 1965 and Lili in 1967, while Antonia lived until 1974. She and Lili's daughter Mariella resided in New Jersey. In a letter to Antonia, Bertalan acted as a mediator, trying to arrange a possible reunion between his sister, his niece and his son:

> A question to you and Malla [Mariella]: Józsi is possibly going on a business trip in May to Washington and New York to attend some mini-computer-symposium. Of course, he would stay with his mother in New York, with whom, as you know, he doesn't always get along very well

(this is no surprise). If you'd be open to see him, he would like to go and pay a visit one day. I warned him that I wasn't sure if you'd be pleased to see him, and I would very much understand if your response were negative. As for me, I get along with him quite well, relatively: for example, when he was here [in Paris] last month, we had a rather friendly exchange. If you don't object him visiting you, please write to me, so I can let him know whether he could call you. If you do object however, and I repeat, I would completely understand your reasons for not wanting to see him, I won't be hurt for a minute, write to me honestly, and in that case, I won't impose.

For reasons unknown to me, this reunion never took place. Whether Antonia and Mariella still felt some resentment toward my father for denouncing his entire family in 1946 while in Cambridge, or they were reluctant to meet someone from a communist country with political views fundamentally different from theirs, will remain unanswered.

It wasn't until 1990 that I first visited the United States. I wish I had known Mariella was still alive, let alone living in New Jersey, but the truth is, at that time I wasn't even aware of Lili having had a daughter, let alone her whereabouts. Had I known, I believe I could have had a much better shot at meeting her than my father had in 1969. If only.

⌒⌒

József was unsuccessful in his attempt to see his aunt and niece on his father's side of the family, but he reunited with his other aunt, Vera's younger sister, whom he hadn't seen in more than two decades. The last time they met was in England in 1946. Marutha was living in Bethesda, Maryland, with her American husband, William Wilson, and their son, Andrew. For Mr. Wilson, a government employee with conservative political views, the mere thought of inviting my father to his home, or even meeting him elsewhere, was completely out of the question. Hence Marutha resorted to some rather adventurous ways, worthy of a spy novel, in order to meet her nephew.

By 1969 the red scare of the McCarthy era was long gone, yet she covered her head with a scarf, hid behind dark sunglasses, and changed taxis multiple times before arriving at a nondescript neutral location far away from her Bethesda neighborhood. She went to great lengths to avoid running into a friend or acquaintance. She wanted to rule out even the slightest possibility of being caught while meeting the black sheep of her family, a communist sympathizer from the wrong side of the Iron Curtain. It wasn't until years later, already divorced from Mr. Wilson, when Marutha felt it was safe to invite my father to her house.

Chapter Twenty-Nine

Lure

AFTER TWENTY YEARS living in the United States, Vera had enough of New York, or maybe America altogether, and decided to move back to Europe. I heard stories that her apartment on East 72nd Street between Park and Madison Avenues was broken into despite its coveted location in the Upper East Side and being situated on a higher floor of a building with a doorman. Crime in New York City was quite rampant those days, and the trauma of someone violating her property must have been hard to digest. Most likely, it was the straw that broke the camel's back, one of several reasons for her decision to move to Rome in 1970.

For the next two years, while she was gradually transitioning from the Big Apple to the Eternal City, looking for an apartment and traveling back and forth, Vera set up residence at the Hotel Eden on Via Ludovisi, a short walk from the Spanish Steps. For me, a child growing up in a communist country, it was a luxury beyond comprehension. She was a distinguished guest, driven to and from the airport by one of the hotel staff in her own car every time she traveled. The hotel also took care of her dry cleaning and ran all kinds of errands for her, as if they were her personal assistants. During my visit in the summer of 1970, my jaw dropped when I noticed that each room had its own color scheme. From furniture fabric to wallpaper, even the towels in the bathroom, everything was a shade of the same color. My room in blue, Vera's in pink. I also remember standing in the lobby listening to my grandmother engaging in a long discussion with a gentleman who I think was the owner of the hotel. Both of them were fluent in Italian, French, German, and English, and they conversed in all four languages, seamlessly switching from one to the next midsentence. It wasn't clear to me whether they tried to upstage each other and flaunt their multilingual proficiency to everyone else in earshot, including me, or if they simply mixed these languages for convenience. When I later mentioned this to my father, he rolled his eyes and said with a smirk on his face that his mother was indeed fluent in several languages, but she didn't speak a single one of them correctly, not even her native German.

Vera had a deep knowledge of art history, and she tried very hard, perhaps too hard, to educate me during my first visit in Rome. While I appreciated her detailed explanation of each and every painting and sculpture in every museum and church we visited, I found it overwhelming and nearly impossible to absorb at the age of nine and a half. After spending the entire day in the Vatican Museum, I was longing for an ice cream in the heat of the Roman summer afternoon rather than trying to remember all the biblical references she mentioned in the Sistine Chapel. My grandmother bought me a journal, and every evening I had to write down all the details about the sights we had visited that day. She became quite upset, thinking I was ungrateful, when I couldn't identify the Doric, Ionic, and Corinthian columns she drew in my journal, or when I didn't recall the subtle differences between Raphael's and Michelangelo's paintings, the nuances she had explained to me while standing in front of these masterpieces. I knew very well how much of a privilege it was to have the opportunity to see some of the most beautiful works of art in the world and learn about ancient Roman history at its birthplace, not to mention having an incredibly knowledgeable grandmother as my private guide. Undoubtedly, she failed to realize that I was too young to fully appreciate and internalize such an intense course in arts and history.

To underscore her disappointment, she often brought up her nephew as an example of an ideal student of hers. She wanted me to be more like him, wishing I had his level of enthusiasm and appreciation. I heard stories of how delighted Andrew seemed when he visited her in Rome and how absorbent he was to all the fine details while listening to her art history lessons. It wasn't until several years later that I first met Marutha's son, already armed with an unhealthy dose of prejudice against him. I detested being constantly compared to this perfect high school student with model behavior, a standard I could never live up to. There was also a fair amount of jealousy brewing in my young mind. I thought it was unjust that I had to compete with him for Vera's affection, an uphill battle, instead of being the obvious favorite as her only grandchild.

Four years my senior, Andrew grew up in Bethesda, Maryland. Compared to Hungary in the 1960s and '70s, his world couldn't have been further from mine. In fact, it was another planet. As a college student in New York, Andrew spent some time studying in Switzerland, from where he visited us in Budapest during the summer of 1977. Much to my surprise, he showed no resemblance to the character my imagination had created and clung to for years. Within minutes of meeting him face to face, my sour feelings, my resentment, and my jealousy all vaporized. I was glad to have met my cousin, a nice person indeed, though he undoubtedly came from another planet.

My grandmother found a beautiful penthouse apartment in Rome, on Piazza dei Santissimi Apostoli, just a couple of blocks from Fontana di Trevi and the Pantheon. It had a rooftop terrace with a panoramic view of the city and a lush Mediterranean flower garden full of bougainvillea and oleander. Although she had a housekeeper, Rita, Vera took pride in meticulously tending to her plants herself. I admired her vast knowledge and passion for history and art, and her flawless taste in everything that surrounded her, including her furniture, home decoration, and wardrobe.

There was no doubt she loved me and had my best interests in mind, yet with every passing year it became increasingly difficult for me to spend my summers in Italy as her guest. The first time I met her in France at the age of four, I found her very intimidating. During my visit in 1970, there was a noticeable uneasiness in the air, and by the summer of 1972, the tension between us became almost too much to bear. No matter how exceptional my table manners were, and they were indeed immaculate by anyone's standards, she always found something to criticize. No matter how much I expressed my gratitude and delight upon visiting beautiful historic sights, museums, or fabulous beaches along

the Italian coastline, in her eyes, I was never enthusiastic or appreciative enough.

Nothing was as awkward as the experience of unpacking my suitcase upon my arrival in Rome. She unzipped my bag, picked up each and
every item of clothing one by one, held it between her thumb and index
finger as if it were contaminated with the plague, and asked me, "What
is this?" I didn't know whether I was expected to answer, or if it was
meant as a rhetorical question to express her horror. Feeling crushed and
humiliated, I would mumble something like "It's a pair of underwear"
or "It's a summer dress," to which she would answer with a follow-up
question: "Who bought this for you?" Of course, she knew it could only
have been my mother.

I tried to explain to her, as well as an eleven-year-old frightened
granddaughter could, the limited availability of merchandise and lack of
fashion choices in my country, but it backfired. She was very well aware
of the concept of "shortage economy," a characteristic of all communist
regimes, and was quick to remind me of the many packages she had sent
over the years, first from New York and later from Rome. I was expected
to have my entire suitcase full of those high-quality items instead of only
a portion of them mixed in with the ones we had bought in Hungary.
In an attempt to defend my mother, I mentioned that I had either out-
grown some of the beautiful presents in Vera's last package, or I haven't
yet grown into them. As soon as I voiced my arguments, I realized it
wasn't about my clothes. It was just another excuse for her to bash my
mother in front of me.

There was another reason I often felt uneasy in my grandmother's
company. It was her sense of entitlement. While she berated me for the
slightest behavioral flaw, she didn't miss an opportunity to make a scene

in a public place. Instead of patiently waiting in line at her bank, she marched right up to the counter. When the clerk dared to remind her it wasn't her turn, she pounded with her hand, her bracelet clinking on the marble counter, and demanded to speak to the manager at once. The entire hall echoed from her loud voice. There were numerous occasions when she sent back her food at upscale restaurants for no apparent reason.

As embarrassing as these incidents were, they couldn't hold a candle to what my cousin Andrew witnessed during one of his visits in Rome as a teenager. Apparently, the two of them were sitting in a restaurant on a rooftop terrace, and Vera sent back her pasta. The waiter brought her another serving, but it failed to meet her expectations again. With a big theatrical gesture, she swung her arm over the railing, throwing the pasta along with the plate off the roof, into the street below.

It was during my stay with her in Rome in the summer of 1972 that my grandmother made an unmasked attempt to lure me away from Hungary and from my parents. "Let me show you something," she said one day as she opened a drawer, revealing carefully wrapped blue-and-white sets of fine, old porcelain. They included coffee cups and teacups complete with saucers, pots, and creamers. "These, among many other beautiful things could be yours, should you agree to leave Hungary for a free country," she said.

Her words rendered me speechless. I couldn't care less about her valuable porcelain, or any other material possession. I loved my parents, and I was content with my life in Budapest. I was old enough to realize some of the obvious differences between Hungary and Western Europe, but too young to even consider giving up the comfort, safety, and warmth of my home. Most importantly, I found it unimaginable to leave my parents for the glamorous allures of a capitalist country, something Vera tried so hard to tempt me with.

⌦

Every September, on the first day of school, we were asked to talk about our summer vacation. One by one, we stood up and shared our adventures with the teacher and our classmates. As much as I liked going back to school, this practice was not my favorite. I always wished we would run out of time before it was my turn, hoping for the bell to ring in the hallway before the teacher called my name.

Most of my classmates talked about spending their vacation at a resort near Lake Balaton, made available and highly subsidized by the company one of their parents worked for, while others described their time visiting relatives in the countryside. For a lucky few, being part of an all-inclusive, organized tour group to the Bulgarian Black Sea opened the door to a foreign country, even if within the Eastern Bloc. Many of my classmates had grandparents living in a small village, and they enjoyed spending most of the summer in a rural environment, so different from the city life we were accustomed to in Budapest. They talked about helping around their grandparents' small-scale subsistence farms in the backyard, feeding chickens and gathering their eggs, baking, cooking, and making preserves using fresh, homegrown produce. Others mentioned bicycling, playing soccer, running around barefoot on dirt roads, and swimming in a nearby stream or pond with neighboring kids from the village.

And then it was my turn to tell everyone how I flew to Paris, where my grandfather took me to the Louvre and to the Jeu de Paume, the museum that housed the most famous French impressionist paintings before Museé d'Orsay opened, and how my French step aunt drove me to Château de Versailles. I also talked about going to Rome to visit my grandmother, who gave me a guided tour of the Sistine Chapel and took me to an outdoor performance of Verdi's *Aida* at the ancient Roman bath Caracalla before heading toward Tuscany. Upon my teacher's encouragement to share further details, I made modest attempts at describing the architectures of Sienna and San Gimignano, the fascinating story of Pompeii, and the experience of swimming in the turquoise lagoons of Capri on the Amalfi Coast.

I intentionally left out the five-star hotels, the luxurious villas with private swimming pools overlooking the Mediterranean, and the elegant restaurants where we enjoyed prosciutto con melone, spaghetti vongole, langouste, and pistachio gelato, to mention some of the delicacies exotic to my Hungarian palate. Most of all, I made a conscious effort not to bring up shopping at Caccetta on Via Piave, where two sales associates fought for my attention while fitting me with quality leather shoes second to none. It was quite a departure from the experience I was accustomed to in Budapest in the early '70s. Due to full employment, the absence of incentives, and a constant shortage of merchandise, customer service was a foreign concept to the retail sector in the Eastern Bloc.

I was torn between two worlds. I knew how extremely privileged I was, and I sincerely enjoyed and valued the opportunity to explore all the beautiful places with my grandparents who happened to live in Paris and Rome, respectively. But I was equally aware of the fact that this was far from the norm. I felt very uncomfortable every time I had to share these adventures with my classmates, as I feared resentment. I was eager to fit in. I hoped they wouldn't envy me too much, and I certainly hoped they wouldn't judge me.

As much as I adored the fashionable, high-quality, and unmistakably Western clothes and shoes my grandmother sent me first from New York and later from Rome, I deliberately avoided wearing them to school. On the very few occasions when my parents and I were invited to dinner or went to a theater and I didn't have time to go home to change, I wore them with reluctance and unease. Instead of a uniform, we all had to cover our street clothes with a blue lab coat at school. It was intended as an equalizer, but it wasn't enough to fully conceal a dress from Saks Fifth Avenue and certainly couldn't hide a pair of fine Italian leather shoes from Caccetta.

Chapter Thirty
Tea

WHEN I SAY I grew up on The Beatles, I mean more than just listening to their music and embracing the culture they represented. The Fab Four also contributed to my early English education. It was in Balaton-világos, at the resort of the Hungarian Academy of Sciences that I heard my first Beatles song. I sat in the grass along with a group of teenagers, one of whom had a reel-to-reel tape recorder. The two official Hungarian radio stations scarcely featured Western pop music, if at all, as it was considered the contagion of imperialist decadence. I was too young to be aware of this, or to remember the exact circumstances, but most likely we enjoyed someone's recordings from Radio Luxembourg, a medium-wave station that played the latest hits around midnight. Assuming you were able to tune into that wavelength, you could record these forbidden tunes. None of us understood much of the lyrics, but we were still taken by storm. As romantic as it may sound, it would be an exaggeration to claim "yesterday" as my first English word. But it was certainly an important one in my initial vocabulary.

My neighborhood elementary school, the one I was officially assigned to, did not offer English classes. My father was determined to find me another school, where English was taught from an early age. This wasn't an easy task in the 1960s. Personal connections are important everywhere, but they were absolutely essential in a country ruled by a communist regime. Knowing the right people in the right places was far more valuable than having money. My father was adamantly against using such personal connections in order to bypass rules, but when my education was at stake, he put his principles aside. Our private pediatrician, also a good family friend, just happened to be on a first-name basis with the pediatrician at the school of my father's choice. Thanks to him, I attended Arany János Általános Iskola és Gimnázium (a combined elementary and secondary school offering education from first to twelfth grades), famous for its English-language program. There were five English classes a week, starting as early as the third grade. In fact, they even launched an experimental program right when I joined, with two playful English classes a week, involving songs and games in second grade. Only a select group was chosen for this program, those of us who finished the first year with perfect grades.

No stone was left unturned in a continuing effort to enhance my English-language skills. In the summer of 1970, I was sent to London for a month to live with a family, partly English, partly Hungarian. György was from Hungary, married to an English lady, Marjory. I spent most of my time with her and their daughter, Alison, who was a couple of years younger than me, and only saw Iain, their older son, in the evenings. When György came home from work, I had the opportunity to speak some Hungarian as an escape from being immersed in a foreign language all day long. It was certainly a very nice gesture from them to host me for a month, and I was old enough to appreciate it, but I don't recall particularly enjoying my stay. It was my first introduction to London, which I liked, and my first taste of English cuisine, which I didn't.

Two years later, I was sent to a summer boarding school that was an incomparably more positive experience and a much bigger boost to my English skills. It wasn't until four decades later that I read the correspondence between József and Vera and realized just how much time and effort went into organizing it. First my father contacted a non-profit British advisory service on independent education to inquire about summer schools in England. Once he narrowed down the options, it took him an entire year to work out the logistics between the school of his choice and my grandmother, who graciously agreed to pay for it. During one of his business trips to London, my father drove to Sussex to visit the school and meet the lady who ran the summer program. The next day, he sent a letter from London to my grandmother in Rome, summarizing his experience as follows:

I visited Miss Eberlie yesterday. She is a nice, typical English, rural, middle-aged spinster who lives with her father, a retired physician, in an old, but cleverly decorated country house. I had a very good impression! She is expecting your letter about the details.

Little did he know, Miss Eberlie was far more than a typical English, rural, middle-aged spinster. As I would learn forty-five years later, she was an intelligence officer at General Eisenhower's headquarters in Normandy after D-Day. For her work in early 1945, assessing the strength and future deployment of the German forces based on information provided by the code breakers at Bletchley Park, she was awarded the American Bronze Star Medal.

After vacationing with my grandmother in Italy, we flew to London for a couple of days, before she dropped me off at Briklehurst Manor, Wadhurst, Sussex, near Tunbridge Wells. At eleven and a half, I was one of the youngest at this international summer school, but fortunately, there was a Spanish girl about my age with whom I shared a room. The rest of the attendees were in their mid to late teens, from Germany, Portugal, Italy, France, and Spain. Some of them shared a language other than English, which was convenient but not the most ideal for them. I, on the other hand, had no choice but to speak English with everyone, which largely improved my vocabulary and helped with my confidence using a foreign language even though I knew I would make mistakes.

This was the first time in my life I found myself in the deep water, without hearing a single word of Hungarian for a month. Despite the challenges it represented, I thoroughly enjoyed every aspect of my stay, much more than I had anticipated. We all had an hour of formal English lesson every day with a tutor, private or in a small group, depending on one's level, and then we spent the rest of the day together, playing croquet, swimming, horseback riding, or other activities of choice, and taking turns completing a few house chores.

We took a very memorable excursion to London, where I was fortunate enough to see the traveling exhibition of Tutankhamen at the British Museum. I wasn't too keen on going to museums at that age, most likely because my grandmother dragged me through way too many, way too young, quizzing me on every detail afterward, but I was thoroughly impressed with the spectacular treasures of this Egyptian pharaoh. I immediately wrote to my parents to make sure they wouldn't miss it when they arrived in London a couple of weeks later.

While I was immersing myself in the English language and country life in Sussex, my parents took a journey through Austria, Germany, and the Netherlands, driving a Lada, the Soviet version of the Fiat 124. They crossed the English Channel on a ferry, visited London, and toured Oundle and Cambridge before picking me up on the last day of my stay at Briklehurst Manor. I was grateful for the opportunity to spend a month at this wonderful summer school, but I couldn't hide my jealousy when my mother talked about the beautiful places she had seen in Holland. More than anything, I envied her for the opportunity to visit my father's alma maters in England. In fact, I was quite upset for not being able to join them in Oundle and Cambridge, the places where József spent his youth, but I understood I couldn't have had my cake and eat it too.

Just like two years earlier in London, English cuisine didn't win me over. One particular dessert stuck in my memory as a sour, soggy disappointment. Gooseberry pie. I have never come across gooseberries anywhere else, neither before nor after that summer in Sussex. Afternoon tea was the only meal of the day I truly looked forward to. I loved this English ritual of drinking a cup of strong, dark tea with milk. It was a world apart from the weak, sorry excuse for a tea my mother used to make at home, flavored with lemon and a hint of sugar. At Briklehurst Manor, afternoon tea was always served with a variety of scrumptious biscuits, real English marmalade, and a fabulous delicacy, an instant favorite of mine, something unavailable in Hungary that time, peanut butter.

Chapter Thirty-One
Deceit

THE YEAR I WAS INTRODUCED to the tradition of English afternoon tea and the game of croquet was also the year of revelations about my parents. I don't remember whether it happened before or after my twelfth birthday, but it was sometime in the fall of 1972 when I accidentally disturbed the hornet's nest with my random discovery.

I was standing in the kitchen, looking at my mother's identity card, which she had left out on the countertop. Actually, it wasn't a card but a little brown, hardcover booklet with pink pages in it, stamped by various authorities. This identity booklet contained one's photograph, signature, personal data, employment records, address of residence, marital status, place and date of marriage, and the names of children, if applicable, with their places and dates of birth. Everyone over the age of fourteen had one of these little brown booklets, and it was mandatory to carry it at all times. One was not to leave the house without it. The police would randomly stop people in the street and ask to see it for no apparent reason, other than to flaunt their power. If it was lost or accidentally left at home, one could potentially be arrested and kept at the police station until a family member, friend, or colleague with his or her valid booklet was available to identify them. As I curiously read every word on those pink pages, I noticed something peculiar. It was the date of my parents' marriage: April 8, 1961. Six months after my birth. Of course, it prompted a series of questions and some rather uncomfortable discussions. To my biggest surprise, my parents offered two different explanations.

First, my father sat me down and told me his version of the story. He began by mentioning that his first wife, Doris, a Scottish lady he had met while studying at Cambridge University during the war, divorced him without his knowledge and consent while he was in prison during the 1950s. He was very much hurt by this and didn't wish to maintain any contact with her after she returned to Scotland. As briefly as he could, my father had already told me about his unjust imprisonment earlier, so I was able to put this piece of information in context.

Then he went on to tell me he had fallen in love with another woman, Zsuzsi, soon after his release from prison. They were engaged, hoping to get married soon, but Zsuzsi defected to the West shortly after the 1956 Revolution. My father said he also made an attempt to cross the border between Hungary and Austria in the summer of 1958 but was captured and thrown in prison for another year for trying to leave the country illegally. After his release, he was under police surveillance, essentially a house arrest, for one more year, during which time he made a living as a translator. He wrote in longhand, and mother Zsófia, a former administrative assistant of Tibor Erdey-Grúz, secretary general of the Hungarian Academy Sciences, typed his translations on her portable mechanical typewriter, often staying up all night in order to meet deadlines. She was indeed an outstanding typist, very fast and accurate. Although she didn't speak a word of English, she quickly learned to type English texts, reading them phonetically.

My father didn't tell me anything about how, when, and where he met my mother, but I assumed it must have been at the Academy of Sciences, since there was an overlap in the time periods they both worked there. He didn't reveal any details about this friendly collaboration with Zsófia turning into an affair, but an obvious mutual physical attraction was implied. He made it very clear to me that the two of them had an understanding about the nature of their relationship. It was to remain casual with no prospect of marriage. In order to fill the gaps my father left in his story, I had to rely on my own speculation. Deep inside he must have known that his chances of reuniting with his fiancée were slipping away. Zsófia must have hoped time would put an even greater distance between Zsuzsi and József than the distance created by geography and history.

And then my mother found out she was pregnant. Apparently, at least according to my father's version of the story, she considered getting an abortion, but her doctor strongly advised against it, saying it could be life threatening due to complications she had suffered from an earlier abdominal surgery. So she decided to have me.

Although my father had no intention spending the rest of his life with my mother despite her carrying his child, he had a change of heart the minute he saw me at the hospital. He said he instantly felt such a deep love for me, a kind of love he had never experienced until then, that he decided then and there that he would have to be fully present in my life. He could not bear the thought of becoming a part-time father who pays child support and only visits with his daughter on occasion. He was determined to be involved in every step of my day-to-day upbringing.

As far as their marriage was concerned, my father told me it was a union of necessity, strictly for my benefit. He made a commitment to me, but not to my mother. In fact, he said they agreed to get a divorce as soon as I was mature enough to handle it. Their priority was to provide a loving, caring, stable childhood for me.

My mother waited for the dust to settle before telling me her version of what happened. Just like my father, she began with the story of her first marriage in order to set the stage. In her early twenties, she had a very intense affair with a man who was married with two children. She said he was the love of her life, and the feeling was mutual. According to my mother, this mystery man, whose name I have never learned, seriously considered leaving his wife and children for her. My mother said she couldn't bear the thought of breaking up a family, so she resorted to desperate measures, hastily marrying another man: Norbert Räth. She was quick to add, not so much in a matter-of-factly way but rather as a hint, that she and the love of her life kept seeing each other in secret for quite a while, despite both of them being married to someone else.

This was the first time I noticed my mother's peculiar way of ever slightly suggesting something instead of saying it out loud in a straightforward manner. It bothered me, increasingly so as I became older, and I never really understood her intention. When she put things in this secretive, mysterious wrapping, I felt as if she wanted to tell me something, making sure I knew but at the same time holding back just enough to suggest it was really not my business. I was equally annoyed and offended by her way of opening doors just enough to take a peek, but not enough to walk through them.

She also mentioned that her lover and his wife later had a third child, a son. My mother believed he was given a name starting with the letter Z in honor of her first name: Zsófia.

Even at the age of twelve, I had serious reservations about this story. Nevertheless, my mother considered it an important piece of background information. Her marriage to Norbert lasted for six years (1947–1953), which I found a surprisingly long time for a union built on false pretenses, assuming it was indeed the case. When I asked why they eventually divorced, my mother said Norbert had a gambling problem and was irresponsible with money.

Then she told me about her ill-fated abdominal surgery. Sometime in the mid-1950s, my mother had appendicitis. By the time she received medical attention, her appendix had ruptured, and the inflammation spread in her abdomen. When they opened her up in the operating room, it was deemed necessary to remove one of her ovaries along with her appendix. She had a terrible infection and an extremely high fever, and she fought her life for days in a delirium. Finally, one of her sisters, Emilia, took matters in her own hands and had her transported to another hospital, where she received better treatment and eventually recovered. In fact, my aunt Emilia would tell me this story several times as I grew up, taking full credit for saving my mother's life. The surgery left my mother with some internal scarring. Although it didn't cause her any discomfort, her gynecologist had serious doubts about her ever being able to have a child.

Naturally, my mother was very surprised when she found out she was pregnant. As it turns out, she had no intention getting an abortion, since she was overjoyed by the prospect of becoming a mother. She was determined to have me by all means, even if she had to raise me alone. She said she made up the story of her doctor advising against an abortion in order to justify her decision. In fact, her doctor strongly advised against her carrying the pregnancy to term. He said it could be life threatening due to the internal scarring she suffered as a result of her previous surgery. He pointed out that her organs were partially attached to the abdominal wall, and should the pregnancy progress, they could tear apart, jeopardizing both of our lives.

Maternal instinct proved much stronger than the doctor's advice. After an easy, uncomplicated pregnancy, in October 1960, Zsófia gave birth to a healthy girl. Me.

As far as the two of them were concerned, she said my father deliberately kept his distance from her during most of her pregnancy, in order to demonstrate he had no intention of marrying her. Once I was born, however, he couldn't stay away from me, and that was when they moved in together. My mother had quite a different outlook than my father did. Against all odds, she believed their relationship stood a chance. She finally persuaded my father to get married for my sake. Of course, she hoped it wouldn't be solely for my sake on the long run.

❧

When I visited my father's stepsister Bobette in Paris in September 2012, she revealed something I had not heard before. As she recalled, it must have been sometime in 1957 that Zsuzsi arrived in Paris and contacted my grandfather Bertalan, in hopes of finding a helping hand. She introduced herself as his son's fiancée and told my grandfather that it wouldn't be long before József joined her. According to Bobette, Bertalan put her up in a hotel in Paris, but only for a short while. He declined to take her under his wing for the long term. Zsuzsi couldn't get a work permit in Paris, so she settled down in Vienna. What were the reasons behind my grandfather refusing to help her? Was he skeptical about Zsuzsi's statements regarding their relationship? Was he questioning my father's chances of leaving Hungary? Bobette didn't know, but she remembered my grandfather mentioning something years later, a detail in the story she found deeply ironic. Apparently, when Zsuzsi defected, she thought she had left her fiancée in good hands, asking a close friend of hers, Zsófia, to take care of József until he himself would be able to escape from Hungary. While enjoying her steak and a glass of red wine at an outdoor café in the 5th arrondissement, Bobette said with a big laugh, "Your mother must have been a very good friend indeed. She took care of him, didn't she?"

☙

An accidental pregnancy leading to a reluctant marriage is a story far too common, as old as humankind itself. Yet it was disturbing to find myself in the middle of it. In all fairness to my parents, I must emphasize something absolutely crucial. I was unplanned, but certainly not unwanted.

Never for a minute did it cross my mind to condemn my father for getting involved with a woman while being engaged to another, all things considered. Nor did I judge my mother for entering into a relationship with a man who claimed to be still in love with his faraway fiancée. I viewed it as a conscious decision between two consenting adults in their midthirties who felt something for each other. Was it lust or love? It is hard to say, but one thing was certain in my mind. There was no victim in this scenario. After all, it takes two to tango.

It was my mother's lie I couldn't digest. It was her dishonest way of handling the situation that left me question her integrity. I didn't blame her for giving in to her maternal instinct and bearing a child, whether planned or unplanned, whether within or outside a marriage. It was the way she misled my father that left me with a bitter taste in my mouth. It was something I have never been able to get past. Her natural instinct was to play the martyr. She told me how she sacrificed herself marrying someone she didn't love, in order to save her lover's marriage. In my mind, it sounded as much of a lie to herself as it was to me. Compounded with her admission to another lie, the one she told my father, her intention was obvious. She was hoping to gain my respect for her as a selfless victim in both cases. Rather than eliciting sympathy for her sacrifice, what stuck with me was her pattern of manipulative lies. Her plan backfired. It didn't draw me closer to her. Instead, it changed my perception of her, and it was a turning point in our relationship. It created the first crack between us, the first of many cracks to come. Cracks that only became deeper and wider with time.

My parents succeeded in sparing me from their marital problems until my discovery and the subsequent conversations it triggered. Once the truth was out in the open, all pretense ceased to exist. The façade they carefully built and flawlessly maintained for twelve years to protect me from reality crumbled in a matter of days.

Chapter Thirty-Two

Lust

JÓZSEF'S AFFAIRS WERE COUNTLESS, shameless, and barely disguised. They started before I was born, well before he married my mother, and continued for two decades. They were blondes, brunettes, and redheads. They were waifs, and they were voluptuous. Some of them were single, some divorced, and some married with children. They were secretaries, fellow scientists, some he worked with, and some he randomly met during his business trips abroad. Whether they were impressed by his mind and personality or simply sought adventure driven by physical attraction, they all showed interest in my father. József had a strong desire to be desired. Once someone said about my father that he ate life with a ladle instead of a spoon. He indeed enjoyed all worldly pleasures, whether it was fine dining, travel, classical music, theater, or the companionship of women. Many women.

Everyone at work—in fact, the entire town—knew about my father's not-so-secret liaisons. He wasn't a good liar. Although he made some attempts to hide his flings from my mother, she was painfully aware of them. She often emerged from her own separate bedroom with swollen, red eyes in the morning, wearing obvious signs of a tearful, sleepless night. My parents never put on a spectacular fight, never slammed doors, and never even raised their voices with each other, but the tension in the air was thick enough to slice with a knife.

One particular recurring pattern is still so clear in my memory, I can almost see their faces and hear their sighs. My father would sit in his armchair reading, and my mother would enter the room, ready to say something. The way he lowered his newspaper with unmasked annoyance, impatience, and utter indifference was hard to miss and uncomfortable to witness. There was a sharp contrast between my mother trying to get his attention and me seeking the same. When he was at home, my father spent almost every waking moment reading something. Whether it was the Hungarian daily, an English-language weekly news magazine, a scientific periodical, or a book of fiction, one would have been hard pressed to find him without some kind of printed material in his hands. Never in my entire childhood did I feel I was disturbing or interrupting him, not even when he worked, correcting his colleagues' dissertations during the weekend. For me, he always made time. No matter how busy or tired he was, he would immediately put aside his literature and look at me with a smile, expressing sincere interest in anything and everything I wished to discuss. My mother couldn't hide her jealousy.

In the early 1970s, József engaged in one of his most heated love affairs, loudly played out in public. This was the first of his many romances I was aware of, becoming a somewhat conflicted accomplice myself. She was everything my mother wasn't: cheerful, positive, decisive, and fashion forward. However, even in my pre-adolescent eyes, her skirts seemed to be just a tad too short and her blouses just a bit too tight and unbuttoned for comfort. There was something about her provocative appearance, loose attitude, and overt sexual confidence I found unsophisticated.

I didn't know then, and wouldn't know later, what to make of my father confiding in me about his extramarital relationships throughout my teens. Being trusted with sensitive information certainly had its appeal, not to mention the special bond our secret alliance created. I felt he treated me almost like an adult, which I welcomed. At the same time, the burden of our conspiracy weighed on my shoulders. There were many times I hoped and wished my parents would get a divorce, but they didn't. Not for another decade.

Chapter Thirty-Three
Vienna

IN 1974 JÓZSEF joined a unique and very prestigious international organization in Austria, founded to promote East-West scientific cooperation during the Cold War.

> In October 1972, representatives of the Soviet Union, United States, and 10 other countries from the Eastern and Western blocs met in London to sign the charter establishing The International Institute for Applied Systems Analysis (IIASA). It was the culmination of six years' effort by US President Lyndon Johnson and USSR Premier Alexey Kosygin, and marked the beginning of a remarkable project to use scientific cooperation to build bridges across the Cold War divide and to confront growing global problems on an international scale. In the 1970s most research organizations focused on national issues. Few encouraged

researchers from different countries or disciplines to work together for the greater good. To achieve its ambitious research vision, IIASA would have to break down the barriers between nations and disciplines...The refurbished Schloss Laxenburg near Vienna was made available by the Austrian government shortly after the foundation of IIASA in 1972...On 4 October 1972, the Institute was officially constituted in London under the auspices of the Royal Society as the International Institute for Applied Systems Analysis (IIASA)...Twelve National Member Organizations (NMOs) from Canada, Czechoslovakia, Bulgaria, East Germany, France, Italy, Japan, Poland, the Soviet Union, The United Kingdom, the United States, and West Germany signed the Charter...Professor Raiffa, an economist from Harvard University, was elected as first Director of the Institute.[58]

Austria joined in 1973, and Hungary became a member a year later. Working at IIASA for the entire year of 1974, József Hatvany was a part of the Systems and Decision Sciences Program as well as a research scholar in the Integrated Industrial Systems Division. He published several papers during his very productive stay in Laxenburg; most notably, he was the lead author of a survey commissioned by IIASA and published in July 1974: *The Present State and Foreseeable Trends in Computer-Aided Design (CAD) as a Major Tool in Industrial, Social and Economic Systems*, in which he and his colleagues explored the considerable influence computer-aided design would have on the future development of industry.

József Hatvany visited twenty-six companies across Eastern Europe, including many in Hungary and eleven more in Japan, where he traveled with his British coauthor, who himself visited thirty-seven all over Western Europe. Their American coauthor went to eleven companies in the United States. The three of them together visited eighty-five organizations and interviewed more than 250 people. The report was republished in an academic journal in 1977 and presented as an invited lecture at the IFIP (International Federation of Information Processing) Congress in Toronto, Canada, with the title *Trends and Developments in Computer-Aided Design*. It was a complete survey on CAD technology in the USA, Europe, and Japan, examining technical aspects as well as administrative ones.

Besides attending conferences, presenting his papers, traveling all over Europe, and visiting Japan and the United States, my father often drove back to Budapest in order to remain involved with his department's work at the Computer and Automation Institute of the Hungarian Academy of Sciences, albeit part time.

Newspapers were as important to my father as bread and butter. He read them religiously every single day. On those rare occasions when delivery failed, it seemed like the world had come to an end. I grew up watching him read the leading Hungarian daily *Népszabadság* (*Liberty of the People*) cover to cover as if his life depended on it. During his travels abroad, his first choice was always the *International Herald Tribune*. Upon his move to Austria in January 1974, he paid extra to have *Népszabadság* forwarded to his address in Vienna. The only problem was that it always arrived a day late, so my father also subscribed to a local paper to keep up with the latest news in the world. Of the two leading Austrian newspapers, he chose *Kurier* over *Kronen Zeitung* for its more left-leaning views.

❦

Nineteen seventy-four was the year when Austria and Hungary abolished the compulsory visa requirement, a first in the divided world. Due to my father's employment status at IIASA, all three of us were given a stamp in our passport, a multiple exit-and-entry permit enabling us to cross the border at any time.

IIASA set us up in a modern, furnished, and fully equipped apartment in a suburb of Vienna just south of the city, where my mother and I joined my father for the second half of the year. It was the first time we didn't sell our old car upon receiving the new one after being on the waiting list for three or four years. Having two cars in the same household was extremely rare for Hungarians in the early '70s, but we couldn't have functioned in our new environment otherwise. My father needed one solely to himself in order to go to work in Laxenburg every day, while my mother drove our second Lada to the neighboring town where I could catch the American International School's private bus that took me to the north end of Vienna. It also gave us independence to go back to Budapest from time to time while my father stayed in Austria and made it possible for my mother to take her sisters and me on a road trip to the Austrian and Swiss Alps during their visit in the summer.

❦

Attending the American International School in Vienna as an eighth grader was quite a departure from the school system I was accustomed to in Hungary. I didn't have to wear the blue lab coat over my clothes, a mandatory feature in Hungarian schools those days. In Hungary we had our own classroom that we shared with the same twenty-five to thirty classmates, coats hanging on the back wall, books stacked in the drawers of a desk we claimed our own for the entire school year. Apart from gym class or the occasional science experiment, we stayed there all day long, and the teachers came to us. At the American school, we went to a different corner of the building for each class while storing our belongings in a locker. It is only logical, as I learned on my first day, that the hallway becomes the social scene, the obvious gathering place amid a loud and somewhat chaotic flow of students always on the move.

I found vending machines and bake sales a nice touch until I faced the consequences. They were to blame for my first unwanted weight gain, along with the impressive amount of Swiss milk chocolate I consumed while living in Vienna, available in every grocery store, too easy to find and too hard to resist.

Being in Austria, we all had to learn some German, but taking two very basic classes per week over four months wasn't enough to build a solid foundation for a new language. However, I picked up a couple of phrases that proved very useful during my stay. One of the first sentences I mastered was *Kein Fleish, bitte!* (No meat, please!). I wasn't a vegetarian, but my first encounter with a hamburger at the school cafeteria in Vienna turned me away from this American staple for life. Next time they served hamburger for lunch, I promptly put my newly acquired German vocabulary to the test.

Although I spent two summers immersed in an English-speaking environment, studying all subjects in English was quite intimidating at first, and of course, the entire curriculum was very different from ours. I found the American school's approach to math problems much easier to digest. To my surprise and my father's great delight, for the first and only time in my life I developed a new appreciation for math. I will be quick to add that it didn't last a minute longer than my stay in Vienna.

My experience in the school choir couldn't have been further from the one in Budapest. Our Hungarian singing teacher had us practice and perform a communist propaganda song encouraging the starving, unemployed proletariat to rise up in arms and fight their capitalist exploiters on the barricades. At the American school we sang John Denver's "Take Me Home, Country Roads." Until then, I had never heard about West Virginia, the Blue Ridge Mountains, or the Shenandoah River, nor did I know why they were "almost heaven." With its catchy tune and pleasant lyrics, it was certainly much more appealing than the militaristic blare about the proletariat. The "barricade song," as we called it, was so outdated and over the top that even we, children of the Eastern Bloc, considered it more fitting for Lenin's Great October Socialist Revolution in 1917 Tzarist Russia.

One of the books we read in English class, John Hersey's *Hiroshima*, completely shook my world and stayed with me forever, both in the literal and figurative sense. I still have the very same 1968 paperback edition on my shelf, and I am convinced the world would be a better place if everyone read it.

History was obviously taught from a very different perspective, but since it was an international school for children of diplomats and other expats from all over the world, teachers encouraged us to express opinions of all shades. As a homework assignment, we had to write a paper about current affairs. I don't recall exactly whether it was supposed be about the Cold War and the divide between East and West or something more specific to each student's own country, but I do remember asking my father for help, which he gladly supplied. In fact, he approached it with such enthusiasm, that I ended up with more than I bargained for. He suggested I write a paper about our political system, arguing for its superiority to capitalism and demonstrating the way it would eventually reach and even surpass the economic growth and prosperity of Western societies. I was understandably nervous presenting this rather rebellious and politically charged paper at an American school in 1974, but to my biggest surprise and immediate relief, my social studies teacher was genuinely interested in my—or, shall I say, my father's—arguments. Although he clearly disagreed, he found it fascinating and sincerely commended me for voicing my opinion. The one lesson I learned from this rather strange experience, even if it makes me slightly embarrassed decades later, was that expressing one's views and daring to be different were encouraged, unlike in Hungary.

Chapter Thirty-Four

Socialism

SOME SAY MY FATHER turned away from politics and decided to focus solely on his scientific career after burning his fingers during the darkest Stalinist era in 1950s Hungary. Others say his views never wavered. I say he evolved. After his release from prison, he undoubtedly put his political aspirations behind him once and for all but maintained a strong opinion and wasn't shy about sharing it.

By the time he helped me write this rather controversial homework assignment in 1974, he had come a very long way from his twenty-year-old radical communist self who abandoned his studies and failed his final exams in Cambridge, severed all ties with his bourgeois family, and returned to a country in ruins hoping to build a new world with his most enthusiastic cheerleader and comrade, a Scottish fiancée in tow. By the end of 1974, he had traveled throughout Western Europe, visited the United States and Japan on multiple occasions, and worked on

international projects with scientists from all over the world. He was very
well versed in global affairs, keeping up with recent events by reading the
International Herald Tribune, The Economist, Time magazine, and *Newsweek* in addition to several Western scientific publications, all of which
widened his horizons. Nevertheless, he remained an outspoken advocate
of a softer, less restrictive version of a system, more socialist than communist, something Hungary proudly called its own in the Kádár regime.
Allowing a limited amount of small private businesses, more opportunities to travel abroad, and having more consumer goods available were
just some of the many amenities we enjoyed, making us the envy of the
Eastern Bloc, the "happiest barracks in the socialist camp."

József's political views often seemed contradictory. He welcomed
certain characteristics of the capitalist system such as incentives, while
he rejected excess. He supported merit-based rewards for motivation at
the workplace but was against growth being the goal at all costs, creating a huge divide between the haves and the have-nots. He thought
capitalism as it was practiced, especially unrestrained, was unsustainable
and would lead to the destruction of society. He liked a system with a
social net and full employment, but he had a disdain for those who took
advantage of it, those who felt there was nothing to obtain by working
more than the absolute minimum required. In fact, he was known for his
spectacular fights with the trade union and human resources at the Computer and Automation Institute every year when it was time to decide
how much bonus each employee should receive. As a head of department, he insisted on rewarding those shooting for the stars. "If someone
doesn't think twice about jumping out of bed at three in the morning to
scribble down a new idea, and doesn't drop the pencil promptly at the
end of business hours when a project's finish line is at arm's reach, that's

what I call a real scientific researcher," said my father once at the dinner table, describing an enthusiastic young colleague of his fresh out of university. He was livid when a union representative tried to convince him that a single mother who didn't have the luxury to work a minute past five o'clock should be given the same or maybe an even bigger bonus than the young fellow who didn't have anyone to take care of. My father argued for a sharp distinction between social benefits, which he thought the single mother rightfully deserved, and an annual merit-based bonus, which he believed should strictly serve as incentive for the ones thriving for excellence.

He was also an outspoken opponent of the so-called five-year-plan, an economic model originally introduced by Stalin in 1928 to boost heavy industry in the Soviet Union. It was a concept adopted throughout the Eastern Bloc, a system that dominated Hungary's entire economy between 1950 and 1990. József often found himself in heated discussions, clashing with heads of various institutions that allocated research and development funds to his projects. In a 1982 TV interview, he voiced his frustration with this outdated Soviet model. He argued against a government-run centralized plan controlling the speed of innovation, making it impossible to stay competitive on the international stage of science and technology:

> We must do something, since it is a nationwide phenomenon that sometimes we suddenly buy a license, localize something, make a new configuration, and other times we just rest on our laurels for a couple of years. We must move beyond this. In fact, computer aided design is exactly the means within industry with which this new design of

manufacturing can be made continuous and perhaps we could even torpedo this old fashioned way of thinking that if we have a good product, it will be good for five years. I think it will be good until the competition comes out with something newer and better, and nobody guarantees it for me that it will happen in five-year cycles. Nowadays in the World market this happens in six-month or one-year cycles.[59]

My father loved to play tour guide, showing his foreign colleagues around Budapest, especially those visiting from the West. He proudly took his guests to the most scenic parts of the city, pointing out sights of historic and architectural interest, even doubling as a museum docent with an impressive knowledge of history, art, and culture. He liked to include a visit to the Opera House or the Franz Liszt Academy of Music, and of course, sampling a generous selection of the local cuisine was always on the agenda.

Undeniably, he himself cherished every opportunity to revisit the most beautiful places in our city, enjoy a ballet or a concert, and indulge in traditional Hungarian flavors at the best restaurants Budapest had to offer. But more importantly, he was on a mission to prove his Western friends wrong. He was determined to show them that Hungary was indeed on the right path, providing a good living environment for its citizens with much less shortage of goods and fewer restrictions than everyone in the West imagined.

József often invited visitors from other countries to our house for dinner. My mother's home-cooked meals were always a huge success. She was a good cook, but it was baking she truly excelled in. Her sour cherry strudel was legendary. Layers of crisp, paper-thin, flaky pastry enveloped a decadent filling of fresh, dark, tart-and-sweet sour cherries and ground walnuts. This heavenly delight, the taste of which will never fade from my memory, was served warm, straight from the oven.

In 2012, I would reunite with one of my father's former colleagues for the first time in four decades. Sitting at a restaurant in California, Andy van Dam, a professor of computer science at Brown University who used to be József's best friend in the United States, if not in the whole world, reminisced about his first visit to Budapest with his wife in the early 1970s: "Debbie and I have the fondest recollections of our times in Hungary, the many great meals we had together, and what is still for us the best dessert we ever tasted in our lives, your mother's sour cherry strudel, never to be equaled, let alone surpassed."

My father's enthusiasm to showcase his country as an example of a successful socialist society resulted in a student exchange program between his old English alma mater and Hungary. In 1969 József traveled to the United Kingdom as a member of a government delegation. While in London, he contacted his former housemaster, Dudley Heesom at Bramston House, Oundle School, where he had spent his teens some thirty years earlier, to see if he could pay a visit. After being granted permission by the British government to receive someone from the Eastern Bloc at the height of the Cold War, the retired housemaster agreed and asked Alan Midgley, his successor at Bramston House, to arrange a group of seventeen- and eighteen-year-old students to meet my father. Upon Alan's request, József delivered a short lecture on life in Hungary, sharing his views on the Cold War with his young audience. At the end of the meeting, he invited Alan to bring a group of Oundelians to Hungary.

In the summer of 1971, three of the most curious and adventurous boys, along with their new housemaster, drove a Volkswagen Beetle all the way from Oundle to Budapest, camping en route as well as in the Buda hills, pitching their tents within easy walking distance from our house. My father spent the week sightseeing with them in Budapest and at Lake Balaton, as well as touring Szentendre and Esztergom in the Danube Bend. He proudly pointed out the abundance of fruits and vegetables at the markets and challenged his guests to find empty shelves in shops, trying to quash Western rumors about our dysfunctional economy and daily struggles. As usual, he took his visitors to a number of restaurants and invited them to our house for a home-cooked meal.

This was the first time Alan and the three boys from Oundle had had a chance to peek behind the Iron Curtain. Later, as they traveled to other countries, it became clear to them that Hungary, with relatively easy access to consumer goods and an impressive selection of foods in particular, represented the exception rather than the rule within the Eastern Bloc.

For Alan Midgley, it was the beginning of a lifelong relationship with Hungary, the first of countless visits and lasting friendships. Together, they hosted two more groups of students from Oundle in Hungary, one in 1972 and another in 1979. In 1985, Alan organized an exchange program between Oundle and a high school in Pécs, in southern Hungary. When my father visited Alan in England the same year, one of the boys from the original group, already in his thirties at the time, came up to Oundle from London just to meet him again.

As much as József tried to show his Western friends the fully stocked shops in downtown Budapest and the large selection of delicious meals in restaurants, he was aware of the shortage economy, an unwelcome feature of all socialist countries. He wasn't blind to the fact that people in the West could buy a car without a three-year wait or that they were given a much wider range of options in general, whether it came to buying clothing or home appliances, or choosing banks or other services. In defense of the political and economic system in Hungary, he always brought up free health care and education, as well as the absence of the homeless and the unemployed, but he admitted the obvious shortcomings, as they were impossible to ignore.

During the '60s and early '70s, my mother would transfer the dripping-wet laundry from the washer to an East German spinning machine. It was the laughingstock of most Hungarian households, a sorry excuse for an appliance that belonged to the "better-than-nothing" category. Although it was equipped with suction cups on the bottom, one had to hold it down to prevent it from bouncing around. I remember the frequent, bizarre sight of my featherweight mother trying to keep it in place by leaning or sitting on it, both of us in tears from laughter. At the end of our stay in Austria, we returned to Hungary with a Bosch automatic washing machine strapped on top of our car. This modern convenience had several programmable cycles, including spinning. The days of my mother wrestling with the East German technical wonder finally came to an end.

Once my father set foot in an American department store, he could never go back to his old days searching all over Budapest for items temporarily or permanently out of stock. For a man who absolutely loathed shopping, it was a relief to walk into a store where he could buy an entire outfit, from business suits to dress shirts, from polo shirts to khakis, from underwear to a trench coat, complete with shoes, belts, socks and ties, available in a great variety of sizes and colors, all under one roof. He told me how impressed he was with the quick, easy, and pleasant experience, not to mention the excellent customer service and complimentary in-house alterations. "I hope my wardrobe will last till my next trip to the United States," he said, only half joking.

My father—the young revolutionary—in Budapest, 1948.
Courtesy of Alan Mackay

The Standard Electric espionage trial in Budapest, 1950.
My father (left) translates for American defendant Robert Vogeler (right),
while British defendant Edgar Sanders (seated in the middle) listens.
Getty Images

With my parents in our backyard in Budapest, 1963.

Bertalan at his apartment in
Paris, 1965.

With Vera in Cannes, 1965.

MIT Professor Steve Coons and my father engaging in a passionate discussion in our backyard, 1976.

My father receiving the Hungarian State Prize for Science and Technology from Cultural Minister György Aczél at the Parliament, 1978.

With my father just days before he left for Toulouse, Christmas 1980.

With Judit in Budapest, 2003.

With Doris on her 89th birthday in Scotland, 2012.

Chapter Thirty-Five
Judit

SHE TOOK AN INSTANT DISLIKE to him before they even met. She had barely warmed her chair when her new boss slid a handwritten note across her desk warning about an important customer: "Hatvany's every word is an order." She was eager to fulfill all reasonable requests by anyone at work, assuming they asked her nicely. The prospect of meeting such a feared, demanding person made her uneasy.

Judit, a young librarian, joined the Computer and Automation Institute in 1974, while my father was away in Vienna. József was a regular at the institute's in-house library. Not only did he heavily rely on their staff to track down certain publications from other libraries for his research, he also kept an extra briefcase there for the sole purpose of bringing home a stack of reading material every weekend. Western news magazines such as *The Economist* and *Newsweek*, and scientific periodicals such as *Computers in Industry* and *Scientific American* were not accessible those days in Hungary. Upon my father's suggestion, the institute's management agreed to subscribe for these valuable resources, but they were not to be taken out of the reading room. József made a special deal with the library. Every Friday afternoon, just before close of business, he would stop by to pick up his second briefcase, packed with these treasures. He read each and every magazine cover to cover during the weekend and promptly returned them Monday morning like clockwork.

At the Computer and Automation Institute, people belonged to one of two camps when it came to their feelings toward József Hatvany. They either hated him with a vengeance or loved him as their idol. There was no middle ground.

Having received that unflattering note about my father just days after joining the institute, Judit was understandably anxious when my father returned from Austria. Once they met in person in early 1975, her worries and reservations quickly evaporated. While he indeed kept her and the entire staff of the library busy, Judit couldn't recall a single occasion when she or her colleagues were ordered around or mistreated. Instead, she described my father's visits as professional, courteous, and appreciative exchanges, often leading to fascinating conversations sprinkled with a healthy dose of humor.

At a family gathering, Judit casually talked about her new acquaintances at work. Upon hearing the name József Hatvany, her cousin's husband, a linguist and university professor, jumped up from his seat in joy. He proceeded to tell everyone about the time he and my father spent together behind bars as political prisoners during the Stalinist era and immediately asked Judit to arrange a reunion between the two of them. She gladly complied. The discovery of their intertwined past made an already-existing friendship grow even stronger, but it wasn't until the late 1970s when it evolved into a romantic relationship.

Judit was different from the other women my father pursued, at least those I knew about. When I first met her, she struck me as a "blue-stocking." There was more to her than met the eye. József was obviously attracted to her intellect as much as he was to her looks. As Judit would tell me several years later, it was my father's extraordinary personality, exceptional wit and talent, open-minded approach to everything in life, honesty, and great sense of humor that made him easy to love. Right from the beginning, it appeared to be a good match.

She was also unique in that she won my grandmother's instant approval. Vera wasn't easy to impress. My father had a rocky relationship with her throughout his whole life. I myself found my grandmother very intimidating and almost impossible to please. The only person I knew of who managed to have a good relationship with Vera was her nephew Andrew. That was until she met Judit.

Chapter Thirty-Six
Diagnosis

IN THE FALL OF 1979, my father suddenly fell ill. He had a high fever and felt very weak and tired. Assuming it was the flu, he decided to stay home and sleep it off. After a couple of days, the fever subsided, but the fatigue was there to stay. For someone who had always been able to get by with less sleep than most of us, it was rather unusual for him to spend the entire day in bed, barely able to emerge from his room for meals. For someone known to have been a true gourmand with a high appreciation of culinary delights of his own country as well as other nations, it was very surprising for him to merely take a couple sips of soup, put down his spoon, and excuse himself from the table.

By the end of the week, he agreed to see a doctor. When his results came back, the hospital called and very apologetically asked him to come back and repeat his blood test. His numbers were so far off the normal levels, they assumed someone made a mistake at the lab. After the second blood test, he was immediately admitted to the hospital.

When I went to visit, my father looked at me with profound sadness on his face, uttering a word so dreadful it still sends chills down my spine. Leukemia. I didn't know much about the disease, but I knew it was incurable. I knew it was a death sentence. His prognosis was dire. The hospital diagnosed him with acute leukemia and gave him two or three months to live. He was about to turn fifty-three, and I had just turned nineteen. It was unimaginable to lose my father so early. I didn't know how to process the unimaginable, and neither did he.

József shared his hospital room with another man, approximately his age, maybe a little older, who had received the exact same diagnosis about a month or two earlier. One day, as I stepped in, I found my father alone in the room, with the other bed neatly made with crisp, clean sheets and the nightstand next to it stripped of all personal belongings. "He died," my father said, and we both knew exactly what this meant for him. His roommate's death put his own mortality in a whole new perspective.

I don't remember whose idea it was, who took the initiative, but after a couple weeks of receiving blood transfusions and some basic medication, someone arranged for my father to be transferred to another hospital. At the National Institute of Hematology, he was put in the hands of Hungary's most respected authority in the field of blood disease, internationally renowned expert Dr. Zsuzsa Hollán. She ordered a series of blood tests, meticulously exploring far more details of my father's disease than the general hospital had, and József was given a new diagnosis: chronic lymphocytic leukemia. While still an incurable cancer, this version of leukemia came with a much better prognosis. Dr. Hollán was very confident telling my father he had five to ten years to live.

Chemotherapy for chronic lymphocytic leukemia was different from most. It was much less aggressive, given in small doses over an extended period of time. My father never lost his hair, and as far as I know, this type of treatment didn't make him violently sick. Nevertheless, it still had unpleasant side effects, leaving him very tired and weak.

After an initial, longer hospital stay, he only had to go in for checkups from time to time, and if his test results didn't satisfy Dr. Hollán, he had to spend a couple days in the hospital, receiving chemo and steroids to restore his energy. It was manageable. He could go on with his life, working, traveling, giving presentations at conferences, publishing papers, mentoring young scientists, doing what he loved. In many ways, his most productive years had just started, as if he were determined to squeeze half a lifetime into those five to ten years he was given.

A few months later, I found myself in a surreal scene. My father knew that leukemia was not a hereditary disease, yet he could not rest until he saw physical evidence, black-and-white proof that I didn't have this terrible fault in my body, dormant, waiting to explode and ruin my life. He asked the hospital to run a very thorough blood test for me, but they declined, since I was perfectly healthy. When it came to his daughter, my father did not take no for an answer. He left no stone unturned when he enrolled me in a school with the best English education in Budapest or when he arranged for me to spend summers in England to further my language skills. As always, he found a way. He slipped some money in one of the nurses' pockets, and she agreed to bend the rules and take the unofficial route.

As bizarre as it sounds, I was sitting in the back seat of my father's car parked behind the hospital, and the nurse quietly slid next to me equipped with a rubber band, gloves, alcohol wipes, a needle, and several vials. When the test results came back the following week, my father could finally exhale. All my numbers were perfect. I was deeply touched by his concern and persistence.

Adjusting to his new reality was rather challenging for József. In less than two months, he lost so much weight that none of his trousers or sports coats fit him. My mother had a sewing machine, and she scrambled to make at least one outfit wearable so he could return to work. I remember my father bringing a pile of clothes to the tailor the following week for alteration.

Working less and sleeping more proved to be the biggest challenge for him. He tried to ignore Dr. Hollán's strict orders and resume his former routine of very little sleep and long hours of work, but it backfired. In a matter of weeks, he admitted defeat, reluctantly accepting the tighter boundaries set by his condition. I recall him saying, "I don't have all this time to waste. We can get plenty of sleep after we die." But for the rest of his life, he scrupulously followed Dr. Hollán's advice, without ever questioning her again.

Chapter Thirty-Seven
Toulouse

IN 1981 JÓZSEF HATVANY was invited to the École Nationale de Électronique et Informatique de Toulouse as a guest professor. He packed all the clothes and personal items he could fit in the trunk of his Lada and embarked on a long road trip with my mother. They took turns driving in treacherous conditions as a heavy snowstorm hit Western Europe in the first days of January. I stayed behind for my midterm exams at Eötvös Loránd University, where I majored in English. After helping my father settle into his furnished apartment in Toulouse and exploring neighboring towns and the foothills of the Pyrenees with him, my mother flew back to Budapest via Paris.

❧

On his first day at the Institut National Polytechnique de Toulouse, József asked his students whether he should teach his postgraduate course in flawless English or in fluent but imperfect French, compromised by the occasional grammatical and morphological mistakes. It goes without saying they chose French. On his way back to the apartment, my father stopped at a bookstore. In addition to an English-French dictionary, he also bought a book on French idioms. He never wrote down his lectures. He preferred speaking freely, using just a couple of handwritten notes to guide him through a chain of thoughts, and he always opened with a joke or a surprising fact to grab the attention of his audience. Despite his seemingly casual way of delivering speeches, he prepared for them meticulously. In Toulouse, he went one step further by including carefully selected French proverbs and even some wordplay in his presentations.

Judit took a leave of absence and joined my father in France for the last four months of his six-month stay. While she had accompanied József on some of his business trips before, it was a true test of their relationship to share an apartment and daily responsibilities with him in a foreign country. Fluent in English and well versed in history, culture, and international affairs, she fit in flawlessly with my father's colleagues and their spouses at conferences and social gatherings.

Before I joined them in July for a vacation in Collioure and visits of such medieval jewels in the Roussillon region as Carcassonne, Cordes-sur-Ciel, Elne, and Albi, Judit and József had spent time in Paris together and toured the Châteaux de la Loire.

As I would learn from Judit several years later, in the spring of 1981 Vera also paid them a visit in Toulouse. Apparently, she was visibly touched when József bought her flowers for Mother's Day. A gesture so trivial it goes almost unnoticed in most households, this was a significant step toward a warmer, kinder, more accepting bond between the two of them. Come to think of it, this bouquet of flowers might have been the very first my grandmother had ever received from her son.

Chapter Thirty-Eight
Split

THE FOUR MONTHS Judit and my father spent in Toulouse served as a successful dress rehearsal for a future marriage, yet it was three more years before they were able start a life together. Rentals were almost entirely in the hands of the local government. While private property existed in the early 1980s, it was as hard to find as it was to afford. The concept of a mortgage, at least as we know it today, was almost unheard of. Most people resorted to exchanging larger, government-owned rentals for two small ones, paying cash for the difference in value. These transactions could become extremely complicated when a real or fictitious third party was involved, especially in cases when someone pretended to move multiple times on paper only, in order to bypass certain regulations and restrictions. According to the old adage, "Hungarians are known to step into a revolving door behind you and come out before you," but resourcefulness alone wasn't enough for those who chose to play by the rules.

Judit was in her late thirties, living with her mother. She was not eligible for a government rental as a single woman, nor was she able to afford to buy a home of her own. She entered into a so-called care contract with an elderly lady, committing herself to look after her as long as she lived in exchange for her tiny apartment. When the lady passed away, with some financial contribution from my father, Judit was finally able to buy a one-bedroom condominium in a nice new building in the Buda hills.

On a Friday afternoon in the spring of 1984, my father sat me down and said, "Tomorrow morning, I am going to move out and go live with Judit." It was long overdue for him to leave an ill-fated marriage. I had been very supportive, rooting for them throughout their five-year journey together, sometimes even covering for my father's unexplained absence, continuing with our long-established pattern of conspiracy. Nevertheless, I was completely taken aback by the way he handled his departure. It was the first and probably only time my father disappointed me.

He told me he had arranged for two young men with a small truck to arrive the next morning to help him pack and transport his personal belongings and a couple boxes of books he intended to take. In order to avoid pointless, lengthy arguments and uncomfortable scenes with my mother, he was only going to tell her at the very last minute, just before the truck arrived.

It was one of the few instances I felt sincerely sorry for my mother. I had a strong disdain for her devious ways of playing the martyr at every turn, weighing me with guilt throughout my life for the countless sacrifices she made for my benefit. Yet on that Friday afternoon, I felt she would have deserved more than waking up the next day to be blind-sided. She should have been given a fair notice, an opportunity to digest such a shock, a chance to have a discussion about it, as pointless as that discussion might have been.

Selfishly enough, I also dreaded finding myself between a rock and a hard place. I felt my father threw me under the bus. "At least give me a chance to escape in the morning," I bargained. "I cannot be a witness to this drama." He agreed—in fact, he encouraged me to leave the house before he and my mother woke up, apologizing repeatedly for putting me in such an awkward situation.

I embarked on a tour of downtown Budapest, walked along the Danube, aimlessly browsed in shop after shop for hours, and had my fair share of coffee and ice cream. In the middle of the afternoon, I finally worked up the courage to go home and face my mother. She was obviously distraught and didn't waste a second before attacking me for having been an accomplice to my father's numerous extra marital affairs at her expense. That fateful Saturday triggered an avalanche that buried the two of us in a thick layer of discomfort for years to come.

I barely knew anyone my age who left his or her parents' nest. Moving away from home during college was the exception rather than the rule. Once I started working in my early twenties, I was dreaming of a place of my own. Exchanging our rental apartment for two very small ones would have been my only hope, but my mother resisted every possible solution I suggested. In her usual, indirect way, she would never tell me what exactly turned her away from the apartments we looked at, nor did she admit she had no intention of leaving her beautifully groomed private backyard in a quiet, secluded neighborhood. More than anything, she was deeply hurt by the implication that I wouldn't need her anymore in my daily life. I felt trapped, and the prospects of gaining my independence looked dim.

Almost immediately after my father moved out, my reasonably good relationship with Judit started to deteriorate. While I knew she hadn't played an active role in plotting my father's less-than-elegant way of leaving us, I couldn't help but associate these events and their unpleasant consequences with her. With József gone, I was confined within the walls of our apartment with Zsófia, and it felt as if I had lost an ally, a protective barrier shielding me from my mother's constant questioning and criticism. I couldn't help but blame Judit. As I perceived it, my access to my father had become scarce and supervised.

In retrospect, my antagonistic feelings for Judit were entirely uncalled for. I must admit, I could also have been more empathetic toward my mother, but what twenty-three-year-old sees the world in subtle shades of gray instead of the harsh extremes of black and white?

It took me several years to fully understand the reasons behind my reservations toward Judit. I had never felt the need to compete for my father's attention with any woman in his life, least of all with my mother. Judit was different. She wasn't just one of his girlfriends, a fling, an affair, like so many before her. When they decided to live together, let alone get married, I found myself in unfamiliar territory. It felt as if someone were trying to climb up to my pedestal, a place I wasn't ready or willing to share. Of course, my father's love for me had never faltered, but in my twenties, I was too insecure to know that. Only in my forties would I fully realize that my resentment toward Judit stemmed from jealousy. Only when I was finally ready to admit it to myself would I apologize for having treated her as an evil stepmother when, in fact, she was neither.

∽

In November 1985, a year and a half after his divorce, József married Judit. They quietly went to the local authorities and singed the papers at the registrar's office in front of two witnesses. My father casually informed me about it a couple days later, when I visited him in his office, the only place where a private conversation was guaranteed. I should have been happy for them, but instead I felt as if another fence had been raised between the two of us. I acknowledged the news as matter-of-factly as I received it but stopped short of congratulating him.

Although József married all three of his wives the same way, without fanfare, without a white dress, without rings, and without guests, the parallels ended with the formalities. Apart from the ceremonies themselves, or lack thereof, these three unions couldn't have been more different from one another.

At twenty-one, he was as blindly in love with Doris, his comrade and biggest cheerleader, as he was with the utopia they hoped to create together in post–World War II Hungary. His dreams turned into a nightmare when he was robbed of five years of his youth by the very regime he had full-heartedly believed in.

A changed man at thirty-four, abandoned not only by his first wife but also by a new flame he called his fiancée, he reluctantly tied the knot with Zsófia, the mother of his unplanned child. As a fully committed father but an emotionally detached husband, he searched for thrills, adventure, and happiness outside his dysfunctional second marriage.

At fifty-nine, he arrived. Not only was he fully accepted and respected in Hungarian academic circles, he made a name for himself as an internationally recognized expert in computer-aided design and manufacturing. As a highly sought-after keynote speaker at conferences around the world, a frequently quoted author of numerous scientific publications, and a recipient of prestigious awards, he no longer had to prove himself to anyone. His political aspirations were distant history, and so were his days of chasing skirts for sport. In Judit, he found an intellectual partner, a lover, a travel companion, someone to confide in and worth coming home to. Knowing very well that his years were numbered, he didn't let his incurable disease cast a shadow over his life, let alone dictate it. He was full of ambitions, plans, and willpower. He ate life not with a spoon, but with a ladle. It wasn't his appetite but his preferred flavor that changed over the years.

Chapter Thirty-Nine
Forecast

EARLIER THAN ALMOST ANYONE ELSE, József focused on, wrote about, and raised awareness of the impact of automation on society, contemplating how it would transform the nature of work and whether it would threaten established, traditional jobs. This awareness, an avid, in-depth interest in the social aspects of his area of scientific research, often ended in controversy, or even in conflict with his colleagues and friends from other countries.

❧

Jakob Vlietstra met my father in 1972 in Ljubljana (then Yugoslavia, today Slovenia), where they attended a newly formed IFIP (International Federation of Information Processing) Technical Committee. For the next three years, they saw each other at regular intervals and worked together on CAD (computer-aided design) and CAM (computer-aided-manufacturing) topics as representatives of various international organizations. Upon his retirement two decades later, Jakob recalled his peculiar relationship with my father as follows:

I appreciated Joe highly for his knowledge, his support, and admired his continuous attempts to establish better relationships between the professionals from the East-West Bloc countries. (At that time the gap was still very, very wide!). I also felt attracted to many of his social views and we quite often got involved in very lively and mind-stimulating debates. The mere fact that open discussions with a supporter of the communist system was becoming possible proved to me that political ideologies, and especially those from Eastern Bloc countries, could be challenged.

At a meeting in May 1975, we were preparing an international CAM-conference when we collided. Joe supported the Japanese invitation for an opening speaker to talk about the virtues of the "unmanned factory." That the conference would be held in Glasgow made me take an opposing position. At the time the Clyde area was struck by numerous closures of the ship building industries and many people were made "redundant". The conflict was emotional, and since I found no support for my view among the other members, I left the organizing committee. Much to my surprise and immense disappointment, I received a letter from Joe some three weeks later. The letter explained his position, made strong accusations against the capitalist system that was responsible for the closures, and concluded that with respect to our past discussions, he assumed my views were more in line with those of the communist countries, than those held by the West. According to him, I merely paid lip service to the company I worked for, and the system that I had chosen to live under while my real views were different. I could have ignored the letter totally, were it not that it had been opened and read by a special security office of Phillips. I was then given a hard time about this whole issue.

My trust in a professional friendship was badly shaken and for some two years I avoided all contacts with Joe. However, in 1977 I was appointed chairman of the committee that was responsible for the work of the CAD and CAM working groups and slowly we began to meet again. The incident was never discussed, but Joe's attitude changed. We never discussed political issues again, but focused heavily on what we were both most interested in: computer science, philosophy and the Hungarian author Arthur Koestler. It was as if our friendship had found a new basis.[60]

In the early 1980s, as part of an international community of scientists, József Hatvany continued his exploration of the economic and social impact of automation. He and his colleagues unanimously acknowledged that a reduction in the overall workforce would become inevitable. They also agreed that automation would increase productivity and incomes, causing the demand for services to grow, which would offset some manufacturing job loss. They theorized that increasing productivity could be liberating, as people would work less for the same output and spend more time on leisure activities. But their views differed on how various nations could facilitate such beneficial change. My father was an optimist. He argued that by the end of the twentieth century automation could enable people to spend less time with incessant work, and more with family, hobbies, cultural activities, and the like. As long as the benefits of increased productivity could be spread fairly across society and not reserved for a wealthy minority, he viewed it as a blessing.

Also in the early '80s, when my cousin Andrew was a law student at Columbia University in New York, my father paid him a visit during his business trip to the United States. "It won't be too long before everyone has a computer in his living room," József said, to which his nephew replied with skepticism: "Why would anybody need a computer at home?"

After finishing his guest professorship in Toulouse, József didn't resume his former role as head of department at the Computer and Automation Institute. Surrounded by a handful of young, talented, and very enthusiastic research fellows, he explored the possibilities and future challenges of computer-aided manufacturing and artificial intelligence.

József Váncza, an engineer fresh out of university, joined his group in the mid-'80s. Almost three decades later, he would reflect on his experience working with my father as follows:

> Joe Hatvany's fame far preceded our first encounter: he was said to be a boss who dragged to the corridor without any ado the desk of a colleague who did not appear fit for his assigned job. This story might have happened (if it happened at all) in the days when he enjoyed still a robust physical stature. When I was seated face to face with him—in retrospect, two years before his early departure—I decided for working under his guidance not because the possibility of such an action was apparently out of question. Indeed, it was impossible not to be fascinated by the intellectual tension that drove him, his relentless quest for passages between theory and practice in production engineering, his command of the wealth of world's literature and culture, his dry wit and sense of humor...
>
> Joe Hatvany had a special bend for technical innovations that had a style. It was in 1985 when, after returning from his US trip, he put a strange-looking white box on the table and said, "This is the computer of the future". That was Apple's new Macintosh machine, fully equipped with a WYSIWYG (what-you-see-is-what-you-get) graphical user interface and an appendage what proved to be a mouse. From this moment on he never ceased to work on his Mac, and before long, to our great pleasure, we were also equipped with such machines.

Chapter Forty

Return

ONCE THEY LEFT HUNGARY in the late 1940s, both of my paternal grandparents made a promise not to go back as long as the communists were in power. I met them in Western Europe throughout my childhood and never expected to see either of them in Budapest. My grandmother was willing to travel as far as the former Yugoslavia in 1969 to meet with her son. She made an exception for the only country in Eastern Europe that broke up with the Soviet Union and wasn't a member of the Warsaw Pact under Tito's leadership.

Bertalan left his homeland in 1938, feeling degraded to a second-class citizen after the first anti-Jewish measures were implemented. He paid a brief visit to Budapest in 1946, hoping to contribute to a newly established democracy, only to be disappointed by increasing communist dominance and Stalinist tendencies. My grandfather returned to Paris and never looked back. However, he remained a Hungarian citizen for as long as he lived.

Unwilling to give up his lifelong habit of enjoying a Scotch or two at home before hailing a taxi and going out on the town, he would wine and dine at expensive restaurants every day, just as he had done in Hungary in the 1930s. By the time he neared his eightieth birthday, Bertalan almost completely depleted his bank account, barely able to pay his rent in the 16th arrondissement. As a foreign national, he wasn't eligible for French health benefits. During his last year, seriously ill, he received treatment at the American hospital in Paris, something he clearly couldn't afford had it not been for the generosity of his niece, Mariella.

Bobette, the most loving stepdaughter anyone could wish for, cared for him in his final days. Her mother, Claire, visited from New York to be by her dying ex-husband's side. When Bertalan passed away in the summer of 1980, Claire brought his ashes to America, where Mariella buried them next to his brother, Bandi, and their sisters Lili and Antonia. The four siblings found a final resting place under the Hatvany memorial on the two sisters' former estate, which they fittingly named Hatvan, in New Jersey. It was Lili's grandson, Anthony Sundstrom, who set up and maintained this beautiful tribute to the family. After his mother, Mariella, died in 2000, Anthony placed her ashes next to Lili, Antonia, Bandi and Bertalan.

∽

My grandfather never had the chance to meet Judit. Although he heard about József's new love interest, he immediately dismissed her as yet another woman who wasn't Jewish. Vera, who was very fond of Judit, tried to persuade him to give her a chance, saying she was a "true dame."

Bertalan agreed to meet her, but by the time József and Judit were planning a visit, it was too late.

As I would learn decades later from Judit, my grandfather dedicated a copy of the second edition of his book, the Hungarian translation of Lao Tze's *Tao Te King*, to József as follows:

"To Józsi. My dear son, if my book's revised edition improved as much as my real life creation, both of us should be satisfied. Warm hugs: your father."

∽

I couldn't believe my ears when my father told me that Vera would come to Budapest over Christmas 1984. It was Judit's idea to invite her, and apparently my grandmother accepted without hesitation. Given how much she hated the communists and having sworn she would never set foot on Hungarian soil until a regime change, it was indeed a surprise.

Knowing how extremely critical my grandmother could be of everyone and everything, my father went to great lengths to show her the best possible side of Hungary in the most flattering light. He booked a room for her on the top floor of a beautiful new hotel on the Pest side of the Danube with panoramic views of the Chain Bridge and the Royal Castle in Buda. They visited museums; dined in the most elegant restaurants the city had to offer; savored traditional Hungarian pastries in historic confectionaries, bringing back prewar memories and old-fashioned charm; and enjoyed a superb performance of Tchaikovsky's *Onegin* at the newly renovated Budapest Opera House.

Vera wrote about her experience revisiting Budapest after thirty-six years, without leaving out the smallest detail. She concluded as follows: "The trip was a great emotion for me, it certainly was worth-while, because I got so much affection, got so spoiled, and everything has been done to make my stay as nice, interesting and comfortable as possible. It was also good to see their life. It is much better than I ever imagined, and after all, the town is beautiful and so well kept. I didn't like some red stars and Russian uniforms, but as Hungary has survived the Turks, I hope it will be free again."

In the summer of 1986, Vera visited Budapest once more. The two of us strolled along the Danube, looked at window displays in Váci utca, the main shopping street in the heart of the city, and browsed in the foreign-language bookstore, which she found very impressive. After enjoying a delicious dessert and an espresso at the famous Café Gerbeaud, I suggested we take a slightly different route back toward her hotel, winding our way through some of the narrowest side streets down-town, lined with beautifully renovated old buildings.

Vera suddenly stopped, and said, "No, I won't walk down this street. A terrible thing happened here, and I can't bring myself to relive that."

It was during the same afternoon, although not exactly then and there, that she told me about a very sad day etched in her memory. Just a few years after the war, she and my father accidentally ran into each other in downtown Budapest. Instead of stopping to greet his mother, he turned his head and passed her as if she were a stranger. My grand-mother didn't offer further details, and I wasn't brave enough to ask. In fact, I didn't even contemplate prying into her past unless she volun-teered. It must have been sometime after August 1947, when József and

Doris arrived in Hungary from England, but before December 1948, when Vera left Budapest. I knew that my father had denounced his entire family in late 1946, severing all contact with them, yet I was still shocked to hear this story.

Was it the painful memory of this incident that prevented her from stepping into that narrow street almost four decades later? Did she witness an unspeakable atrocity there during the war? Was she hiding from the Nazis in an apartment in that very street before they raided the building and marched her off to the Budapest Ghetto in November 1944?

∽

On her last day in Budapest, Vera pulled me aside and gestured toward my father, who was out of earshot, and said, "He doesn't look good, your father. He really doesn't."

Fighting back tears in an effort to keep our conversation between us, I replied, "Yes, I know."

As I later saw them standing next to each other, it struck me that József looked almost as old as his eighty-year-old mother, when he had yet to see his sixtieth birthday. His thick, black, hard-to-tame waves had given way to a head of finer, straighter, steel-gray hair. He was very thin and frail. His bony shoulders were pronounced under his sports coat, further emphasized by a slightly hunched posture. As much as he considered it a waste of time, he had to take a nap every afternoon in order to get through the day. Vera's remark sent shivers down my spine, and I was convinced we had the exact same thing on our minds, a terrible thought neither of us could say out loud. What if she outlived her son?

Chapter Forty-One

Munich

In January 1987, two weeks after her eighty-first birthday, my grand-mother was found dead, lying on the floor of her Rome apartment, holding a burned-out cigarette between her fingers.

The winter of 1986–87 was exceptionally harsh in most of Europe, with the coldest temperatures I had ever experienced in Hungary. The deep snow and frozen ground in Munich prohibited the removal of Erich Hesselberger's gravestone, thus delaying the funeral until early May, when Vera's ashes could be placed next to her father's.

It was the first time I met my great aunt Marutha, who at seven-ty-five looked considerably younger than her age. She didn't speak any Hungarian, and I noticed a strong German accent in her English, even though she had left her native country well before the war and didn't return until her sister's funeral half a century later. Her son Andrew, whom I first met exactly ten years earlier in Budapest, when he was a college student, had matured into a very confident and decisive thirty-year-old. It was strange to see him as the only person tearing up during the memorial service.

When we all sat down with an attorney after the ceremony to review Vera's last will, I was completely taken aback upon hearing the following clause:

> If my granddaughter, Maria Helga Hatvany, survives me,
> I give, devise and bequeath unto her...provided...(1) that
> at the time of my death she shall have reached the age of
> twenty-five (25) years, and (2) she shall not at such time
> be a permanent resident of the Soviet Union, Poland,
> Hungary, Rumania, Czechoslovakia, Albania, China, East
> Germany, Bulgaria or any other country which is then or
> was at any time a signatory of the so-called Warsaw Pact.[61]

I was twenty-six and living in Budapest, therefore not eligible for as much as a crumb. My father received a negligible amount of cash, a slap in the face rather than a generous gesture. At her own discretion, Marutha decided to give me a triangular wall mirror in an ornate silver frame with VH engraved in it.

As Andrew told me, perhaps in an attempt to soften the blow, Vera had spent most of her money by the time of her death, leaving almost nothing behind.

I sincerely couldn't care less about the material implications, or lack thereof. What truly shocked me were the conditions I was required to meet in order to be considered a beneficiary of my grandmother's will. It was the principle that left me with an incredibly bad taste in my mouth.

On our way back to Budapest, my father told me he was invited to be a guest professor at a university in Washington, DC, for the school year of 1987–'88. He went on to describe his future rental the university was going to provide for him and Judit, being especially enthusiastic about the swimming pool that came with the apartment. He suggested I planned my visit for fall or spring instead of the winter so I would be able to take full advantage of this lovely feature.

As our plane was about to touch down at Ferihegy Airport, I couldn't hold back my tears anymore. It was utterly surreal to hear him talk about the apartment, the swimming pool, and the best time for me to visit them in America when it was so evident that the walls around him were rapidly closing. I wanted to scream something from the top of my lungs, something so obvious as "You won't be alive by then!" but of course, I couldn't. When he asked why I was crying, I had to come up with an excuse in a split second, without having a chance to think it through. I said I was upset about going home, facing my mother, and being trapped with her without much hope of having my own place in my midtwenties.

As soon as those words left my lips, I felt extremely ashamed and selfish talking about my problems, which were petty, minuscule, and incomparable to his. In retrospect, I think my father might have seen through it, but he was smart enough not to tell me.

Chapter Forty-Two
Despair

Soon after his mother's funeral, József Hatvany embarked on a very demanding business trip to the United States. It was astonishing he would even consider such a thing in his condition. He was in no shape to get on a transatlantic flight, let alone give lectures at a conference and attend various meetings when even prolonged standing posed a challenge for him.

A longtime colleague and good friend of his told me a story that happened on another business trip they took together about a year earlier. He recalled my father delivering a speech with his usual high energy and enthusiasm, grabbing the attention of his large audience with a sprinkle of humor and captivating presentation style, only to look for an empty conference room afterward where he could lie down on a table in complete exhaustion.

This time, a quick nap wasn't going to work. In the middle of his lecture, József collapsed on the podium and was rushed to the hospital with life-threatening stomach bleeding.

Ever since he was diagnosed with chronic lymphocytic leukemia in the fall of 1979, his physician, Dr. Zsuzsa Hollán, kept his optimism alive by suggesting he would be a good candidate for some of the latest experimental treatments for his disease. In fact, it was my father who helped translate the entire procedure for installing and operating the equipment for bone marrow transplants at the Institute of Hematology in Budapest, where he was a regular, with the rare privilege of a private room with its own bathroom and telephone. He often used his time during chemotherapy treatments to read the English documents regarding these procedures and dictate his Hungarian translation into a tape recorder. He even asked me once if I was willing to be his bone marrow donor, assuming I proved to be the right match. "Before you say yes, I must warn you, it is a very unpleasant, painful operation for the donor as well as for the recipient," he said as he described a bone marrow transplant step-by-step. Of course, I agreed without hesitation, but as much as he hoped to be one of the first patients to benefit from this brand-new surgery in Hungary, it never happened.

It was at the American hospital where they stopped his stomach bleeding that he first heard the unforgiving truth in black and white. They said he had reached a point where no treatment, no new medicine, and no experimental procedure would help.

Judit met him at the Budapest Airport with an ambulance. On their way to the hospital, my father told her what the American doctors said to him. They both cried. I had never seen my father cry. Men of his generation and with his upbringing were not supposed to cry.

For about a month, I visited my father in the Hospital of Hematology every single day. To spend some time alone with him I went during my lunch break, as Judit visited on her way home from work. It was quite obvious to me that my father was saddened by the tension between Judit and me, but he tried to be very diplomatic about it, and so did I. It was also obvious that he didn't want to take sides. Neither Judit nor I expected him to do so.

Every time I knocked on the door of my father's room, I held my breath, waiting for a reply, wondering whether I would find him alive or his bed would be empty. He was in a terrible condition, skin and bones, wasting away, unable to get out of bed on his own. However, his mind was crystal clear. He was in full possession of his mental capacity to the day before his last. He religiously read his favorite newspaper, *Népszabadság*, every day and listened to the news on a small transistor radio that was within arm's reach on his nightstand. There were no TVs in Hungarian hospital rooms those days.

Up to his last week, he regularly conducted staff meetings with his closest colleagues sitting on the edge of his bed or on the windowsill. He reviewed the drafts of their publications, talked to them about future projects, the direction of scientific research, and upcoming international conferences. Despite all odds, somehow he managed to maintain a flicker of hope in his heart to the very end. He never complained. In fact, he didn't even like to talk about his situation or prognosis. He would rather engage in conversations about me, my life, Hungary's political future, world events, and, of course, his work.

With an ailing János Kádár, general secretary of the Hungarian Socialist Workers' Party, a regime marked by his name and lasting for more than three decades was slowly inching toward its end. *Glasnost* and *perestroika* gave us a peek into a new era to come, replacing a crumbling, outdated one. While my father welcomed the first signs of openness and restructuring from the Soviet Union, an ideology that later became synonymous with Gorbachev, he still seemed to be loyal to the status quo. Or was he? I vividly remember my attempt to argue for "good capitalism," the political and economic system associated with the Scandinavian countries, expressing my longing for a society that would successfully combine the best of both worlds while maintaining freedom and democracy.

Much to my surprise, my father, who had always been eager to engage in arguments just about any topic, didn't seem particularly keen on having this debate with me. I sensed that my criticism of the Kádár regime and admiration for the Scandinavian model didn't sit well with him. His usual way of responding would have started with an extensive history lesson, followed by a carefully compiled list of arguments for and against both sides, and finally making his case with ample reasoning. Instead, all he said was "It's not so simple, my little angel." There was an undeniable level of sadness and resignation in his voice. I still recall the expression on his face as he said it. I wonder if his sadness and unwilling-ness to discuss this topic stemmed from the realization that I was closer to the truth than he would have ever liked to admit, or he was simply sad to see his daughter distancing herself from his long-held views.

I have never known anyone who loved life as much as my father did. I have never seen anyone hanging on to the last drop of life with such hope and determination as he did, despite doctors telling him there was no cure, despite him knowing that all odds were against him.

On July 10, everything shifted. The minute I saw him, I could tell he was in more distress than ever before. For the first time, he didn't try to hide he was suffering. For the first time, there was no trace of optimism flickering in his eyes. He couldn't sit up without help anymore, and he couldn't stand up at all. He was connected to tubes, catheters, and mon-itors, physically barely existing. For the first time, I noticed complete resignation on his face and in his voice. He looked at me with an expres-sion equally sad and angry and said, "It's all shit." It took me every bit of concentration and effort to fight back tears. I held his hand for a while, kissed him on the cheek, and waited for him to fall asleep.

Chapter Forty-Three
Silence

JULY 11, 1987 fell on a Saturday. When I arrived at the hospital, I knocked on his door, fearing, as I had been every single day for a month, that there would be no answer. On this warm, sunny morning, there was silence.

As I slowly opened the door and stepped in, I saw my father lying in the bed, still connected to monitors. He was struggling for air. The sound of his loud wheezing sent chills down my spine. He didn't react to my presence, to my words, not even to my gentle touch. I felt the urge to run down the hallway in a desperate effort to find a nurse or a doctor, but I immediately realized I couldn't have helped him, and neither could anyone else.

This was the point of no return. Defeated and helpless, I sat down and held his hand. It was surprisingly cold and damp, a very strange sensation etched in my memory forever. I talked to him even though I knew he wouldn't hear me. I don't know how long I sat there. I knew it was the last time I was going to see him, so I wanted to stay as long as possible, but after a while, I just couldn't listen to his terrible wheezing anymore.

As I was about to leave, a very nice nurse came in. I asked her if my father received painkillers, and she assured me he was given enough to be comfortable, and he wasn't suffering at all. I believed her. She asked me if I wished to take his watch and other personal items with me. I said, "No, just give them to his wife. She will come later, I assume." I gave the nurse my home number, asking her to call me when *it* happened. I didn't want to learn it from Judit. I said, "When you call, please make sure you ask for me in case my mother answers the phone." I didn't want to hear it from her either.

She said, "Of course. I will make sure I do so."

I couldn't bring myself to stay at the hospital and watch my father die, but I also dreaded the thought of going home, as my mother was the last person on earth I wanted to be with. I realized there was no place where I could hide from reality. Learning about my father's death secondhand, especially from my mother, was not an option. I felt I had to go home so I wouldn't miss that terrible phone call from the hospital, the official confirmation of the inevitable. I desperately tried to hold on to the one and only thing I could control. Sobbing inconsolably, I drove home, barely able to see the road through a heavy curtain of tears.

"Did he die?" my mother asked quite matter-of-factly as I entered the house.

"No, not yet, but any time now," I said. I really didn't want to talk to her or even be in her presence.

Instead of comforting me, she went on a rampage, bringing up one bad memory after the other, pointing out my father's infidelities throughout their entire marriage. I was livid. All I needed was a shoulder to cry on, a hug, a little sympathy, and a few kind words. After all, I was about to lose the most important person in my life, and it would happen far too early for both of us. Instead of the warmth, sense of calm, safety, and reassurance only a mother could provide under these circumstances, I had to listen to degrading stories about my father while she portrayed herself as the victim, the ultimate martyr. To add insult to injury, she berated me for sobbing so hysterically, saying I should pull myself together. What was already the worst day of my life, she managed to make it even worse. I have never felt as lonely as I did that afternoon.

And then the phone rang. I ran to answer it before my mother could. The nurse first carefully verified she was indeed talking to me and then said the time of my father's death. She didn't actually say the words "he died"; she just said the time of the day it happened. Before I even had a chance to ask, she repeatedly and rather convincingly assured me that he had been given an ample dose of painkillers and didn't suffer. The minute I hung up the phone, my eyes went dry. I ran out of tears. I wasn't able to shed another one until his funeral three weeks later.

August 4 was the first cool, drizzly day after a long, hot, and sunny period, setting the tone for József Hatvany's funeral. The idea of a grave, a physical reminder of his life, did not appeal to my father. He considered it a burden for his survivors, something we would feel obligated to visit and maintain. Spreading his ashes in a ceremony was the perfect fit for my father's personality. Given the number of adversaries József had made over the years, I was surprised and touched to see a crowd of 150 strong gathering at the cemetery.

My mother chose to stay away. She said she would feel humiliated standing there, surrounded by people who knew about my father's numerous affairs, all guilty by association, not to mention having to face some of his former mistresses in person. Most of all, she had no desire to meet my father's widow, Judit. I felt terribly alone without a single relative by my side, yet her absence turned out to be a relief rather than a void.

I hadn't cried a single tear since my father's death. For most of the ceremony I held it together, but after a touching speech, when everyone was quiet and his ashes were spread by a swoosh of a fountain with soft classical music playing in the background, I felt as if I were suddenly kicked in the stomach. My brain knew it was irreversible the minute I left my father's hospital room on July 11, but this was the moment when it really sank in. He was gone. Forever. I started sobbing uncontrollably. My whole body was shaking, and I felt a trickle of cold sweat running down my back.

Just when I thought I was completely alone in my pain and misery, Judit put her arm around me. This seemingly small gesture was the first step in the direction of repairing our fragile relationship.

⚭

About a year before his death, my father traveled to Israel for a scientific conference. Upon returning to Hungary, he told me something that took my breath away. Standing in front of the Western Wall in Jerusalem, he said a prayer in Hebrew, one he remembered from his childhood.

"You did what? I thought you were an atheist," I said in disbelief.

"I am, and I always will be," he replied. "It was the ancient history of that place that resonated with me. It was much more powerful than I expected. Suddenly, I was overwhelmed with emotions. Saying a Jewish prayer, in Hebrew nonetheless, came naturally."

For József Hatvany, Jewish identity didn't equate with religion. It was a feeling of connection with something more than himself: his culture and ethnicity. As I write these lines, I realize I am the exact same age as my father was when he stood in front of the Western Wall in Jerusalem. Maybe it's time I put a menorah on the mantle as a tribute to my heritage, and for a sense of belonging.

Chapter Forty-Four
Waves

WHAT REMAINS? What is our legacy? Must we make a visible, public contribution to society in order to leave our mark? Is it only by a touchable object, a sculpted or painted piece of art, a scientific discovery, or a groundbreaking innovation that our existence becomes noteworthy? Are there other ways to make a lasting impact on people's lives, and if yes, can they be equally or even more important?

My great-grandmother Fanny renovated a palace in Budapest and furnished it in a lavish baroque and rococo style. A sizable room was dedicated solely to her exquisite porcelain collection. The palace suffered considerable damage during World War II, most of her belongings were taken either by the Germans or the Russians, and the whereabouts of her legendary porcelain remain a mystery.

Yet Fanny left behind something much more valuable and lasting than her carefully selected, priceless objects. Instead of a material heritage, she handed over her vast knowledge of art and history to her young granddaughter while they traveled together in Italy. She ingrained a deep appreciation of culture and beauty in Mariella, who in turn became a highly respected art history teacher in America without any formal education in the subject. Many years after her death, Mariella's students at Solebury School remembered her as their beloved teacher whose impact reached far beyond the classroom. She gave them a taste of old-fashioned European sophistication and encouraged her students to travel and open their hearts and minds to different nations and cultures.

As a self-made Orientalist, Bertalan Hatvany spent years traveling in Asia during the 1920s and '30s. He returned with an incredible collection of ancient Chinese and Indian sculptures. Most of them were looted at the end of the war, their fate, similar to the fate of his mother's porcelain, remains unknown. My grandfather published two books, one of them earning him an honorary doctorate from the University of Pécs. While both reveal an immense knowledge of Asian history and culture and contemplate deep philosophical questions, his books only reached a narrow audience even at the time of their first release. By the turn of the twenty-first century, the studious work of an exceptional intellect would almost entirely fade into oblivion.

Yet Bertalan left his mark in ways beyond his wildest dreams. As cofounder and sole sponsor of the literary periodical *Szép Szó*, he played a key role in promoting Attila József, one of Hungary's most brilliant poets, by giving him a platform to publish his work. He also taught me something I carry and live by: the importance of asking questions. "It's only when we shed our fear and embarrassment to ask questions that we learn new things, and expand our horizons," he once said to me.

It was Bertalan who planted the seeds of appreciation for ancient history and art in his stepdaughter while traveling with her in London, giving her guided tours of museums, and it was he who introduced Marie-Françoise (Bobette) to renowned Egyptologist Jean Leclant. In 2014, Bobette established the Jean Leclant Foundation, in memory of her late husband. Prix Jean et Marie-Françoise Leclant is a prize awarded annually to support archaeological research in the Nile Valley.

József Hatvany's legacy cannot be confined into one compartment, or filed under one category. While his obituaries and memorial tributes that appeared in various Hungarian and international newspapers and scientific journals yield a very impressive list of his professional accomplishments, they only highlight one facet of his life:

He was a member of many scientific committees in his country, including the Hungarian Society of Mechanical Engineering, as well as prestigious organizations abroad, most notably the International Federation for Information Processing (IFIP) and The International Academy for Production Engineering (CIRP). He was the author or coauthor of more than 170 scientific papers and served on the editorial boards of international scientific publications such as *Computer-Aided Design*, the *International Journal of Man-Machine Studies, Computers & Graphics, Computers in Industry*, and *Robotics and Computer-Integrated Manufacturing*. He received several awards, including the Gold Medal for Development of Technology from the Hungarian Society of Mechanical Engineering in 1977, the Silver Core Award from IFIP the same year, the State Prize for Science and Technology, the highest Hungarian honor for engineers in 1978, and gold medals for outstanding inventions from the Hungarian Academy of Sciences in 1978, 1980, and 1982. The Computer and Automation Institute presented him with the Benedikt Prize in 1983, and in 1984, he became a titular professor of the Budapest Technical University. In 1985, he received an honorary doctorate from the École Nationale de Électronique et Informatique de Toulouse, and in the same year, the US National Academy of Engineering elected him a foreign associate, the first from Hungary.

As one of the pioneers in automation, especially in the field of computer-aided design and manufacturing, his early research and innovations by all means represented cutting-edge technology. His design of the graphical display unit in the late 1960s was indeed groundbreaking. Half a century later, they would remain important building blocks for emerging new technologies, even as their relevance fades.

Fortunately, József Hatvany didn't limit his scientific career to technological innovations. He was equally or even more interested in examining and foreseeing the impact of automation and robotics on society. As computers evolved, so did his questions about the ways they would affect our lives. In his early days at the Computer and Automation Institute, he focused on how computers control tools and machines. In the next phase, he explored how humans control these computers, and before long, his attention shifted to the inevitable consequences of automation, when computers gradually replace humans. He did not see robotics as the evil enemy—in fact, he believed technology would improve the quality of life, giving factory workers the chance to work shorter hours and spend more time with leisure activities. He also thought it was the responsibility of each and every country's administration to provide a strong social net that would support a new work-life balance.

Toward the end of his career, he directed his attention to the engineers, the creative minds on the other side of the computer. He wasn't blind to the potential problems posed by artificial intelligence (AI), yet he maintained a very optimistic outlook, even more so than in case of the factory workers. He thought AI would help skilled professionals instead of making their jobs obsolete, especially if societies provided and encouraged a strong educational program for the next generation, with an emphasis on creative thinking. It is hard to measure the extent to which he would be proven right or wrong many years later, but asking these questions and trying to find solutions to these problems remain as relevant as ever.

József Hatvany was also known as a mentor to numerous talented research fellows of a younger generation. As long as they could keep up with his extremely demanding, sometimes harshly critical style of work, he took them under his wing. At the height of the Cold War and under strict embargo, he opened doors for them to participate in international conferences, publish their work in foreign periodicals, and study in a Western country. He showed them an exceptional work ethic, a relentless drive, and an appetite for knowledge, values they themselves would carry and pass down to the next generation.

In 2000, the Mechanical Engineering Faculty of Miskolc University established the József Hatvany Doctoral School for Computer Science and Engineering. Many years later, some of its founders would still call themselves "Hatvany students."

Members of the laboratory that grew out of his former research group in the 1980s recalled my father teaching them the importance of participating in the international arena. More than thirty years later, this group would boast an impressive number of representatives in the prestigious organization CIRP.

Those who knew my father, whether on a professional or personal level, all carry a part of him. If I had the power to choose one thing to remain, to live on, it would be his courage to dream. No matter how many times or how hard his dreams were crushed, he dared to dream again and again.

As for me, I have been carrying a little secret all my life, a secret no more. Every time I fly over the ocean, I look for whitecaps. When I catch a glimpse of them dancing on top of the waves, they always bring a smile to my face. I see something that remains invisible to others. I see the salt.

Acknowledgments

"You should write a book about this" was a recurring response from many of my friends and acquaintances upon hearing the story of my father's life in a nutshell. I am thankful to everyone who encouraged me.

I was ecstatic when I found my father's long-lost first wife, Doris Hatvany, in Scotland. It was Raymond Budd, a former colleague and friend of hers, who made it possible for me to meet her.

My French friend Christine Perrotin helped me reconnect with my step aunt, Marie-Françoise (Bobette) Leclant, after I had lost contact with her. When I reunited with Bobette in Paris, her entertaining stories about my grandfather Bertalan filled in missing pieces of the puzzle I was trying to put together.

Many of my father's former colleagues from around the world were kind enough to share their personal memories and gave me permission to use them. I am very thankful to Jakob Vlietstra for taking the initiative to contact a large group of scientists, encouraging them to send me anecdotes about József Hatvany. I would also like to thank Géza Haidegger for mailing me photocopies of my father's publications, all 170 of them. I had them bound into eleven volumes once I found a bookbinder in California who was willing to handle thousands of loose pages in A4 format. I am grateful to József Váncza, not only for sending me a very interesting collection of stories about my father, but also for writing in immaculate English, complete with citations, as if he were submitting a scientific paper. I was honored and touched to receive such personal and emotional notes as Professor Hiroyuki Yoshikawa sent me from Japan. My lunch conversation with Professor Andries (Andy) van Dam was one of the most personable interviews I conducted over the years. It was also highly entertaining. Of all my father's coworkers and friends, László Nemes was the closest to him for many years. I met him in my teens and twenties in Hungary, but we lost contact with each other after he moved to Australia and I moved to the United States. We reunited in New Zealand in 2013, and we have been in regular email correspondence ever since. He shared countless anecdotes with me, including funny, light-hearted ones as well as details of his professional relationship with my father, always keeping it honest, sparing any sugar coating. For László's invaluable contribution, I cannot thank him enough.

I would like to thank my cousin Andrew Wilson for sharing his mother's (Marutha's) memoirs with me, along with many old letters, documents, and photos left behind by my grandmother Vera. Some of them served as revelations, based on which I had to reevaluate my story and rewrite entire chapters. I am very thankful to my second cousin, Lili Hatvany's grandson Anthony Sundstrom, for the endless supply of stories, old family letters, and photographs I received from him. Before

2014, we had never heard about each other. Since then, he proved to be one of my most valuable sources. I would like to thank my father's third wife, Judit Petróczy, for her immense help from the conception of this project. Among many documents, letters, photos, and anecdotes, she sent me József Hatvany's correspondence with his former classmate András Nagy. These handwritten letters my father sent from Cambridge immediately after the war played a pivotal role in my initial research and helped me find Doris.

Last but certainly not least, I am incredibly grateful to my husband, Bruce Elder, for being my biggest cheerleader from the very first day I embarked on this journey. Every time my confidence started to slip away, every time doubt seemed to take over, he helped me surmount the obstacles. I often used him as my test audience, reading excerpts to him, and he always gave me his honest opinion and suggestions. I couldn't have dreamed of anyone more supportive being at my side.

Bibliography

REFERENCES:

1   Hatvany, J. *Dreams, Nightmares and Reality*, in: *CAPE'83 Conference Proceedings*, North-Holland Publ. Co, Amsterdam, 1983, p. 10. With the permission of Elsevier.

2   Sundstrom, Mariella. *Happily Hungarian*. [Manuscript], 1995, pp. 7–9.

3   ibid. p. 10.

4   ibid. p. 10.

5   Rozsics, István. *Hatvany Lajos az író és az irodalompolitikus* [*Lajos Hatvany the writer and the literary politician*], in: *A Hatvanyak emlékezete* [*The Memory of the Hatvanys*]. Hatvan, 2003, p. 26.

6   ibid. p. 28.

7   Vermes, Gábor. *The October Revolution*, in: Völgyes, Iván. *Hungary in Revolution*, University of Nebraska Press, Lincoln, 1971, p. 49.

8   Lendvai, Paul. *Hungary Between Democracy and Authoritarianism.* Columbia University Press, New York, 2012, pp. 57–58.

9   Molnos, Péter. *Elveszett Örökség [Lost Heritage].* Kieselbach Galéria, Budapest, 2017, p. 354.

10 Korzim, Erika. *Emlékezés a Hatvanyakra [Remembering the Hatvanys]*, in: *A Hatvanyak Emlékezete [The Memory of the Hatvanys].* Hatvan, 2003, p. 11.

11 Sundstrom, Mariella. *Happily Hungarian* [Manuscript]. 1995, p. 6.

12 ibid. p. 16.

13 ibid. p. 24.

14 Wilson, Marion. *Memoirs* [Manuscript]. 2011, pp. 1-3.

15 ibid. p. 10.

16 ibid. pp. 14-16.

17 ibid. pp. 20-22.

18 József, Attila. *Thomas Mann üdvözlése [Welcome to Thomas Mann]* (Translated by Vernon Watkins). Excerpt. https://www.mathstat.dal.ca/~lukacs/ja/poems2/jozsef-eng.htm#18.

19 *Hatvany Lili búcsú partyja [Lili Hatvany's Farewell Party]*, in: *Futár*, Budapest, 1938, p. 14.

20 Sundstrom, Mariella. *Happily Hungarian* [Manuscript]. 1995, p. 29.

21 ibid. pp. 24–26.

22 Dawkins, Richard. *An Appetite for Wonder—The Making of a Scientist.* HarperCollins, New York, 2013, pp. 119–120. Copyright © 2013 by Richard Dawkins. Used by permission of HarperCollins Publishers.

23   Hausner, Gideon. *Justice in Jerusalem.* Waldon Press, New York, 1997, p. 132.

24   ibid. pp. 133–134.

25   ibid. p. 135.

26   ibid. p. 140.

27   ibid. p. 141.

28   Korzim, Erika. *Emlékezés a Hatvanyakra* [*Remembering the Hatvanys*], in: *A Hatvanyak Emlékezete* [*The Memory of the Hatvanys*]. Hatvan, 2003, pp. 11–12.

29   Hausner, Gideon. *Justice in Jerusalem.* Waldon Press, New York, 1997, pp. 141–145.

30   Sundstrom, Mariella. *Happily Hungarian* [Manuscript]. 1995, p. 24.

31   *Swiss Embassy Report*, in: Ungváry, Krisztián. *The Siege of Budapest.* Yale University Press, 2005, p. 350.

32   *School Play*, in: *The Laxtonian.* Oundle School Archives, 1944, p. 10.

33   Molnos, Péter. *Elveszett Örökség* [*Lost Heritage*]. Kieselbach Galéria, Budapest, 2017, p. 373.

34   Pálóczi-Horváth, George. *The Undefeated.* ELAND, London, 1993, pp. 120, 134.

35   ibid. pp. 135–137.

36   ibid. pp. 148–149.

37   ibid. p. 154.

38   Pécsi, Vera. *A Standard-ügy 1949-1989* [*The Standard Case 1949-1989*], a TV documentary film, 1990, Excerpts.

39   ibid. p. 2.

40 Vogeler, Robert A. *I Was Stalin's Prisoner.* Harcourt, Brace and Company, New York, 1952, pp. 136–137, 183.

41 ibid. p. 192.

42 Pécsi, Vera. *A Standard-ügy 1949-1989* [*The Standard Case 1949-1989*], a TV documentary film, 1990, Excerpts.

43 ibid.

44 Pécsi, Vera. *The Standard Electric Trial,* in: *The Hungarian Quarterly,* Vol. XLII, No. 162, Summer 2001, pp. 2–3.

45 Pálóczi-Horváth, George. *The Undefeated.* ELAND, London, 1993, p. 223.

46 *Court Documents in József Hatvany's Case,* 1952–1960, Excerpts.

47 ibid.

48 Pálóczi-Horváth, George. *The Undefeated.* ELAND, London, 1993, p. 277.

49 *Court Documents in József Hatvany's Case,* 1952–1960, Excerpts.

50 ibid.

51 ibid.

52 ibid.

53 ibid.

54 ibid.

55 ibid.

56 Hatvany, J. *Are Displays Good for Us?,* in: *Proceedings, 10th National Symposium on Information Display,* Arlington, Virginia, 1969, p. 57.

57 Hatvany, J. *Hogyan maradhatunk rabszolgáink urai?* [*How can we remain the masters of our slaves?*], in: *Élet és Irodalom,* Vol. 13, No. 5, 1969, Excerpts.

58 *History of IIASA*, 2018, Excerpts. https://www.iiasa.ac.at/web/home/about/whatisiiasa/history/history_of_iiasa.html.

59 Bartha, Béla. *Interview with József Hatvany*, in: *Szellem a palackból?* [*Genie from the bottle?*], a TV program on scientific research in Hungary, 1982.

60 Vlietstra, Jakob. *32 Years of Information Processing—A Farewell Address and Legacy*. Hilversum, The Netherlands, 1992, pp. 30–31.

61 *Last Will and Testament of Vera Hatvany*, January 15, 1975, pp. 4–5.

Other Sources:

Bencze, Géza, and Kornélia Sudár. *A Hatvani Cukorgyár Története 1889–1987* [*The History of the Hatvan Sugar Factory 1889–1987*]. Hatvan, 1989.

Boulger, Francis W. *József Hatvany 1926–1987*, in: *Memorial Tributes—National Academy of Engineering*, Vol. 4, Number 34, Washington, DC, 1991, pp. 125–128.

Computers in Industry, Special Issue: József Hatvany Memorial, Vol. 14, Numbers 1–3, Elsevier Science Publishers B.V., The Netherlands, May 1990.

Fejtő, Ferenc. *Budapesttől Párizsig* [*From Budapest to Paris*]. Magvető, Budapest, 1990.

Földes, Anita. *Átéltem egy évszázadot—Utolsó interjúk Fejtő Ferenccel* [*I Lived Through a Century—Last Interviews with Ferenc Fejtő*]. Scolar, Budapest, 2013.

Hatvany, József. *Eötvös Loránd*. Művelt Nép Könyvkiadó, Budapest, 1951.

Hatvany, Lajos. *Urak és Emberek* [*Lords and Men*]. Szépirodalmi Kiadó, Budapest, 1963.

Hatvany, Lajosné and István Rozsics. *Hatvany Lajos levelei* [*Lajos Hatvany's Letters*]. Szépirodalmi Kiadó, Budapest, 1985.

IIASA (International Institute for Applied Systems Analysis) Library.

Koncz, E. Katalin. *A hatvaniaktól a Hatvanyakig—Kísérlet egy nagyvállalkozó család pályájának elemzésére* [*From the hatvanis to the Hatvanys—An attempt to analyze the path of an industrialist family*]. 1983 [Manuscript].

Nemes, László. *Laci emlékei* [*Laci's memories*]. 2021 [Manuscript].

Oundle School Archives.

Trinity College Cambridge Archives.

Witness testimony given by György Pálóczi-Horváth in front of the United Nations General Assembly, London, March–April 1957.

Zimler, Tamás (ed.). *Hatvany József Emlékére* [*In Memoriam of József Hatvany*]. Tertia, 1999.

(Unless otherwise noted, Hungarian citations translated by Hatvany, Helga).